SOUTHWESTERN INDIAN JEWELRY

CRAFTING NEW TRADITIONS

DEXTER CiRiLLO

Photography by

ADDISON DOTY

RIZZOLI
NEW YORK

FOR MY HUSBAND, DENNIS
AND FOR ALL OF THE SOUTHWESTERN INDIAN
JEWELERS—PAST, PRESENT, AND FUTURE—
WHO BRING BEAUTY INTO THE WORLD.

First published in the
United States of America in 2008
by Rizzoli International Publications, Inc.
300 Park Avenue South
New York, New York 10010
www.rizzoliusa.com

Text copyright © 2008 Dexter Cirillo
Photography copyright © 2008 Addison Doty
See page 231 for additional photographer credits.

2008 2009 2010 2011 / 10 9 8 7 6 5 4 3 2 1

Printed in China

ISBN: 0-8478-3110-8
ISBN 13: 978-0-8478-3110-4

Library of Congress Control Number: 2007942633

Project Editor: Sandra Gilbert
Production Manager: Kaija Markoe
Designer: Susi Oberhelman
Map Illustrator: Rodica Prato

PAGES 1 Jesse Lee Monongya, Navajo, Hopi. 14k gold turtle,
reverse side (front cover and page 138), with diamonds.
Collection of Marcia Docter.
2–3 Lee A. Yazzie, Navajo. Sterling silver
belt buckles with Lone Mountain turquoise. Left, collection
of Hiroumi Imai; right, collection of Erik VanItallie.
4 Kee Yazzie Jr., Navajo. Sterling silver stamped vessel with
lid and coral. Courtesy of the artist.
5 Darryl Dean Begay, Navajo. Sterling
silver Clovis point bolo tie with Morenci, Ithaca Peak, and
Bisbee turquoise and Mediterranean coral. The bolo represents
the Protection Way, a Navajo ceremony. The designs on the tips
symbolize prayers. Collection of Donald and Noël Neely.

CONTENTS

Preface: The Southwest   6

Introduction: Modern Design Influences   10

CHAPTER 1

SILVER AND METALWORK   24

CHAPTER 2

LAPIDARY ART   96

CHAPTER 3

OBJECTS AND
SCULPTURAL JEWELRY   166

Notes   220

Glossary   225

Suggested Readings   230

Artists   232

Jewelry Sources   234

Acknowledgments   236

Index   238

THE SOUTHWEST

first visited New Mexico in the summer of 1965 to train for the Peace Corps. Over the course of the summer, we traveled to many of the Pueblos between Albuquerque and Taos to work in the health centers, and to attend a dance whenever time allowed. It would be ten years before I would return to New Mexico as director of a university conference on minority literature. In 1978, I made my third trip to New Mexico to interview Native American writers for my book *The Third Woman–Minority Women Writers of the United States*. They say three times is the charm, and it worked for me. For thirty years now, the Southwest has been my other home from wherever I've lived—California, New York, and now Colorado.

What is the Southwest? It's Indian Country—Arizona, New Mexico, southern Utah, and Colorado. It stretches into western Texas and southern California. The Southwest encompasses the Colorado Plateau and Mesa Verde. The Southwest is ancient. It has been home to the Anasazi, now called the Ancestral Pueblo people, who built astonishing villages and cliff dwellings in Mesa Verde over one thousand years ago. This region includes hundreds of petroglyph fields ranging in age from 300 to 2,500 years old, where different tribes recorded the events of their day. New Mexico's Chaco Culture, which flourished from the 800s to the 1100s, still baffles archaeologists with its massive stone buildings of multiple stories and its complex roadway system that connected prehistoric communities to each other.

The Southwest is also multicultural. Spain ruled from 1598 to 1821, followed by Mexico from 1821 to 1846. In 1846, the Mexican-American War began, and ended in 1848, when the United States took over the region. Throughout four centuries of European and American government, the Native American cultures of the Southwest have managed to survive, sustain their traditions, religions, ceremonies, and art.

Of the many tribes in the Southwest, the Navajo Nation is the largest with close to 300,000 members. Their reservation of approximately 27,000 square miles spans New Mexico, Arizona, and southern Utah. The Navajos call themselves *Diné*, which means *The People*. I have used the name *Navajo*, because it is more familiar to general readers.

The Pueblo tribes are defined by language group and have lived in permanent stone and adobe villages in the same location for hundreds of years. Known for their rich ceremonial life, the Pueblo cultures have excelled at pottery, weaving, and jewelry. The Spanish named the tribes *pueblos* after their word for town. There are nineteen Pueblos in New Mexico: Zuni, Acoma, and Laguna to the west; Isleta to the south of Albuquerque; and fifteen Pueblos that line the corridor of the Rio Grande River Valley: Jemez, Zia, Santa Ana, San Felipe, Cochiti, Santo Domingo, Nambe, Pojoaque

OPPOSITE: Cliffs near Ghost Ranch in Abiquiu, New Mexico.

Tesuque, Santa Clara, San Ildefonso, San Juan, Sandia, Picuris, and Taos. In 2005, San Juan Pueblo changed its name to its traditional name of Ohkay Owingeh. I have used the more recognizable name of San Juan Pueblo.

Arizona has twenty-one federally recognized Indian tribes, including the Hopi, who live on three mesas north of Flagstaff. Their village of Old Oraibi, located on Third Mesa, has been continuously inhabited since 1100 A.D. In addition to the Navajos and the Pueblo tribes, there are the Apaches: the Jicarilla and Mescalero of New Mexico, the Chiricahua of southern New Mexico and Arizona, and the western Apache bands in Arizona.

The Southwest is also where turquoise, the centerpiece of Southwestern Indian jewelry, is mined. Turquoise has been used in jewelry since prehistoric times and is revered by all of the Southwestern tribes for its beauty and religious significance. Turquoise is identified by the mine from which it comes. I have indicated when possible the type of turquoise used in a specific piece of jewelry. Nevada, New Mexico, Arizona, and Colorado have produced some of the world's most spectacular turquoise. Nevada is home to such legendary turquoise mines as Lone Mountain, Royston, Blue Gem, Lander Blue, No. 8, Fox, Indian Mountain, and Red Mountain. In Arizona, the famous mines include Kingman, Bisbee, Morenci, Castle Dome, and Sleeping Beauty. Colorado's well-known mines are King's Manassa, Leadville, Villa Grove, and Cripple Creek. And in New Mexico, the Cerrillos, Tyrone, Santa Rita, and Hachita mines have all produced turquoise appreciated by artists and collectors alike.

THE ENDURING ATTRACTION of Southwestern Indian jewelry is the glimpse it offers into other world views. Artists draw on their heritage for motifs that may range from the flora and fauna of the Southwest to designs taken from textiles and pottery to more esoteric concepts, such as *Kachinas*, the spirit intermediaries between the Hopi and their deities. Kachinas are part of the rich ceremonial life of the Hopis, and they are often portrayed in jewelry. Terms like Kachina are defined within the text, as well as in the glossary.

Many of the jewelers profiled here have won awards for their work at annual Indian market competitions. The Santa Fe Indian Market is the largest of the competitions in the Southwest, but it is mirrored on a smaller level by the Gallup Inter-Tribal Indian Ceremonial in Gallup, New Mexico; the Eight Northern Indian Pueblos Arts and Crafts Show held each year at a pueblo in northern New Mexico; the Heard Museum Guild Indian Fair and Market in Phoenix, Arizona; and the Museum of Northern Arizona's Annual Hopi, Navajo, and Zuni Festivals of Arts and Culture in Flagstaff, Arizona. In 1992, the Eiteljorg Museum of American Indians and Western Art launched its first Indian Market in Indianapolis and is now the largest Indian market in the Midwest. The various juried markets have become showcases for artists to demonstrate their best work; they have also sparked cross-cultural exchanges among artists, blurring the lines of tribal styles of jewelry. I mention key awards and fellowships that jewelers have won, because they represent a significant accomplishment on the part of the artist. Noteworthy regional Indian markets and galleries are listed in the Jewelry Sources on page 234.

Southwestern Indian Jewelry–Crafting New Traditions charts the evolution of contemporary jewelry from approximately 1970 to 2008. Of the eighty-eight featured jewelers from eighteen distinct tribes, twenty-eight appeared in my 1992 book *Southwestern Indian Jewelry*, and sixty artists are new. Predictably, it was impossible to carry everyone forward. Instead, I have included a handful of standard bearers, who are an integral part of the historical continuum of Southwestern Indian jewelry for their creativity, innovations, and craftsmanship. All of the outstanding jewelers who appeared in the first book are listed on page 232. Many

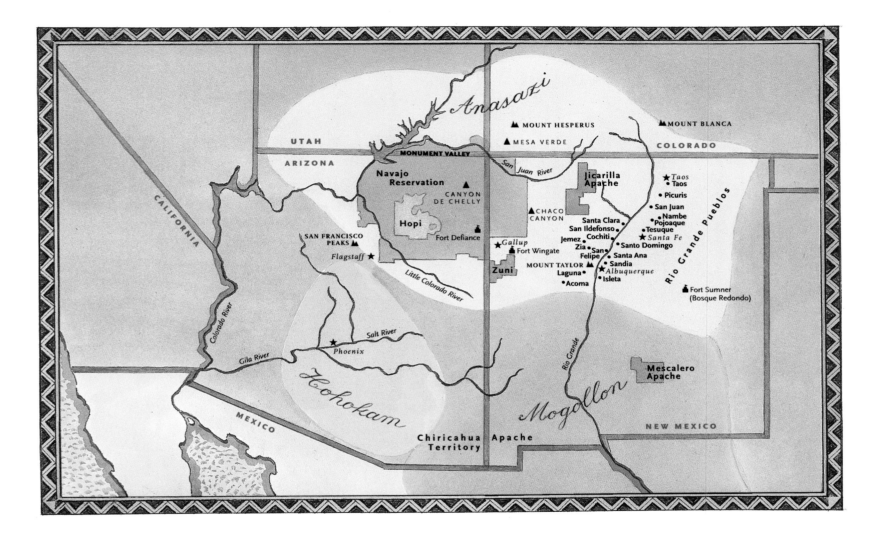

deserving jewelers could not be included because of space limitations. Their omission does not in any way reflect on their art or accomplishments.

It is impossible to look to the future without visiting the past. Each chapter provides a historical context for viewing the ongoing artistic achievements of contemporary Southwestern Indian jewelers. Throughout, artists speak about their creative processes, their inspirations, and their techniques. All of the personal statements, unless otherwise noted, have come from interviews I conducted with the artists in their studios, on the reservations, and wherever else we arranged to meet. Once again, it has been a privilege to observe and document how Southwestern Indian jewelers craft their traditions for the next generation.

Modern Design Influences

Att the Heard Museum Indian Market in March of 2006, Darryl Dean Begay, a young Navajo jeweler from Gallup, New Mexico, won several prizes for his jewelry, including one for a jewelry box entitled *Fathers of Inspiration*. That same summer, the box was awarded the Best in Category at the Gallup Inter-Tribal Indian Ceremonial in Gallup, New Mexico. "The box is a tribute to Charles Loloma and Kenneth Begay, who were the pioneers of modern contemporary Native American jewelry," Darryl Begay says.[1]

Charles Loloma graces one side of the round box, sporting sunglasses and an open shirt with the Hopi village of Old Oraibi and the San Francisco peaks in the background. On the other side of the jewelry box, Kenneth Begay is depicted as a traditional Navajo man in front of an ancestral home known as a *hogan*. The lid of the box has a cornstalk handle surrounded by the four sacred mountains of the Navajo.[2] On the interior of the box, Begay has carved a Hopi *kiva*, a ceremonial chamber, replete with murals. On the inside of the lid are images of jewelry by Loloma and Begay. Loloma is represented by the *Corn Maiden* pendant, the *Badger Paw* pin of his clan, and his famous height bracelet of stones inlaid at various angles, while Kenneth Begay's legacy is symbolized by the three-stone belt buckle with clean, elegant stampwork radiating out from the center—a style that would earn him the title, "Father of contemporary Navajo jewelry."

ABOVE and **OPPOSITE:** Darryl Dean Begay, Navajo. Sterling silver tufa-cast box with the following turquoise: Lone Mountain (top of lid and side), Easter blue and Morenci (inside), Godbur (bottom), Bisbee (in Badger paw), and Blue Gem (bottom of lid); also Mediterranean coral and opal. Private collection.

RiGHT: Kenneth Begay,
Navajo. Sterling silver necklace
with Bisbee turquoise.
Stamped KB. Collection of
Martha H. Struever.

OPPOSiTE: Kenneth Begay.
Sterling silver necklace
and bracelet with Morenci
turquoise, circa 1950s.
Chiseled design simulates
braiding. Private collection.

KENNETH BEGAY AND CHARLES LOLOMA are historic figures in Southwestern Indian jewelry as the founders of contemporary jewelry. In their respective ways, they influenced generations of jewelers to experiment with new materials, designs, and techniques. Both men were reared in traditional ways. Begay grew up on the Navajo Reservation under the tutelage of his father, a medicine man and practitioner of the Beauty Way Ceremony. Charles Loloma was a member of the Badger Clan at Hopi and participated throughout his life in ceremonies in his native village of Hotevilla.

Kenneth Begay began as a blacksmith, taking his first course in silversmithing from Fred Peshlakai at the

Fort Wingate Vocational School for Native Americans in Fort Wingate, New Mexico, in 1938. The program was part of a crafts initiative sponsored by the United States government to promote traditional techniques and good design to counteract the growing commercialization of Indian jewelry in the 1930s. Peshlakai was the son of Slender-Maker-of-Silver, one of the first Navajo silversmiths. In 1933, Peshlakai had demonstrated traditional Navajo silversmithing at the Chicago World's Fair, and it was those techniques that he taught at Fort Wingate. More than three decades later, in 1976, Kenneth Begay wrote, "We started learning with copper, filing, and chiseling—and then went on with silver. We used scrap silver and melted it down the old way at a forge and hammered it out into the shapes we needed. We learned to make our dies out of steel. . . . Fred Peshlakai taught us the old Navajo style that he learned from Slender-Maker-of-Silver. I like that style and still work in it."[3]

Though sheet silver was available to silversmiths by the 1930s, Peshlakai used ingot silver and coin silver in his own work into the 1950s. He also appears to have been one of the first silversmiths to sign his work, signaling the importance of the individual artisan. Peshlakai's approach resonated for Begay, who would teach traditional techniques of silversmithing to his own students from 1968 to 1973 at Navajo Community College in Many Farms, Arizona.

In 1946, Begay went to work with John Bonnell at the White Hogan shop in Flagstaff, Arizona, beginning an eighteen-year relationship. Bonnell was not a silversmith himself, but he had a keen sense of design and hired Navajo silversmiths to work for him making jewelry and objects that combined elegant shapes with Navajo stampwork. In 1950, Bonnell moved the White Hogan to Scottsdale, Arizona, and took Begay with him. "Begay received a regular salary and was allotted a percentage of company profits; this financial inducement allowed Begay the freedom to experiment with, and enhance, his artistic abilities. Such arrangements

soon became more common in the region and provided native silversmiths . . . with the means to advance economically and artistically."[4]

Bonnell's philosophy was bound to a single principle: Native jewelers should make jewelry with the same tools their predecessors had used fifty years earlier. Keep the jewelry simple, unfettered, and pure. He abhorred the popularization of non-native motifs of bows and arrows on tourist jewelry; similarly, he disliked the trend toward overly ornate designs that had begun to characterize Navajo jewelry in the 1930s and 1940s.[5] Kenneth Begay was a master metalsmith with a creative imagination strongly influenced by his traditional background. In Begay's jewelry, this translated into a balance between silver, stone, and bold but unpretentious designs. Begay introduced ironwood, a dark brown hardwood, into his jewelry in the 1950s. He also began signing his jewelry, still an unusual practice among silversmiths in the 1940s. "I began marking my jewelry in 1951 or 1952 using a KB as my mark," Begay wrote. "While I worked for the White Hogan, I stamped it with a small hogan."[6]

In collaboration with Bonnell, Begay made flatware sets, plates, boxes, goblets, ecclesiastical chalices, and vessels of various kinds, moving Indian jewelry beyond just personal adornment into the arena of pure metalsmithing. Despite his success with the White Hogan, Begay did not, however, like to draw attention to himself. "Kenneth didn't like to talk about himself to anyone. It was the way he was brought up as a Navajo," his son Harvey Begay recalls. "Don't draw attention to yourself. Don't stand out."[7]

Kenneth Begay's legacy is, perhaps, most enduring in the work of Harvey Begay. "I am definitely influenced by my father, but everything I know is not a direct continuation of Kenneth. I had to break away and do my own thing."[8] Over the last thirty-five years, Harvey Begay has created a body of work that blends tradition with modernism and exemplifies how beautiful pure design can be.

OPPOSITE: Harvey A. Begay, Navajo. Sterling silver bracelet and necklace with Lander Blue turquoise. The shell motif has been chiseled and filed. Private collection.

15

BELOW: Charles Loloma, Hopi. Sterling silver Corn Maiden pendants set with turquoise, coral, wood, fossilized ivory, gold, and lapis. Circa 1980. Courtesy of Wheelwright Museum of the American Indian, Santa Fe.

OPPOSITE: Charles Loloma. Sterling silver height bracelet and ring with mixed inlay and gold accents. Collection of Marcia Docter.

If Kenneth Begay shunned publicity, Charles Loloma found himself in an international limelight for most of his life. A muralist, painter, and ceramicist before becoming a jeweler, Loloma had a meteoric rise to fame the moment he stepped outside his village of Hotevilla on the Hopi Reservation in northern Arizona. He traveled to France, Spain, Italy, Egypt, Colombia, Peru, Japan, and Korea. Loloma studied ceramics at Alfred University in New York State. In 1962, he became the first director of plastic arts at the newly established Institute of American Indian Arts in Santa Fe, New Mexico.

Like Begay, Loloma benefited from seminal people in his life. He studied painting in high school with Fred Kabotie, a renowned Hopi painter. In his junior year in 1938, Loloma attended the Phoenix Indian School where he studied art with Lloyd Kiva New, a Cherokee artist and one of the founders and first director of arts at the Institute of American Indian Arts in Santa Fe. The next year, Loloma and New traveled together to San Francisco where Loloma had been selected to participate in a Native arts exhibit as part of the 1939 Golden Gate International Exposition. There Loloma met René d'Harnoncourt, acting director of the Federal Indian Arts and Crafts Board, who would arrange for Loloma's inclusion in the milestone exhibition, *Indian Art of the United States*, at the Museum of Modern Art in New York City in 1941.

Many years later, Loloma writes that he began working in silver: "I am not versed in the exact date that I started working in jewelry, but my guess is it was in 1947 when I was a student at Alfred University. I was working in pottery and silver."[9] Loloma moved to Scottsdale, Arizona, in the mid-1950s to become part of Lloyd Kiva New's recently developed Kiva Craft Center for artists and designers. Surrounded by a stimulating coterie of artists, including the architects Paolo Soleri and Frank Lloyd Wright, Loloma began making jewelry in earnest.

From all the avenues of his experience—his travels, the world of fine art, fashion, and architecture—Loloma gleaned ideas and found inspiration, translating those ideas through the vernacular of his Hopi culture. Loloma's greatest legacy for future generations was his sense of color and his use of different stones. He broke with the traditional pairing of silver and turquoise to incorporate myriad different stones and colors in his jewelry, opening the door to the contemporary era of Southwestern Indian jewelry. "I had formal design and color training at Alfred University, and you have to look at how materials fit together and balance each other," Loloma said. "I feel that I have to make each

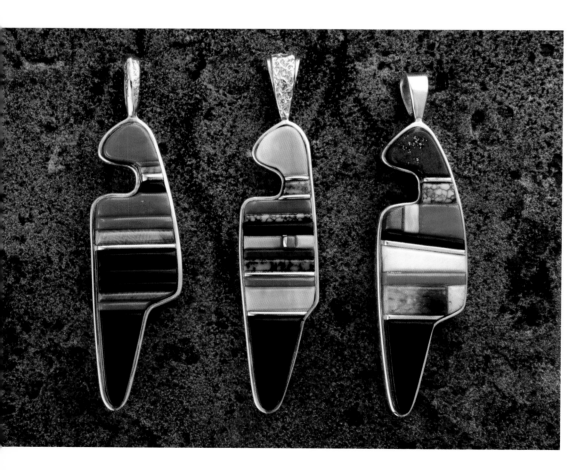

material interpret itself as richly as I can by the amount of that material that I use."[10]

With jewelry as his new palette, Loloma reflected the changing colors of the Southwest landscape with ironwood, lapis, coral, malachite, fossilized ivory, and turquoise. He created abstract Kachina faces in his bracelets and carved Corn Maidens as stylized female figures that he inlaid with stones. Loloma popularized the use of gold, and he inlaid the underside of bracelets and rings with brilliant colors to reflect his philosophy that inner beauty resides in everyone. Loloma introduced sculptural inlay into Southwestern Indian jewelry, placing stones at jagged right angles to their metal base to mirror the rugged topography of the Southwest. The name "Loloma" translates as "many beautiful colors." Throughout his career, Loloma made jewelry true to his name.

Georgia Loloma, his widow, reflected on his legacy in 2006: "As an artist he had the inspiration to follow his own dream of creating beautiful art. He will be remembered by those who knew him well as a man who was committed with devotion to his Hopi responsibility as an elder of the Badger clan. He was a genius of design with sensitivity to all the elements of his creations, and he had the inner strength to create his ideas. . . . he taught that real success is finding your own designs within yourself."[11]

BY THE MIDDLE OF THE 1970S, both Kenneth Begay and Charles Loloma were on the national radar screen. In April 1974, Jack Peterson produced a documentary on Loloma for public television, the first in a series he would do on American Indian artists. That August, *Arizona Highways* magazine published its now-famous Indian jewelry issue, charting the early history of Southwestern Indian jewelry and nominating contemporary Native American jewelers to its newly created Hall of Fame. This landmark issue included an essay and photographs by Jerry Jacka. "Joseph Stacey, the edi-

tor, had the foresight to represent Indian culture through its art. He literally opened the floodgates for *Arizona Highways* to do feature articles on Native American art," says Jacka.[12] Jacka would go on to photograph five complete issues of *Arizona Highways* and publish numerous articles for the magazine, becoming an authority on contemporary Southwestern Indian art in his own right.[13] "By 1977, I realized there was a real movement going on in contemporary jewelry, and I proposed the idea to *Arizona Highways*," Jacka said. The result was the April 1979 issue entitled "The New Look in Indian Jewelry." Using Hopi and Navajo models, Jacka photographed the "new" jewelry in the timeless landscape of Monument Valley, officially documenting that the contemporary period in jewelry inspired by Loloma and Begay had, indeed, come of age.

THE GENERATION OF JEWELERS following Kenneth Begay and Charles Loloma began their jewelry careers in the mid-1970s. Born after World War II, they inherited some of the mobility and educational opportunities the G.I. Bill had afforded their parents. The Civil Rights movement of the 1960s also increased opportunities for Native Americans to attend colleges and vocational schools, expanding their career opportunities and life experiences. When the post-World War II generation turned to jewelry, they were a bit older and brought a more sophisticated world view to their art. They have been making jewelry for over thirty years now, and their impact on the evolution of jewelry making is just now becoming apparent. Two such artists, who have introduced new design concepts into contemporary Southwestern Indian jewelry, are Yazzie Johnson, Navajo, and Gail Bird of Laguna Pueblo and Santo Domingo Pueblo heritage.

In February 2007, the Heard Museum in Phoenix mounted an exhibition entitled *Shared Images–The Jewelry of Yazzie Johnson and Gail Bird.* The only other time the Heard Museum had dedicated an exhibition to a single jeweler was in 1978, when it presented a retrospective of

Charles Loloma's jewelry. At the time of his show, Loloma was fifty-eight years old and internationally renowned. A generation later, in 2007, Johnson and Bird were similar in age to Loloma and had also worked for more than thirty years to create an original body of work that warranted a museum retrospective. *Shared Images* included forty-three of the thematic concha belts for which Johnson and Bird have become well known. Seen together for the first time, the belts were striking examples of a new direction in Southwestern Indian jewelry that Johnson and Bird inaugurated in 1981 when they won the Best of Show at the Santa Fe Indian Market for a concha belt entitled *Petroglyph Migration*. In place of the oval or round shape of traditional concha belts, each concha had a distinct asymmetrical shape. The

designs in the individual conchas were also varied and consisted of overlay figures, stampwork, and unusual stones. The belts represented conceptual works of art in which each part had been designed to support a given theme. The themes of the belts ranged from serious to humorous. Some belts were designed around southwestern art forms, such as their 1982 *Pottery Maker Belt,* or the *Basket Belt* created in 1983. Others, like the 1988 *Road Signs Belt* and the *Route 66/Tourism Belt* made in 1995, were more whimsical.

In 2006, Johnson and Bird designed a belt entitled *The Crawling and Flying Insects Belt,* or the *Heebie Jeebies Belt,* incorporating designs adopted from Mimbres pottery and southwest petroglyph motifs into the individual conchas. A microcosm of the insect world, there are snails in the first concha, a petroglyph centipede and worms formed by the coral in the second, and a butterfly in the third. Wasps, grasshoppers, caterpillars, worms, and more butterflies complete the other conchas. In some cases, the stones form the body of the insect. The techniques used to fabricate the belt include tufa casting, overlay, stampwork, appliqué, and awl work. The stones in the belt consist of jaspers, agates, Yowah and Boulder opals from Australia, palmwood, and petrified wood with accents of turquoise and coral.

Johnson and Bird first met each other in Utah in 1960. Johnson is Navajo, and Bird is Laguna Pueblo on her mother's side and Santo Domingo Pueblo on her father's side. Bird attended high school in California and studied at the University of California in Berkeley. Johnson went to Utah State University in Logan where he took his first courses in jewelry: classes in casting and in forming metal. In 1965, he joined the army for three years and served a tour in Vietnam. After the military, Johnson joined Bird in California and took his only other course in jewelry making, a metalsmithing course at San Francisco's California College of Arts and Crafts in 1969. Otherwise, Johnson is a completely self-taught jeweler.[14] In 1972, they both attended the University of Colorado in Boulder on scholarships, where Johnson pursued art and Bird took a liberal arts curriculum.

Bird designs the jewelry that Johnson fabricates. She makes dozens of sketches for each piece of jewelry before she arrives at a design they both agree upon. For his part, Johnson is an accomplished metalsmith, capable of portraying the flora and the fauna of the Southwest in meticulous detail through overlay or stamping. While they work primarily with pre-cut stones, Johnson does his own lapidary work when it is required to complete a design. Johnson and Bird have studied the prehistoric cultures of the Southwest, as well as the historic development of metalsmithing among the Navajos and the Pueblo cultures. Johnson keeps a notebook of pottery, textile, and petroglyph motifs that he has sketched to use in designs, many of which appear on the underside of buckles.

Since 1981, Johnson and Bird have produced at least one belt each year for the Santa Fe Indian Market that is a cumulative statement about experiences they have had that year, or that speaks to a specific theme they wish to explore. Some belts reflect personal experiences. Johnson and Bird are farmers when they are not jewelers. They live in rural New Mexico and actively farm five acres of land and tend to seventy fruit trees. No strangers to the animals that inhabit northern New Mexico, Bird designed a belt in 1996 with the lighthearted title, *The Game Refuge.* "That was the year a mountain lion wandered through our fields; a bear climbed a tree on the adjacent property; deer, elk, and skunks visited the cornfield and orchards; bats flew through the trees, and Yazzie stopped me from walking under a broken limb with three raccoons sleeping on top," Bird explains.[15] The belt depicts bear, elk, a bat, skunks, mountain lions, rabbits, deer, and crows. The stones selected evoke the actual habitats of the animals portrayed, either by their color or the natural patterns within the stone. Despite the asymmetrical shape of each concha and the multiple designs, the belt is unified by the monochromatic tones of the agates, jaspers, and opals.

In a catalogue essay for the 2002 exhibition, *Changing Hands: Art Without Reservation I* mounted by the American Craft Museum in New York City, Bird wrote, "In the 1960s and 1970s, Kenneth Begay and Charles Loloma concurrently broke away from stylistic Indian fashion—in Begay's case by simplifying and clarifying metalwork, and in Loloma's by incorporating new materials, which expanded the color range of his work, and by utilizing abstraction of shape, scale, and depth. Both set standards of creativity and excellence by respecting the past; both used that respect and knowledge to enlarge the scope of Indian jewelry."[17] Bird could as easily be describing the contribution she and Johnson have made to contemporary Southwestern Indian jewelry—that of moving jewelry from craft into art. Their legacy is evident in the multitude of stones that proliferate in Southwestern Indian jewelry and in the thoughtfulness jewelers give to their pieces. It has become a convention for an artist to formally name a piece of jewelry that has a personal or cultural theme. Also, it is a given that contemporary jewelers have mastered the technical challenges of metalsmithing and lapidary work. What is at their fingertips now is the challenge of crafting new traditions, which Johnson and Bird unconsciously did in 1981 when they initiated the next generation of excellence in Southwestern Indian jewelry.

WHAT IS SO CAPTIVATING about Southwestern Indian jewelry? For one, it is singularly beautiful. The many colors of turquoises, corals, greens, and purples are magical. Southwestern Indian jewelry is also authentic. In our post-modern age of instantaneous communication, there is something comforting about a piece of jewelry that has been handcrafted by labor-intensive hammering, filing, stamping, grinding, and polishing. There is an individual behind the process, who has thought about the way stones relate to each other and has created an artful design that causes us to look a second time. In that moment of reflection, we witness the transformation of tradition into art.

In 1981, a year after they received a fellowship from the Southwestern Association for Indian Arts, Johnson and Bird made their first pearl necklace, combining pearls with coral. This was another innovation in their jewelry, as they crossed the bridge into the arena of fine jewelry. "We were the first jewelers to make a point of trying to use quality pearls," Bird says.[16] Self-educated, Bird is adept at grading pearls and has bought multiple pearl strands, taking them apart and sorting the pearls for quality, size, and color. She and Johnson have chosen naturally colored unusual pearls for their jewelry: Japanese Biwa pearls when they were available, multi-shaped coin and keshi pearls, mabe and blister pearls, and striking South Sea and Tahitian pearls. Johnson and Bird have also introduced the use of small bezel-set stones, which they call satellites, to artfully enhance the color of the pearls, coral, onyx, or other stone beads they use for their necklaces.

CHAPTER 1

SILVER AND METALWORK

In June 2005, New Mexico state officials and leaders of the Navajo and Mescalero Apache tribes attended the inauguration of the Bosque Redondo Memorial at Fort Sumner State Monument in Fort Sumner, New Mexico. Like other war memorials, the Bosque Redondo Memorial is a somber reminder of a watershed event in Navajo history—the "Long Walk," when over eight thousand Navajos were removed from their ancestral homeland in the Four Corners area of the Southwest and forced to walk hundreds of miles across New Mexico to the Bosque Redondo Indian Reservation near Fort Sumner. The Navajos called Bosque Redondo *Hweéldi*, the place of suffering, and they were imprisoned there from 1864 to 1868. Almost 400 Mescalero Apaches were also imprisoned with the Navajos. Bosque Redondo, Spanish for 'a circle of trees,' signaled the end of decades of fierce conflicts, raiding, and war that had raged throughout the Southwest in the nineteenth century between Spanish and Mexican settlers and the Utes, Comanches, Apaches, and Navajos. Mexico had assumed power from the Spanish in 1821, the same year the Santa Fe Trail opened up commerce to the Southwest from the eastern United States.

Landscape seen from Third Mesa, Hopi Reservation, Arizona.

In 1846, the United States declared war on Mexico in a dispute over the Texas-Mexico border, starting the two-year Mexican-American war. On February 2nd, 1848, the United States signed a peace treaty with Mexico in the small town of Guadalupe Hidalgo, north of Mexico City. As a provision of the treaty, Mexico ceded fifty-five percent of its territory to the United States, including Arizona, California, New Mexico, and parts of Colorado, Nevada, and Utah. The Guadalupe-Hidalgo treaty also established the Texas-Mexican border along the Rio Grande River. Suddenly, the floodgates of westward expansion were thrown open

under the umbrella of Manifest Destiny, further exacerbating the cultural clashes among the region's inhabitants. In 1863, Kit Carson, a trapper, scout, Indian agent, and soldier, began a campaign against the Mescalero Apache in southern New Mexico, eventually moving more than 400 members of the tribe to Bosque Redondo. The next year, Carson launched his "scorch and burn" battle in the Navajo homeland, destroying crops, livestock, orchards, and homes in an effort to force the Navajos to surrender and be relocated to eastern New Mexico. By the end of that summer, close to 9,000 Navajos began the long walk to Fort Sumner on the

Bosque Redondo Indian Reservation, where they would be confined until June of 1868.

If Bosque Redondo represents a nadir in Navajo history, it also offers some of the first written records of Navajos working with silver. In his book *Navajo Silver*, published in 1938, Arthur Woodward cites several newspaper accounts from 1864 that mention the skills of some Navajo silversmiths: " . . . the warriors themselves fabricate saddles, and bridles, and buckles, buttons and clasps of silver which are tasteful ornaments to their finely fitting cloth and buckskin dresses."[1] Navajos also learned blacksmithing from the soldiers, a skill that allowed them to make counterfeit metal ration tokens. It would later help them make tools for silversmithing as well. In 1853, Captain Henry L. Dodge, the newly appointed Indian Agent for the Navajos, had arrived at Fort Defiance, Arizona, with a blacksmith and a silversmith on his staff, who most probably demonstrated their crafts to the Navajos.

Atsidi Sani was the first acknowledged Navajo silversmith. Between 1853 and 1858, Sani (the Old Smith) was said to have learned blacksmithing from a Mexican blacksmith. Most of the oral histories state that he learned to work in silver after Bosque Redondo.[2] Sani would teach the craft to several of his sons and his younger brother, Slender-Maker-of-Silver, who also learned from Atsidi Chon (Ugly Smith). Chon was also mentioned in the oral histories as the person who taught silversmithing to Lanyade, the first Zuni, in the early 1870s. Lanyade in turn taught the craft to a Hopi man named Sikyatala in the late 1890s. By the beginning of the twentieth century, only three decades after Bosque Redondo, silverwork had spread throughout the tribes of the Southwest.

In 1868, the Navajos were released from Bosque Redondo by the U.S. Army and began their journey back to their homeland in the Four Corners region, their numbers spanning more than ten miles. (The Mescalero Apache, who had voluntarily surrendered and never felt they were captives at Bosque Redondo, had slipped out one night and returned to their lands in southern New Mexico in 1865.) A rare photograph of Slender-Maker-of-Silver shows him wearing a military jacket, most probably given to him at Bosque Redondo. The year 1868 also marked the beginning of silverwork as a Navajo art form. First Phase jewelry lasted from 1868 to 1900 and was characterized by uncomplicated designs on a field of silver. These designs reflected the rudimentary tools of the time: cold chisels and files for stamping, incising, and rocker engraving.

In 1885, Slender-Maker-of-Silver, also known as Peshlakai (which means silversmith), posed for the famous photograph by Ben Wittick, holding his jewelry: a concha belt, a horse bridle, and a silver-bead necklace with a naja pendant. As ubiquitous as this photograph is in the histories

LEFT: Peshlakai, Navajo, at twenty-eight years of age. Courtesy of National Museum of the American Indian, Smithsonian Institution, Washington, D.C.

Navajo Silver Smith

of Southwestern Indian jewelry, it illustrates the pristine quality of First Phase silver jewelry. In 1893, Peshlakai traveled to the Chicago World's Fair to demonstrate and sell his silverwork, which was already in high demand. A respected leader of the Navajos, Peshlakai was the grandfather of Carl Gorman and the great grandfather of R. C. Gorman, two eminent and internationally known Navajo artists of the twentieth century. Slender-Maker-of-Silver had three wives, all sisters, and nineteen children, including Fred Peshlakai, who would become well-known as a silversmith in his own right and as Kenneth Begay's first instructor.[3] By 1900, Peshlakai "had as many as ten Navajo assistants working for him in Crystal [New Mexico], melting and pouring silver, and pounding out Mexican silver coins, all crowded into the long stone barn that he had converted into a factory. In addition to the silver bead or squash blossom necklaces, bracelets, rings, and concha belts, Peshlakai was called upon to make more difficult objects than most other silversmiths attempted: ornate canteens, complete bridles, intricate unconventional necklaces—all of silver, with no turquoise used."[4] A pioneer of Navajo silverwork, Slender-Maker-of-Silver died in 1916.

The soldiers, who were stationed at Fort Wingate and Fort Defiance to maintain the peace after Bosque Redondo, provided coins to the Navajos to use for silver. They also commissioned the silversmiths to make tobacco canteens out of the coin silver as mementos of their tour in the Southwest. The silversmiths melted the coins into ingot bars, or slugs of silver. The silver was then hammered into thinner sheets so jewelry could be made. They also hammered coins flat to serve as buttons, which were attached in long rows to the sides of their pants and to their bandolier bags, after the Mexican style of the day. During Bosque Redondo, Navajo women were encouraged to wear full skirts and short blouses, which they decorated with silver coin buttons. When the U.S. government passed a law in

1890 prohibiting the disfigurement of coins, the Navajos switched to Mexican pesos, which they used for another thirty years. Sheet silver would not be widely available to silversmiths through the traders until the late 1920s.

In the twenty-first century, there are a number of Southwestern Indian silversmiths who make jewelry in the *revival style*.[5] Inspired by First Phase silverwork, the *revivalists* consciously strive to preserve and perpetuate the designs and techniques of their predecessors. They utilize the same methods of making jewelry as the early silversmiths, and they base their designs on historic pieces, creating traditional jewelry that evokes a bygone era. Cippy CrazyHorse, Mike Bird-Romero, and McKee Platero are three accomplished silversmiths who exemplify the enduring attraction of the revival style. For more than thirty years, they have each sustained a level of excellence and consistency in their jewelry that has become a touchstone for the new generation of silversmiths.

CrazyHorse did not turn to silversmithing until he was twenty-eight years old. Prior to that, he had attended college at Eastern New Mexico University, served in the Navy, and worked as an electrician's assistant on the Cochiti Dam Construction Project. In 1974, he had an accident while working on the dam that left him without a job and opened the door for him to become a silversmith. In 1975, he formally changed his name from Quintana to CrazyHorse. Although he is primarily self-taught, CrazyHorse grew up observing the jewelry collaboration of his parents, Terecita and Joe H. Quintana. "My mother would design pieces for my father to make, and she would hold him to the design," CrazyHorse recalls with a chuckle.[6]

Joe H. Quintana, who died in 1991, was one of five silversmiths working at Cochiti Pueblo when John Adair published *The Navajo and Pueblo Silversmiths* in 1944. Among many styles of jewelry he made, Quintana was noted for his *ketohs*, or bowguards, wrist guards worn to protect against

OPPOSITE: Slender-Maker-of-Silver, circa 1885. Photograph by Ben Wittick. Courtesy of Palace of the Governors.

BELOW: Narbona Primero, sub-chief of the western Navajo, 1874. Courtesy of Palace of the Governors.

LEFT: Clyde Peshlakai's family, circa 1948. Courtesy of Palace of the Governors.

the snap of a bowstring. Ketohs typically have a decorated silver plaque attached to a leather band that goes around the wrist. A shipyard welder during World War II, Quintana transferred his skills in metalworking to silversmithing when he returned home to Cochiti Pueblo. After World War II, Pueblo silversmiths did benchwork for production companies in Santa Fe and Albuquerque, making Indian jewelry for the tourist trade. Irma Bailey, one of Quintana's employers, writes, "In 1966, he became the number one silversmith in my new shop on the Old Town Plaza in Albuquerque, 'Irma's Indian Arts & Pawn.'"[7] During the five years Quintana worked for Bailey, from 1966 to 1971, he was free to create his own jewelry from silver and stones made available to him. "Joe had the green light. He worked on his own and did whatever he wanted," CrazyHorse states. Although Bailey closed her shop in 1971, she continued to support Quintana, collecting more than 600 pieces of his work, 100 of which constituted the retrospective exhibition, *Joe H. Quintana, Master in Metal: Selections from the Irma Bailey Collection,*

mounted by Santa Fe's Museum of Indian Arts and Culture in 2004. The exhibit affirmed Quintana's place in the history of southwestern silver jewelry.

Like his father, CrazyHorse has become a standard-bearer for "Pueblo style" jewelry, which he defines as less decorated than its Navajo counterpart. He melts scrap silver to cast his ingots, and he makes many of his own dies and stamps. His work is characterized by simple, bold designs that he chisels into the silver. A very traditional man—he served as Governor of Cochiti Pueblo in 2006—CrazyHorse models his jewelry after the style of the early Navajo and Pueblo silversmiths. He domes out the shape of the conchas by hammering the silver into a concave hole in a log stump. He stamps and chisels repeating designs onto the perimeter of each concha, leaving the center of each medallion either plain or decorated with a single design. He uses repoussé for the raised curved pattern on the buckle of his concha belt. CrazyHorse calls the design a 'moustache' design because it resembles a moustache.

OPPOSITE: Joe H. Quintana, Cochiti Pueblo. Sterling silver bowguards. Collection of Liss and Radcliffe.

navajo canteens

Cody Sanderson, a metalsmith of Navajo, Hopi, Pima, and Nambe descent, updates the traditional Navajo canteen style by adding repoussé rivets that are reminiscent of World War I army tanks. He creates a central flower motif out of curved repoussé corn leaves—a design that was popular on early Navajo ketohs or bowguards. Kenneth Begay also popularized the corn leaf design in his jewelry. Repoussé is a technique of creating a raised design by hammering the metal from the opposite side. In 2007, the National Museum of the American Indian, Smithsonian Institution, named Sanderson a visiting artist as part of their Native Arts Program.

Collection of Sam and Judy Kovler.

LEFT: Cippy CrazyHorse, Cochiti Pueblo. Sterling silver crosses. Courtesy of the artist.

RIGHT: Cippy CrazyHorse. Brass and sterling silver concha belts. Courtesy of the artist.

The brass concha belt by CrazyHorse dates from the mid-1970s and is a clear nod to the historical antecedents of silverwork. Adair cites evidence that the Navajos and Zunis were making objects from brass and copper as early as the mid-1830s. They procured the materials by melting down pots and pans most probably obtained through trade with the Mexicans and the Plains Indians. With the arrival of traders to the American Southwest, brass and copper wire became accessible to Native artisans, who would manipulate the metals into simple bracelets and earrings. Another source for brass came from ammunition shells. According to Paula Baxter and Allison Bird-Romero, "the first Hopi metalsmiths used brass cartridge cases or discarded scraps to make both tools and decorations."[8]

Mike Bird-Romero, a silversmith from San Juan Pueblo (also known officially as Ohkay Owingeh since 2005), has been recognized for his original interpretations of classic designs. "I try to uphold the traditional way of making jewelry, because it's important not to lose the process," Bird-Romero states. "People today don't understand how much goes into the old style."[9] Of Taos Pueblo heritage on his father's side, Bird-Romero grew up at San Juan Pueblo in a family of artists. Luteria Atencio, his grandmother, was a distinguished potter, and his mother, Lorencita Bird, was a respected authority on Pueblo-style weaving and embroidery. As a child, Bird-Romero became interested in jewelry by watching established silversmiths Julian Lovato, Mark Chee, and Anthony Duran work. The three silversmiths were from, respectively, the Santo Domingo Pueblo, Navajo, and Picuris Pueblo tribes, but all three had married women from San Juan Pueblo and lived there during Bird-Romero's youth. "I knew their kids and played with them," Bird-Romero recalls. "After a while, I began to watch their fathers making jewelry. Julian Lovato taught me that the key to everything is heat. If you know how to control the heat [from soldering], you can do anything."

One of Bird-Romero's signature styles is the multiple-band bracelet in which he fabricates individual bangles of plain silver or multiple silver drops and then joins them together in a process called sweating, soldering one element at a time to the next. The number of bangles is determined by the center stone. The abalone bracelet, for example, is a nine-row design, while the dinosaur bone with Royston turquoise dictates an eleven-row design.

A collector of high-grade turquoise, Bird-Romero credits Teal McKibbon, a Santa Fe art dealer and collector, with sparking his love for good stones. "She hired me in the mid-1970s to repair historic jewelry that museums would bring her," he says. "I started a collection then of what I call 'shoebox' turquoise, big old stones that matched the museum pieces, but that we couldn't necessarily identify." Such a stone is the centerpiece of the arrow pin, inspired by early twentieth-century tourist jewelry.

Bird-Romero also made traditional concha belts for McKibbon in the late 1970s that she sold to Ralph Lauren. "Teal always wore real traditional jewelry and lots of it," he says. "One day, Ralph Lauren saw her and followed her across the street, asking where she got her jewelry. After that, a bunch of us worked for her to make jewelry for the Ralph Lauren stores, including Cippy CrazyHorse and McKee Platero. That whole 'Santa Fe' look came from Teal." In 2002, the Indian Arts Research Center of the School of American Research (SAR) awarded Bird-Romero a prestigious King Fellowship. After his fellowship, Bird-Romero made a pair of spurs that he donated to SAR's collection for future generations of jewelers to study.

Like CrazyHorse and Bird-Romero, McKee Platero crafts jewelry that has its roots in historical silversmithing. Platero comes from a long line of traditional Navajo silversmiths, who cast their silver in ingot bars and were known for their deep stampwork. "They all did cast and stampwork," Platero says. "My grandfather, Anastascio Luna, worked for

OPPOSITE: Mike Bird-Romero, San Juan Pueblo, Taos Pueblo. Sterling silver bracelets and pins. Stones in bracelets, clockwise (from top left): dinosaur bone and Royston turquoise; Lander Blue turquoise; and abalone shell. Stones in pins (left to right): an unidentified piece of turquoise; and Persian turquoise. Collection of Allison and Mike Bird-Romero.

C. G. Wallace in the 1920s and 1930s. He didn't sign any of his pieces unfortunately. All of the great masters are gone."[10] Platero is known for his use of rocker engraving as a decorative element on his jewelry. Rocker engraving is a painstaking process of moving a chisel back and forth across metal to produce a design. The First Phase silversmiths used rocker engraving to embellish silver in the absence of more sophisticated tools. For Platero, silversmithing is also about working with reflected light. A trained painter, he studied painting with friends and took courses at Navajo Community College (now Diné Community College) in the 1970s. He uses stamping, incising, and rocker engraving to create different planes in the surface of the silver to catch fields of light.

While Platero's bracelets look "traditional" at first glance, he is noted for his unique and often humorous designs. An avid gardener, Platero incorporates images of various insects into his jewelry, stating simply, "My jewelry reflects my garden. Insects are the true owners of the world. They were the first to arrive. Man was the last to arrive. We are still of the earth, and we have to take care of the natural world. We must return to exalting the earth."[11] Underlying Platero's use of images from nature, which may appear whimsical on the surface, is his deep understanding of Navajo religious and cultural beliefs. In *Diné bahanè—The Navajo Creation Story*, as translated by Paul Zolbrod, insects were the first inhabitants of the first world and were called "the Air-Spirit People. . . . For they are people unlike the five-fingered earth-surface people who come into the world today, live on the ground for a while, die at a ripe old age, and then leave the world. They are people who travel in the air and fly swiftly like the wind and dwell nowhere else but here."[12]

A traditional Navajo, Platero says, "Making jewelry is a profound experience, because you are exalting nature." Platero signs his jewelry with three dots to represent Orion's Belt. "I saw the constellation as a child. It has always been there, and its permanence is beyond humanity." Platero has

the same reverence for turquoise, which he describes as "a piece of the sky." Unlike many contemporary artists, Platero rarely participates in Indian markets, and he does not enter his jewelry in competitions.

Perry Shorty, a Navajo from Shiprock, New Mexico, is one of the younger generation of silversmiths working in the revival style. He has made a conscious effort to go back and craft jewelry, using the techniques and materials employed by early Navajo silversmiths. He says, "I have to admire the first silversmiths' ability to fabricate jewelry with

OPPOSITE: McKee Platero, Navajo. Sterling silver bracelets with repoussé and stamped designs. Collection of Martha H. Struever.

ABOVE: McKee Platero in his studio, outside of Gallup, New Mexico.

OPPOSITE: Perry Shorty, Navajo, in his studio, Shiprock, New Mexico. Shorty pours melted coin silver into an ingot mold.

TOP RIGHT: Perry Shorty. Coin silver bracelets. Stones in bracelets: Blue Gem turquoise (left and center) and Royston turquoise (right). Courtesy of the artist.

BOTTOM RIGHT: Perry Shorty. Coin silver bracelets. Courtesy of the artist.

what little they had."[13] Shorty makes his jewelry from coin silver, utilizing coins that were designed by Charles Barber, the sixth chief engraver of the U.S. Mint from 1879 to 1917. Barber executed many designs over his career, the most famous, perhaps, being the Liberty Head nickel. "Coins remain in circulation for only about twenty-five years," Shorty points outs. "I like 'slickers.' These are coins that have been worn smooth by use."

While millions of Barber coins were in circulation at the beginning of the twentieth century, Shorty admits it is a challenge to find them more than one hundred years later. When he does, with the help of friends who scout antique shows across the country, he melts the coins down and pours them into an ingot mold and then hammers the bar into a sheet of silver. A bracelet may take twelve to fifteen 50-cent coins. These coins are 90 percent silver and 10 percent copper. As a comparison, sterling silver is an alloy of 92.5 percent silver and 7.5 percent copper. The higher copper content of the coin silver jewelry deepens the color of the silver. Shorty says, "I try to study and look at a lot of old jewelry. I like to touch it and get a feel for it. Every piece I make will include a traditional design. The difference is I've been able to refine my techniques and improve the look." The style of Shorty's jewelry is evocative of Navajo jewelry from the 1930s and 1940s with its combination of repoussé, stampwork, appliqué, and twisted wire motifs. Shorty is well-known for his deep stamp and file work achieved with stamps and tools he makes himself. He uses twisted wire to set off the central Blue Gem turquoise stone in his bracelet that is perfectly matched to the other stones.

Shorty began making jewelry by helping his mother, who was unemployed and needed to make money to support six children. He recalls, "It was the 1970s, and jewelry was big. I was nine or ten at the time. When she got a job, she quit making jewelry." In 1986, when Shorty turned back to jewelry, his mother still had her tools, which she passed on to

him. From 1986 to 1990, Shorty worked at the Thunderbird Supply Company in Gallup, New Mexico, selling supplies to jewelers and asking them about their work. "I would have asked more questions, if I knew what I know now," he says. Shorty learned silversmithing by trial and error, and was encouraged by his father-in-law, Bill Malone, who ran the historic Hubbell Trading Post in Ganado, Arizona, for many years. "Bill helped me set prices, and he always bought pieces for the trading post." Malone also introduced Shorty's work to art dealers and museums. At Hubbell Trading Post, Shorty met Raymond Yazzie through his wife Colina, who worked there. Yazzie is a well-known Navajo jeweler, celebrated for his fine inlaid jewelry (see Chapter Two). "Raymond taught me how to cut and grind stones," Shorty says.

In 1990, Shorty quit his job at Thunderbird and entered his jewelry at the Gallup Ceremonial. Christopher Cates, a jewelry dealer from Albuquerque, bought everything Shorty had made for the show and would buy seventy percent of Shorty's work over the next three years. Shorty entered his first Heard Museum Indian Market in 1991 and his first Santa Fe Indian Market in 1993. In 1994, he received a fellowship from the Southwestern Association for Indian Arts. "By Sunday of my first Indian Market in 1993, I had only sold two or three small pieces," he recalls. "Gail Bird and Marti Struever came over to see my work. Marti bought a necklace and Gail ordered one. Marti also invited me to do a show with her in Chicago." Martha Hopkins Struever—a Santa Fe art dealer, collector, author, and former owner of the Indian Tree Gallery in Chicago from 1976 to 1983—has been running Indian Art Travel Seminars for close to thirty years, taking collectors to remote areas in Arizona and New Mexico to visit the studios of Native American artists. She began the program in 1979 from her gallery, and she has been instrumental in educating collectors about the history and process behind Native American jewelry, pottery, and weaving. Struever invited Shorty to present a demonstration

of his jewelry making for her seminar participants, which he has done now for over a decade. "Marti opened the door for me," Shorty says. A man of devout faith and Pastor of The Door Church in Shiprock since 2002, Shorty is very modest about the attention he has received from an international clientele. "I never expected to be at this place," he says. "I owe God all the credit for whatever ability I have to do what I do."

WHILE NAVAJO SILVERSMITHS appear to have been few in number before Bosque Redondo, the Navajos had a long history of trading with the Spanish and the Mexicans for brass, copper, and silver adornments. The long Spanish presence in the Southwest, inaugurated by Juan de Oñate's *entrada* into New Mexico in 1598, was well-established by the middle of the nineteenth century. Because of their isolation from the centers of commerce and culture in Spain and then Mexico, the Spanish colonists had become self-sustaining, depending upon their own resources to make the goods they needed for survival. They crafted their own furniture and religious objects for home altars, which they decorated with emblems from their Spanish heritage: pomegranate and floral motifs, rosettes, and crescent shapes—designs originally of Moorish heritage that had become part of the Spanish aesthetic during the almost 800-year Moorish occupation of Spain, lasting from circa 711 to 1492. Mexican blacksmiths made the stamps that leatherworkers, *plateros* (silver workers), and tin smiths utilized to decorate their objects, and they were, most probably, the ones who taught the Navajos to make their own stamps.

Many of the designs that the early Navajo silversmiths adapted from Mexican leatherwork and silverwork have endured to the present. They include scalloped edges, embossed rosettes and leaf motifs, crescent shapes, and punched holes—patterns that have adorned concha belts for over a century. The history of the concha (Spanish for shell)

the Mexican period. In the eighteenth and nineteenth centuries, both Spanish and Mexican men wore trousers and jackets adorned with pomegranate-shaped silver beads, which the Navajos integrated into the squash blossom necklace. Similarly, they adapted the half-crescent *naja,* which was a protective talisman originally attached to the bridle of a horse, into a pendant suspended from the beads.[15]

At the height of its popularity in the 1970s, the squash blossom necklace was synonymous with Southwestern Indian jewelry. Allison Lee, a Navajo silversmith, recalls that he started making jewelry at age fourteen, helping his mother make squash blossom necklaces during the boom in Indian jewelry.[16] Even though the style began to fall out of vogue by the late 1980s, Lee continued making squash blossom necklaces. He has won numerous awards at the Santa Fe Indian Market for his creativity within a traditional form, including the use of 14k gold in place of silver. For Lee, the squash blossom necklace represents family. "The blossoms on either side are the offspring, and the naja symbolizes a family hugging. The crescent shape is like arms coming out to embrace the family."

As a classic Navajo style, the squash blossom necklace has been variously interpreted. Vernon Haskie substitutes ten prayer sticks for squash blossoms and a fabricated Navajo dancer for the naja in his 18k gold necklace. Haskie states that the inspiration for the necklace came from a Fire Dance he attended at a winter Navajo healing ceremony. "I saw two girls dancing toward each other back and forth, while a little boy was drumming on a wedding basket turned upside down. The girls each had rattles, which the doll depicts."[17] The miniature dancer wears a traditional squash blossom necklace and a not-so-traditional diamond concha belt and carries dance rattles inlaid with turquoise. Her hair is pure 18k yellow gold, and her face is 18k white gold. The title of the necklace is *Keeping My Culture, Tradition, and Language Alive.*

can be traced back to the eighteenth century when fur traders introduced European brooches through trade to American Indian tribes in the East. The fur traders later carried the round and oval brooches west to trade with the Plains Indians, who in turn adapted the shape to oval disks they attached to a leather strip to adorn their hair. The Navajos further transformed the style into a concha belt worn around the waist.[14]

Before the Southwest became an American territory in 1848, Spain ruled the region from 1598 to 1821, followed by Mexico from 1821 to 1846. Spanish styles carried over into

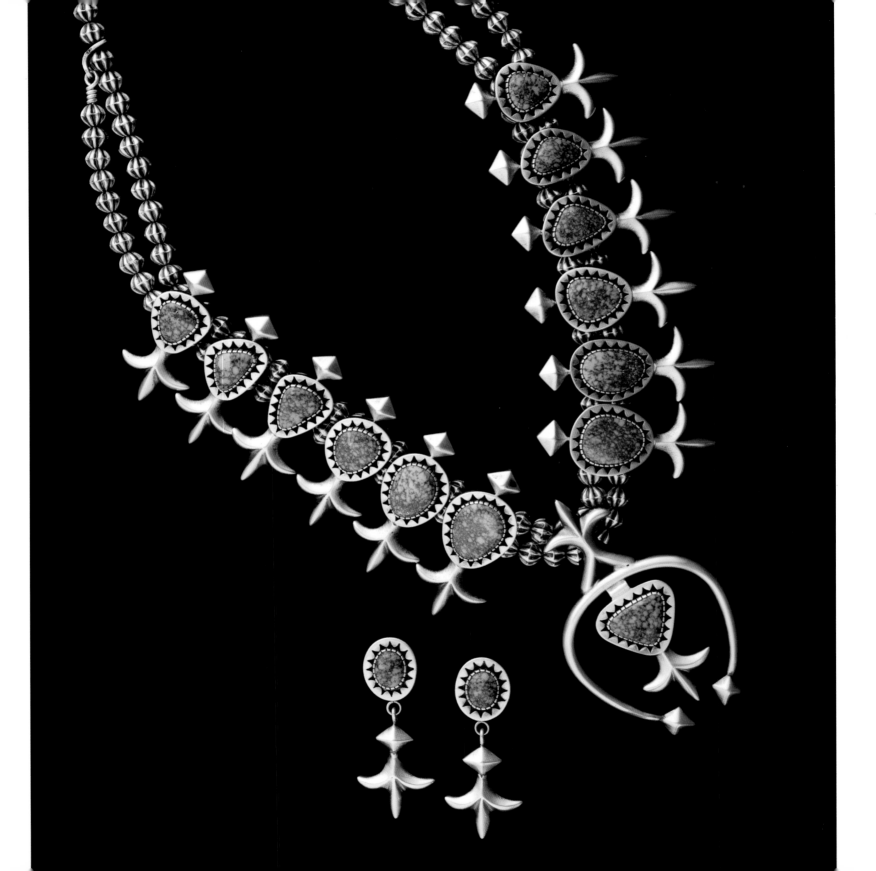

LEFT: Allison Lee, Navajo. Sterling silver squash blossom necklace with natural Lone Mountain turquoise from the Turquoise Museum, Albuquerque, New Mexico. The pomegranate pendants are attached to a double row of sterling silver stamped beads. Courtesy of the artist.

RIGHT: Vernon Haskie, Navajo. *Keeping My Culture, Tradition, and Language Alive.* 18k yellow and white gold necklace with turquoise, coral, and diamonds. Courtesy of the artist.

TEXTILE DESIGN

Navajo jeweler Benson Manygoats creates a necklace with a miniature Navajo loom as the pendant. Entitled *Grandmother's Love and Joy*, the loom has a reversible textile design and is complete with a batten and a spindle whorl for the yarn. A small ladybug crawls up the side of the loom. As a child, Manygoats spent summers with his grandparents in the Chuska Mountains, where he would observe his grandmother weaving outdoors on a traditional loom. The necklace won the 2007 Best of Jewelry award at the Heard Museum Indian Market in Phoenix. Fabricated in 14k gold, the loom pendant and beads are inlaid with turquoise, coral, lapis, sugilite, jet, and mother-of-pearl.

Below: Navajo women weaving, spinning, and carding in Monument Valley. Courtesy of Palace of the Governors. Right: Courtesy of the artist.

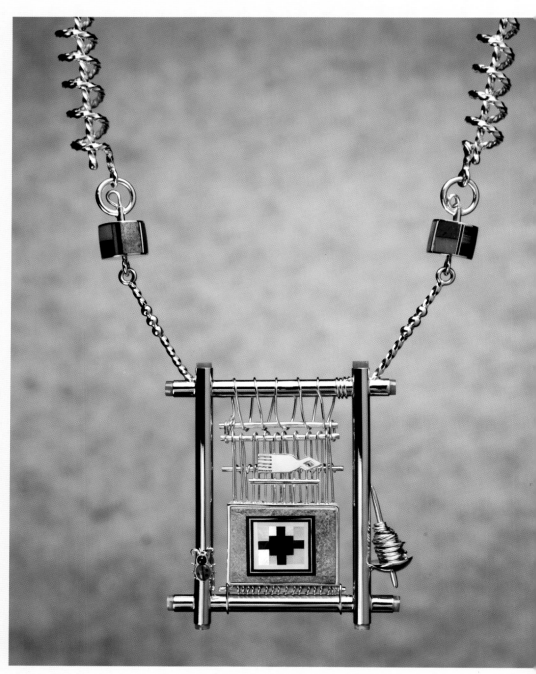

BOSQUE REDONDO ALSO MARKS the official beginning of trading posts in the Southwest. After their release in 1868, the Navajos walked more than three hundred miles from Bosque Redondo back to a reservation established by treaty with the U.S. government. *Diné Bikéyah*, or the Navajo homeland, is approximately 27,000 square miles and spans part of northeastern Arizona, northwestern New Mexico, and southern Utah. "Trading posts in the Southwest were offspring of the reservation system," according to Frank McNitt. "These small unfortified stores replaced the old trading forts after warring or nomadic tribes were confined, with more or less success, within reservation boundaries. No one planned it that way; the posts were a logical answer to a felt need."[18]

By the 1880s and 1890s, trading posts were springing up across the Navajo reservation, located in remote areas where goods were unavailable to the local population. Trading posts served as the local general store, post office, and bank. From single wagons to tents to permanent buildings, trading posts were the nucleus for business and social interactions. The arrival of the railroad to the Southwest in the 1880s spurred a new market for Native arts and crafts, expanding the role of the trader to art consultant.

The history of the early traders on the Navajo Reservation has been well documented. Famous traders, such as Juan Lorenzo Hubbell, C. N. Cotton, and J. B. Moore, conjure up a romantic past in the West. Their names are synonymous with such colorful places as the Hubbell Trading Post in Ganado, Arizona, that was named a National Historic Site by the U.S. Park Service in 1967. Hubbell, Cotton, and Moore have earned their places in history through their influence on the evolution of Navajo weaving, an art form that has contributed many design motifs to Southwestern Indian jewelry.

Moore and Hubbell set the stage for twentieth century trader/artist relationships by their intimate interaction with Navajo weavers and their profound impact on the direction of Navajo weaving. Moore and Hubbell influenced design

by providing weavers with patterns to incorporate in their blankets and rugs. Moore, who ran the trading post in Crystal, New Mexico, favored motifs from Oriental rugs popular in the first decade of the twentieth century. He introduced diamonds, crosses, terrace designs, and arrows within borders into Navajo weaving. Moore was the first trader to publish a mail-order catalogue to market the weavings in the East. He also controlled the quality of the wool by having it cleaned and processed in the East.

Hubbell commissioned drawings of early Navajo blanket styles for weavers to reproduce. Paintings and drawings by E. A. Burbank and other artists of the time can still be found on display at the Hubbell Trading Post. The art depicts classic banded styles and striking crosses against a deep red background known as Ganado red. Considered a "traditional" Navajo style today, the Hubbell Ganado textile

ABOVE: Hubbell's Trading Post, Ganado, Arizona. Lorenzo Hubbell is seated in the center. Photograph by Ben Wittick. Courtesy of Palace of the Governors.

was instantly popular among tourists, who bought them at the Fred Harvey shops along the Santa Fe Railroad route. By the beginning of the twentieth century, the American trader was intrinsically involved in the evolution of Native American art by dictating designs, providing materials, and creating an audience for the art.

Hubbell and C. N. Cotton were among the first traders to see the commercial possibilities of silverwork. Cotton arranged for a Mexican silversmith named "Thick Lipped Mexican . . . living at Cubero, to move to Ganado and, with other silversmiths brought from Mexico, to teach the craft to men in the Ganado region," according to Frank McNitt.[19] J. B. Moore added silverwork to his mail-order catalogue around 1906, listing concha belts, bracelets, horse bridles, and squash blossom necklaces for sale, though apparently he did not enjoy much success and dropped silverwork in his 1911 catalogue.

To silversmiths, traders supplied tools that previously had been unavailable—rolling machines, fine pliers, emery wheels, and lapidary sticks. Improved tools and materials spurred the new art of silverwork to develop quickly and to become a source of income for both the silversmith and the trader. As more and more tourists ventured west by train, the market for authentic Native American crafts and souvenirs burgeoned, further sealing the symbiotic relationship between trader and artisan.

In the early twentieth century, Southwest traders were the lifeline to the outside world. They supplied artists with

ZUNI CLUSTER WORK

Although Jennie Vicenti did not enter her first Indian Market until 1996—the year she and her husband, Ed Vicenti, moved back to Zuni—she has been making jewelry for over thirty years. Vicenti learned by observing her parents, Anita and Buddy Hattie. She has become well-known for her needlepoint, petitpoint, and cluster-style jewelry. After high school, the Vicenti's left Zuni to further their education. Ed Vicenti received a degree in electronics from Arizona State University in 1968 and worked for IBM for twenty-eight years, while Jennie Vicenti pursued a career in nursing. Since their return to Zuni, Ed Vicenti has made a lifetime commitment to serve as Head *Kachina* Priest for the tribe.[23] Well-known for her cluster-style jewelry of domed-shaped stones placed in contemporary silver settings, Jennie has received many awards, including the 1997 Centennial Award from the Arizona State Museum in Tucson. Like many contemporary jewelers at Zuni, the couple often collaborate, signing both their names on the jewelry. The earrings are set (from top) with Sleeping Beauty turquoise, coral, and Demali turquoise.

Courtesy of the artist.

tools and raw materials, and they sold the finished products. Traders influenced the designs. They also established the pawn system, where an individual could leave his jewelry as security against his purchases.[20] C. G. Wallace was one such trader, who transformed jewelry making at Zuni Pueblo in the first half of the twentieth century.[21] Wallace arrived at Zuni Pueblo in 1918 to find only a handful of silversmiths producing Navajo-style jewelry. Over fifty years later, there were hundreds of Zuni artisans making jewelry in a variety of styles that ranged from channel inlay to cluster work to petit point and needlepoint designs. "I made up my mind that I'd have every man, woman and child working—and by the time I left just about all of them were," Wallace said.[22] Zuni jewelers became known for their intricate lapidary work, which Wallace supported by providing them with grinders and carving tools, as well as top-quality turquoise from some of the best mines in the Southwest.

In design, Wallace encouraged Zuni artisans to produce jewelry that would resonate with a commercial audience. He influenced carvers to incorporate fetishes into necklaces that could be worn. Leekya Deyuse, who died in 1966, became famous under Wallace's tutelage for his stylized rounded animal carvings that found their way into many jewelry forms. Wallace also favored designs that he felt were authentic to Zuni culture, such as the Rainbow and Knife-Wing figures or the ubiquitous dragonflies and butterflies that appeared on Zuni pottery. As emblems of the spring and summer rains that insure a good corn harvest, butterflies decorate the tablita headdresses worn by women in the social dances, while dragonflies are part of the iconography painted on different Kachina masks. Leonard Martza, an employee of C. G. Wallace's in the 1950s, has continued to make "classic" butterfly pins and is noted for his use of unusual stones and color combinations.

Among contemporary jewelers, butterflies and dragonflies have been popular motifs for pins, because they speak to

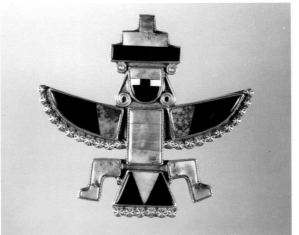

ABOVE: Leekya Deyuse, Zuni. Five-strand coral bead necklace interspersed with 216 carved turquoise animal fetishes, circa 1930. Private collection.

LEFT: Sterling silver Zuni Knife-Wing mosaic pin inlaid with turquoise, red abalone, white shell, and jet. Courtesy of Palace of the Governors.

49

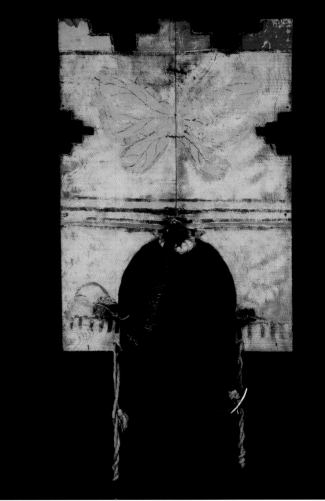

OPPOSITE: Inlaid Zuni butterfly pins, from the C. G. Wallace collection, circa 1940s. Private collection.

LEFT: Hopi tablita with Kachina motif.
RIGHT: Hopi tablita, reverse side, with butterfly motif. Courtesy of the School for Advanced Research.

tradition and the natural world, at the same time offering creative design opportunities. Liz Wallace (no relation to C. G. Wallace), a jeweler of Navajo-Washoe-Maidu ancestry, has become well-known for her butterfly pins that are set with high-quality natural turquoise stones. "The vintage butterfly pins with all turquoise stones were so rare and so collectible, I decided to make one myself," Wallace says.[24] She made her first butterfly pin in 2000 with a rare piece of turquoise from the No. 8 mine in Nevada, immediately selling it to a collector.

Immersed as a child in the jewelry-making world of her parents, Kathryn Morsea and Alan Wallace, Wallace began making jewelry in 1996 and entered her first Indian Market in 2003. From her father, a master of inlay, she learned lapidary skills and was introduced to the greater world of fine jewelry design through *The Master Jewelers* by A. Kenneth Snowman, which included chapters on Art Nouveau and Art Deco. Wallace was mentored by Bob Bauver, a jeweler and restorer of Native American jewelry and the author of *Navajo and Pueblo Earrings–1850-1945*. This association deepened her appreciation for historic techniques of jewelry making. In 2004, she took a course in blacksmithing at the Turley Forge Blacksmithing School in Santa Fe. "I wanted to understand the earliest phases of Navajo silver and make my own tools, as the first smiths had done," she recalls.[25]

Besides her fascination with historic Navajo silver, Wallace has pursued her interest in the Art Nouveau Period (1890-1914) with its emphasis on curvilinear floral and leaf patterns. More recently, she has experimented with *plique-à-jour*, a technique of enameling she learned from Bauver, in which thin filigree silver or gold wires or pierced plates are filled and fused with glass enamels to create translucent designs, perfect for the wings of her latest insect pins. "Nature is the ultimate artist," Wallace says.

The natural world has been a constant source of inspiration to jewelers. Charles Supplee replicates the way ants build their hills in his elegant bracelet. In one area of the

dad were good friends, and she used to give him jars of garnets."[26] In place of garnets, Supplee has placed rubies in the mouths of the ants. He fabricates the bodies of the ants from 18k gold. To cast the bracelet, he carved the anthill backwards with an ant on the inside of the bracelet, crawling up to the surface with another stone.

ONE OF THE ENDURING attractions of Southwestern Indian jewelry is the window it offers into the ceremonial life of the Hopi, Zuni, Navajo, and Rio Grande Pueblo tribes. Artists have taken motifs from their respective cultures and integrated them into jewelry that is unique in American culture. Some examples include corn, Corn Maidens, rain and cloud symbols, lightning bolts, rainbows, the sun, petroglyphs, turtles, butterflies, dragonflies, feathers, horned toads, eyedazzler rug patterns, arrows, *Yei* figures (Navajo holy people), and Kachinas. These subjects have been interpreted in countless ways by jewelers over the last century and inform many of the pieces presented in this book. For more traditional tribal members, there have been taboos about portraying ritual figures. On the other hand, art has been a way of perpetuating culture. C. G. Wallace understood the attraction of such subjects to an Anglo-European audience and encouraged jewelers to work within their tradition.

Four Corners region near Kayenta and Garnet Ridge on the Navajo Reservation, ants kick up garnets to the surface of the ground as they excavate to build their nests. For decades, Navajos have "harvested" the garnets and sold them to traders. The traders in turn have sold the garnets to European watchmakers to use as jewels in watches.

Supplee grew up across the road from the Hubbell Trading Post in Ganado, Arizona. His father had been a park ranger at Canyon de Chelly and a close friend of Dorothy Hubbell, the wife of Lorenzo Hubbell's son, Roman. Supplee recalls the period: "Dorothy Hubbell had jars of garnets. The Navajos would go into the desert and get garnets and take them to Lorenzo to trade for groceries. Dorothy and my

The Zuni Fire God figure is one such example. This pin depicts all the attributes of the Fire God, one of the principle figures in the Zuni Shalako ceremony. "The *Shalako*, a winter ceremony held in late November or early December, is the major ritual performed at the Pueblo of Zuni," according to Tom Bahti. "Usually referred to as a house blessing ceremonial it is a forty-nine day re-enactment of the Zuni emergence and migration myths. In addition, it is a prayer for rain, for the health and well being of the people, and for the propagation of plants and animals."[27] The body of this Fire God figure is painted black and then dotted with the directional colors: yellow for the north, blue for the west, red for the south, and white for the east. The underworld is black and the sky above is multicolored. The Fire God carries two cedar sticks in his hands for making fire. Over his shoulder is a fawn skin filled with cornmeal that he will sprinkle for blessings. His head is adorned with feathers of different birds, and he wears turquoise ketohs and a turquoise necklace. Shalako culminates in a dramatic all-night ceremony that embodies fundamental Zuni religious beliefs about birth, death, and regeneration.

Like the Zuni Shalako ceremony, many of the dances carried out at the Pueblos in the Southwest are prayers for renewal and regeneration. Many of the dances center on corn, the indispensable food of Native American cultures for close to 10,000 years. Santo Domingo Pueblo holds the largest corn dance in the Southwest every August fourth. The women wear turquoise tablita headdresses with cutout cloud designs, symbolizing the sky from whence the rain will come. The men wear dance shell necklaces with mosaics of turquoise, another emblem of water and fertility. Men and women carry small branches of evergreen, a symbol of eternal life. "The [corn] dance, as with all Southwestern ceremonials," Bahti states, "is a combination of song, drama, dance and poetry which forms a prayer for rain, bountiful harvest, the propagation of animals and plants, and the well-being of the pueblo and all those who attend."[28]

Within Southwestern Indian tribes, the Zuni Shalako ceremony and the Santo Domingo Corn Dance are but two of hundreds of ceremonies that form the rich cultural life of the tribes and provide jewelers with endless subject matter to draw upon for designs. Corn is a popular motif with multiple symbolic references. In the Navajo Creation Story, First Man and First Woman were created by the wind from a white ear of corn and a yellow ear of corn respectively. A newborn Hopi child receives a perfect ear of corn as a gift. Corn pollen has been used for blessings and for protection throughout Southwestern tribes.

Darryl Dean Begay uses Lone Mountain turquoise to represent the earth in his stylized gold, tufa-cast cornstalk pendant entitled *Harmony*. "I'm the type of artist who thinks traditionally and my art expresses what I feel," Begay says. "I think our living culture is still strong enough to carry on the prayers of our ancestors. To live in balance and harmony (*hózhó*) is my foundation, and throughout my career, my artwork will always relate to it."[29] At the top of the pin, Begay has carved two hummingbirds. "Hummingbirds are sacred birds that bring blessings. These tiny birds are leaders and our medicine men use their feathers in ceremonies. I like them because they are absolutely amazing."[30]

Tufa is a porous rock (also known as tuff) made of volcanic ash and found on the Navajo Reservation and parts of the Hopi Reservation. It is a soft stone, which is relatively easy to carve, and its rough surface leaves a textured impression on metal. Contemporary jewelers have become highly sophisticated in carving designs into tufa, using dental tools in some instances to get very fine detail. Jewelers also take pride in digging their own tufa stone from well-kept secret sources. The process of digging, carving, casting, and finishing a piece of jewelry from tufa is very labor intensive. The casting requires that the artist cut a mold and then halve it, carving the design, air vents, and sprue hole into one side of the stone. The two sides must fit tightly together so the molten silver or gold poured through the sprue hole will fill in the design. The final step is to remove any redundant metal, smoothing uneven edges before the piece is polished. The first documented examples of cast work among the Navajos appear in the 1870s.

White Corn Mother is the title Steve Wikviya LaRance has given to his gold tufa-cast bracelet composed of ninety-five Australian opals. The bezels for the opals are carved into the design of the bracelet. "The Hopi naming ceremony is very important," LaRance says. "The matrons in a family bestow the names. During the ceremony, they select a perfect ear of white corn and rub it gently against the baby's chest. After the

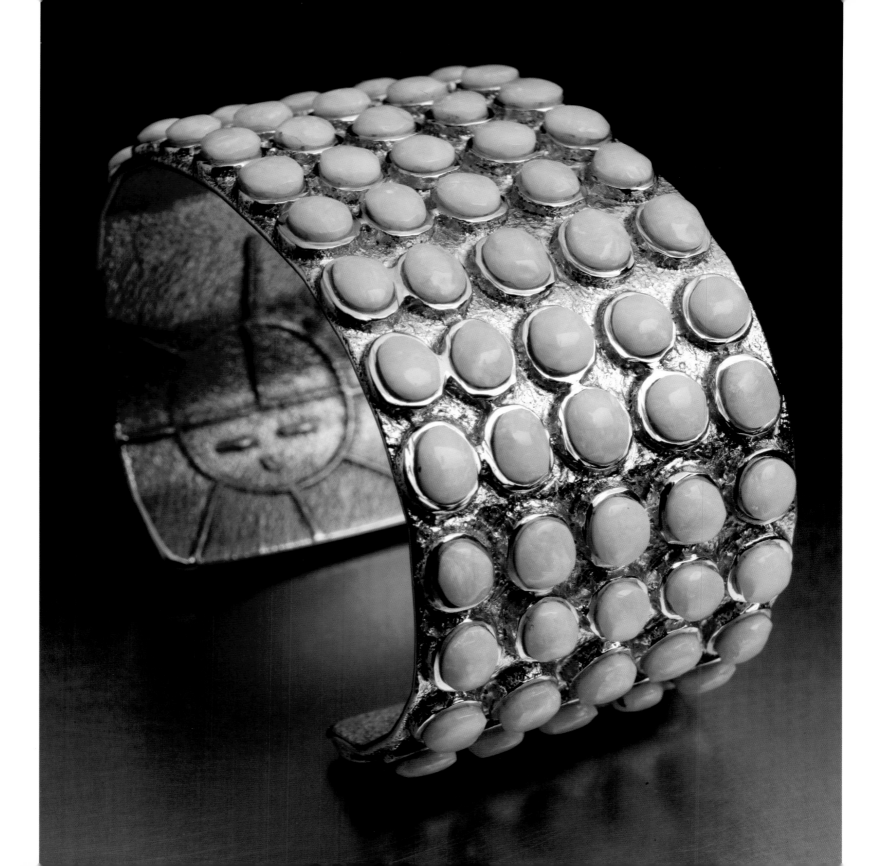

naming, they give the ear of corn to the parents to keep for the child. This represents the Corn Mother who will sustain and nourish the child throughout life."[31] LaRance received his Hopi name, Wikviya, from his godmother, which translates to "blessing and bringing of the animal spirits."

WHILE THERE IS A TENDENCY to view traders and trading posts as relics of a frontier past, they continue to be a vital part of the story of Southwestern Indian art. In 1931, the United Indian Traders Association was founded to foster good relationships among traders, artists, and arts and crafts dealers, as well as to promote and preserve authentic handmade Native American art. In 1997, the organization disbanded and has preserved its legacy with an oral history project housed at Northern Arizona University. The oral history project includes collected papers and oral interviews from forty-four traders in the Four Corners area. The Web-based project is entitled *Traders: Voices from the Trading Post*.[32]

Joe Tanner, a descendant of Mormon pioneer Seth Tanner and a trader for over fifty years, is representative of many contemporary traders in the Southwest. His family has "been continually trading among the Navajos since 1872."[33]

A SHALAKO NECKLACE WITH MUDHEADS

Preston Monongye designed and cast this necklace in tufa. The multistone inlay work was done by Veronica Poblano from Zuni Pueblo. Poblano (see Chapter Three) worked with Joe Tanner when she was a teenager, inlaying jewelry designed and cast by Monongye. The Mudheads, also known as *Koyemshi*, are clowns who participate in Hopi and Zuni ceremonies. "According to Zuni migration legend, ten koyemshi were born of an incestuous union. The figures have misshapen heads with knobby bumps for ears and hair and are depicted as clay-red or mud-colored, wearing a black kilt and bandana."[34] The male dancers who impersonate the Mudheads cover their bodies with red clay and wear masks with lumpy protuberances on their heads. Early American traders in the Southwest saw the headdresses and body paint and dubbed the dancers Mudheads. While the Mudhead often acts like a clown, he has multiple roles. He can cure illness, "be a magician, a dance director, a warrior, a messenger, a sage, or a fool."[35]

Collection of Joe E. Tanner, Gallup, New Mexico.

Tanner developed wholesale and retail markets in Navajo weaving, wool, jewelry, and piñons. In jewelry, Tanner has been especially influential. Early in his career, he worked at Zuni Pueblo, where he provided jewelers with silver, stones, and designs for jewelry. He then bought back the finished product to sell. "I had found a group of people that had incredible talent, incredible willingness to work hard," he said. "Well, my secret was I've always had a great feel for design and simplicity and elegance." As Tanner found new markets for Zuni jewelry, he hired Navajo silversmiths to do silverwork, which he would then take to Zuni Pueblo to have inlaid with stones. He insisted that artists sign their work and represent it as theirs, not Tanner's. He entered special pieces in the annual Gallup Ceremonial, winning ribbons and recognition for his jewelers.

In 1964, Tanner met Preston Monongye, who passed away in 1987 and has been widely recognized as one of the most innovative designers in contemporary Indian jewelry. Tanner said, "He was just an absolute genius. He was a painter. He was a potter. He was a sculptor. But most of all he was a jeweler." As a child, Monongye was adopted by the Hopi family of David Monongya, who lived in Hotevilla on Third Mesa on the Hopi Reservation. Monongye attended school on the Hopi Reservation and grew up in a traditional Hopi family. He became fluent in the Hopi language. In 1936, at age nine, Preston apprenticed with his uncle, Gene Pooyouma, from whom he learned the basics of silversmithing, which included melting down Mexican pesos to use for silver.

When Joe Tanner invited Monongye to move to Gallup to become his lead silversmith, Monongye was already an accomplished master of tufa casting. "My idea was to take this tufa texture that came onto the silver and mix it with some sophisticated Zuni inlay," Tanner said. "Monongye would design the jewelry, make the silverwork, and dictate the color. I hired a complement to him right away." The "complement" was Ted Klaus, a German illustrator, who created

color charts for the jewelers at Zuni to follow when they inlaid the pieces that Monongye designed.

In 1969, Tanner hired Lee Yazzie and other members of his family to work in his store, Tanner's Indian Arts, in Gallup, New Mexico. One of thirteen children, Yazzie grew up with his siblings in a one-room hogan south of Gallup. Although both of his parents were silversmiths, Yazzie learned the basics of silverwork in a high-school course at Fort Wingate Boarding School. He attended Brigham Young

ABOVE: Preston Monongye, Mission, adoped Hopi. Tufa-cast parrot jar with Lone Mountain turquoise and coral. Inlay by Lee A. Yazzie, Navajo. Circa 1974. Collection of Joe E. Tanner, Gallup, New Mexico.

University but was forced to drop out for surgery on a congenital hip deformity. During his recovery in 1969, he helped his mother with her silverwork, and he went to work for Joe Tanner. Recalling the opportunity Tanner gave him at the time, Yazzie says, "Joe has a great ability to recognize talent. He saw in me that I had something worth developing, and he pursued that."[36] Tanner arranged for Yazzie to study stone cutting with Harold "Cal" Johnson, one of his cutters, in Globe, Arizona. From Johnson, Yazzie learned to cut cabochons, stones cut in a circular or elliptical shape that are then individually polished before they are set.

In 1970, Tanner brought Monongye and Yazzie together. Although Monongye did his own lapidary work, he concentrated primarily on designing and casting his jewelry. For five years, from 1970 to 1975, Yazzie inlaid a number of Monongye's pieces. "When I started inlaying, it was natural to do the domed or raised inlay," Yazzie says. "It was different from the Zuni flat style at the time." The domed inlay, sometimes called a "padded" or "pillow" inlay, enriched the drama of Monongye's designs and would become a signature of Yazzie's style. Tanner, in the meantime, continued to submit their jewelry collaborations and their individual pieces at the annual Gallup Inter-Tribal Indian Ceremonial, garnering multiple ribbons for both artists.

In 1974 and 1975, Yazzie won the coveted Best of Show award at the Gallup Inter-Tribal Indian Ceremonial. He would win a record Best of Show for the third time in 1987. Gene Waddell, a turquoise broker and Indian art dealer, who has worked with Lee Yazzie since 1980, says, "Lee is a unique jeweler because he excels at both metalwork and inlay. He works with the best stones and appreciates fine turquoise, perhaps, more than anyone I know."[37]

In 2006, Waddell sold a concha belt by Yazzie on the secondary market. The belt had been made in 1975 and was unique because each concha has a stone inset with a different design, as opposed to a repeating single design. This was an innovation in 1975 that has since become popular among younger artists. Yazzie's buckle designs have become more complex over the years. Using two sheets of silver, he constructs the buckles with space for his domed inlay of stones on the sides and the top. In place of stamps, he chisels the lines of his patterns with a file.

"I see so many designs all at once that I have to sketch everything out," Yazzie states. "I try to harness what I see in my mind, even if it's just to capture a fragment of a design." For Yazzie, creativity grows out of his faith. He is president of the local branch of the Mormon Church in Tohatchi, New Mexico. "The most important thing is to render service to others," he says. "That's when you relax, and that's when the ideas flow. I have ideas I may never complete."

LIKE CHARLES LOLOMA and Kenneth Begay, Preston Monongye opened the door to the modern era of Southwestern Indian jewelry. "In the early 1960s, people identified Indian jewelry by tribe. Preston mixed up the styles and turned the jewelry into art," Jesse Monongya says of his father. "He was the bridge from just the craft of making jewelry into the art of making jewelry. He stepped outside

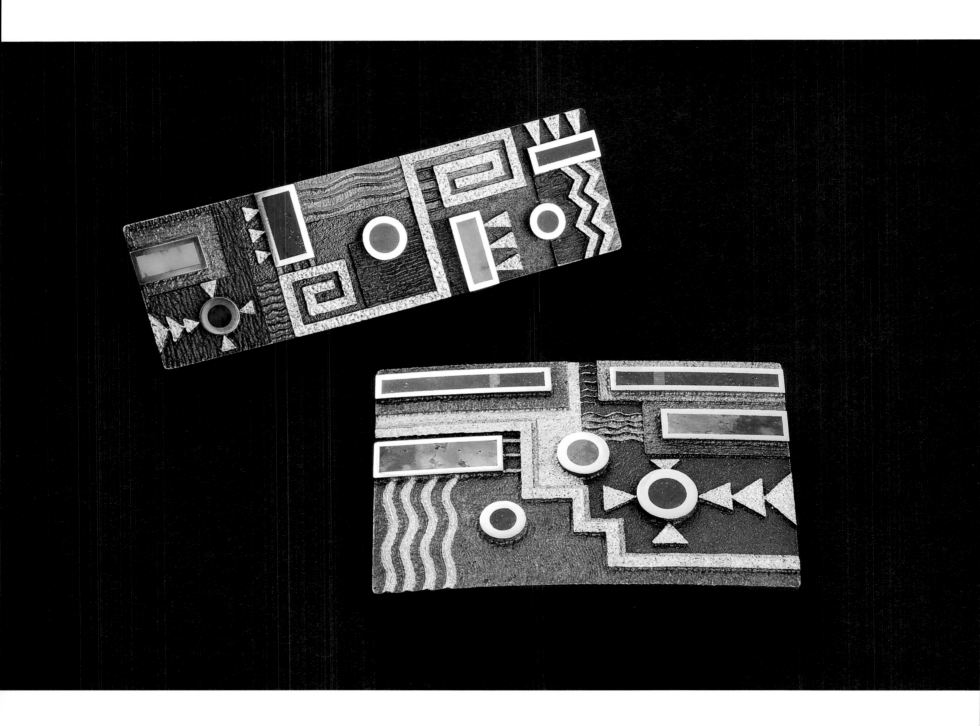

boundaries."[38] Monongye's legacy has been evident in the popularity and creativity of tufa-cast jewelry among contemporary jewelers.

Ric Charlie, acknowledged as a consummate tufa carver by other silversmiths, credits Charles Loloma with introducing him to the artistic possibilities of Native American jewelry. "I was a student at Tuba City High School in Arizona in 1975, and our teacher invited Charles Loloma over to give a slide lecture on his work," Charlie says. "He drove up in his expensive car, looking like an artist. Loloma and Monongye were out there creating great jewelry, but there wasn't a Navajo really doing contemporary tufa work. I wanted to be the best there was so I took that journey."[39] Charlie had always wanted to be an artist, excelling in ceramics, drawing, and jewelry in high school. He attended Mesa Community College on a football scholarship, where he studied art, taking courses in lost-wax casting and drawing. In 1980, he sold his reel-to-reel tape player for 40 ounces of silver, beginning his career in jewelry.

Charlie uses dental tools to carve intricate and stylized designs of Yei figures on his belt buckles. Yeis are the Navajo Holy People. They are the teachers and spiritual protectors of the Navajo and are represented in ceremonies by Yeibichai, males wearing masks to impersonate the holy figures. Yeibichai is also another name for the Night Chant, a nine-day healing ceremony in which many Yeis appear. In jewelry, Yeis are usually abstract figures without a specific religious reference. "I grew up in a traditional way," Charlie says. "Even though my grandparents and parents only spoke to us in English, we still went to all the Navajo ceremonies. When I do the Yeibichai figures, I'm inspired by a powerful out-of-body experience I once had, where I found myself in Monument Valley surrounded by Yeis on all the buttes, looking out over the mesas and valley to protect the area."

Charlie has perfected a technique of applying different colored patinas to his designs, creating jewelry that has

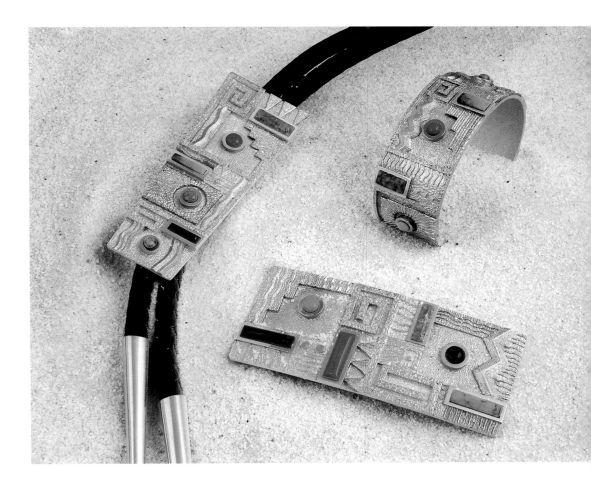

a painterly quality. On the back of his buckles, he often carves a scene of Monument Valley, a place of spiritual and personal significance to Charlie. In 2007, Charlie won the Best of Classification in jewelry at the Santa Fe Indian Market for this buckle, bolo, and bracelet with patinas of colored gold. Charlie alloyed 18k gold to create yellow, white, rose, and green gold, which he then inlaid with different stones to create the stylized Yei masks.

Darryl Dean and Rebecca Begay have become well-known for their tufa-cast work. In 2006, they won the Best

OPPOSITE: Ric Charlie, Navajo. Sterling silver tufa-cast belt buckles with multicolored patinas. Courtesy of the Faust Gallery.

ABOVE: Ric Charlie. Tufa-cast bolo tie, bracelet, and belt buckle, with 18k yellow, white, rose, and green gold, and inlaid with stones. Courtesy of the Faust Gallery.

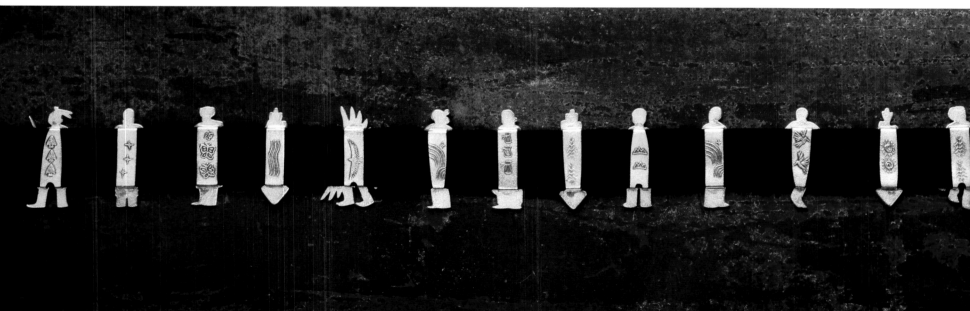

of Division at the Heard Museum Indian Market for their collaborative concha belt entitled *Taos Pueblo Trading Center*. They capture the pluralistic spirit of the great Taos trade fairs of the eighteenth and nineteenth centuries by depicting the Plains Indians, Pueblo Indians, and Navajo Indians who would converge in the fall to trade with each other. The Plains Indians would trade buffalo hides for Navajo blankets, while the Pueblo tribes would trade their corn, beans, and squash for hides and dried meat. Cornstalks separate each group of three conchas, emblems of the Blessing Way. On the reverse side of each concha, they have carved symbols that reflect the identity of the figures. The male dancers and Navajo warrior have an arrowhead, a symbol of protection. The female dancers are represented by butterflies or hummingbirds. The Navajo medicine man has a bag for corn pollen to be used in ceremonies. Water and sun symbols adorn the back of the cornstalks.

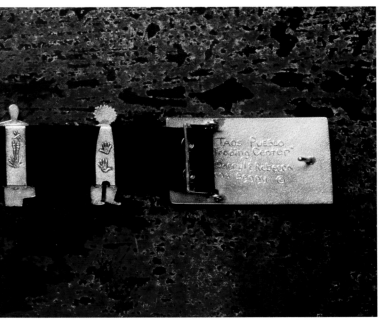

Darryl Begay began making jewelry in 1997, learning tufa casting from his uncle, Bobby Begay, and lapidary work from Raymond Yazzie. In 1999, he entered his first Santa Fe Indian Market. He has taught tufa casting to his wife, Rebecca, who has a degree in art education from Northern Arizona University. Darryl and Rebecca Begay have each received the Goodman Fellowship from Santa Fe's Wheelwright Museum of the American Indian in 2002 and 2006, respectively.

Darryl's two figures are cast in 18k gold. The male figure entitled *Grandfather* represents Begay's late grandfather,

Whitehair Begay, a Medicine Man. "He was one of the greatest influences on me growing up," Begay says. The female figure, named *The Maiden*, represents Changing Woman/White Shell Woman, a central figure in the Navajo Creation Story. Changing Woman was the first mother of the Navajo. She created the four original clans of the Navajo. Associated with the seasons and the earth, Changing Woman grows old and then young again in a cyclical fashion.

Within Navajo tradition, the deities, the four directions, and the four sacred mountains that circumscribe the

OPPOSITE, LEFT: Rebecca
T. Begay in her studio in
Gallup, New Mexico, carving
designs into tufa stone. She
wears her *Circles* pendant with
Lone Mountain turquoise
and sugilite. The Navajo lady
bracelet, with Number 8
turquoise, and eagle-wing
ring are by Darryl Begay.

OPPOSITE, RIGHT: Darryl
Dean Begay in his studio
in Gallup, New Mexico,
carving tufa. He wears his
ring with Lone Mountain
turquoise. The bracelet with
Lone Mountain turquoise
is by an unknown artist.

LEFT: Darryl Dean Begay. 18k
gold tufa-cast figures: on left,
with Bisbee turquoise; on
right, with Morenci turquoise
and coral. Private collection.

spiritual and physical home of the Navajo—all are represented by stones and shells used in jewelry. To the east in Colorado is Blanca Peak, the dwelling of White Shell Woman. Mount Taylor to the south in New Mexico is Turquoise Mountain, and the directional color is blue. The San Francisco Peaks in Arizona to the west are associated with abalone and the color yellow. Jet, a hard black stone, is associated with the north and Hesperus Peak in Colorado.

RIGHT: Marian Denipah, Navajo, San Juan Pueblo, and Steve Wikviya LaRance, Hopi, Assiniboine, at Santa Fe Indian Market, 2007. Denipah has on her sterling silver tufa-cast bracelet with gaspeite and Sleeping Beauty turquoise, and 18k tufa-cast gold pendant inlaid with gaspeite, coral, and sugilite. LaRance wears his tufa-cast bolo tie with Number 8 turquoise.

OPPOSITE: Steve Wikviya LaRance. Sterling silver and coral concha belt. Courtesy of the artist.

Steve Wikviya LaRance and Marian Denipah are a husband and wife team who dig their own tufa on the Hopi Reservation and collaborate on much of their jewelry. Denipah studied modern dance, painting, and photography at the Institute of American Indian Arts, graduating in 1983. She also holds a BFA in painting and photography from Northern Arizona University. She did not begin making jewelry until her mid-thirties, when she and LaRance moved to Flagstaff, Arizona. There she shared a studio with Ric Charlie for five years, learning the techniques of casting from him. "It's the texture and rawness of tufa that is so beautiful," Denipah says. "I can draw in it. It's an easy transfer from painting to tufa."[40]

LaRance moved a lot as a child since his father was in the military. He moved from Moenkopi on the Hopi Reservation to Colorado, California, and Guam. When he was twelve, the family returned to Moenkopi, where he went to school and spent time with his grandfather, a religious leader from Hotevilla. Immersed in the Hopi culture, LaRance learned how to carve Kachina dolls and learned to make bows and arrows. LaRance began his career as a sculptor, carving Hopi themes into marble and alabaster. When he and Denipah met in the late 1970s, she encouraged him to spend more time on his art. An arts advocate, LaRance has divided his time between sculpture and jewelry; he is also a consultant with various museums and the National Park Service on Hopi arts and culture.

Both LaRance and Denipah carve molds, and whoever carves the mold signs the mold. LaRance does the pouring for the jewelry, and Denipah does more of the finishing work. Of his work, LaRance says, "I have one foot in the past, but I'm trying to move toward the future."[41] The title of his tufa-cast concha belt with coral is *Hopi Stars*. "When the Spanish arrived, they thought our star motifs were crosses. A lot of our important ceremonies are based on stars. They guide us on when to have ceremonies," he says.

ANTHONY LOVATO HAS REVIVED the art of tufa casting at Santo Domingo Pueblo, a pueblo known best for mosaic, shell, and stone beadwork. Lovato uses tufa from the Hopi Reservation for his spirit pendants that have become his signature pieces. On each pendant, Lovato folds a piece of silver over the side of the body to represent a blanket or a cloud. For his faces, he uses stones that lend an ethereal quality to his figures.

Like many jewelers from Santo Domingo Pueblo, Lovato started selling jewelry when he was twelve under the portal of the Palace of the Governors in Santa Fe. The portal is a long covered sidewalk that borders one side of the plaza in Santa Fe. Native American vendors draw lots for a space each day to sell their work. When Lovato was fifteen, he began making jewelry under the tutelage of his mother, Mary Coriz. "I knew what my career was going to be," he says. A 1978 graduate of the Institute of American Indian Arts with a major in metals and a minor in museum studies, Lovato worked at the Museum of Northern Arizona from 1978 to 1981, taking more courses in jewelry at Northern Arizona University. In 1982, he moved back to Santo Domingo to be close to his culture. "In our culture, we pray for the whole world," Lovato states. "The Easter dances, the Corn Dance, they are for rain and a good harvest and for food for the world. These ideas go into my spirit pendants, as I make them."[42]

Lovato acknowledges the influence of Chiricahua Apache sculptor Allan Houser and Charles Loloma on his work. Loloma's Corn Maiden pendants particularly inspired Lovato, a member of the Corn Clan at Santo Domingo Pueblo, to create his Corn Spirit pendants in which he carves cornstalk images on the body of the figure. Images of stars, hands, and clouds also adorn the bodies of his pendants, as well as bears, deer, horses, and eagles.

Eddie Two Moons Chavez uses tufa to cast his pendant entitled *Geronimo's Repatriation*. The large pendant of the necklace contains 512 carats of natural Morenci turquoise, which Chavez acquired in 1988. "I wanted to wait until I had the right piece of jewelry before I used it," he says.[43] That moment came in 2004, when the various bands of the Apache united to petition Congress to repatriate the remains of Geronimo to Arizona for burial. A Chiricahua Apache, Chavez portrays the homecoming ceremony that the Apaches will have when Geronimo is laid to rest. On the bottom right are three Apache couples dancing around the fire and the wickiups. The smoke from the bonfire rises up to become Geronimo's face. On the left is an Apache Crown dancer who leads the procession. Above the corn and cloud designs is an eagle carrying prayers to the Creator, who is represented by

BELOW: Anthony Lovato, Santo Domingo Pueblo. Sterling silver tufa-cast spirit pendants. Courtesy of Desert Son of Santa Fe.

LEFT: Eddie Two Moons Chavez, Chiricahua Apache. Sterling silver tufa-cast necklace with 512 carats of natural Morenci turquoise. Courtesy of the artist.

ABOVE: Geronimo, Chiricahua Apache, March 1905, Washington, D.C. Photograph by Delancy Gill. Courtesy of Palace of the Governors.

the sun's rays emanating in all directions. On the backs of the bezels are Apache sun symbols inset with Apache garnets from the San Carlos Reservation in Arizona. Geronimo's portrait is depicted on the clasp.

Better known, perhaps, for his fine art jewelry, Chavez has carved the various elements of Geronimo's homecoming in tufa. He engraves details on the figures, making sketches that were overlaid on the silver as a template. Chavez studied over thirty portraits of Geronimo from his private collection to come up with a drawing that is true to Geronimo's spiritual character, as well as his place in history.

KACHINA FIGURES ARE ALSO POPULAR subjects for contemporary jewelry. Kachinas are part of the complex ceremonial life of all the Pueblo tribes. Paula Baxter and Allison Bird-Romero give the following definition of these ethereal beings:

"Katsinas are sacred beings of the Pueblo peoples, and their physical representation on earth comes from the men who dance in Pueblo ceremonies; each dancer wears a combination of mask, body paint, and costume that replicates an individual Katsina spirit, a holy force of nature that brings some benefit to humanity. These sacred intermediaries between the gods and the Pueblo peoples visit the pueblo villages at certain times of the year, bringing gifts—such as Katsina dolls, representations of Katsinas carved from cottonwood that are painted and adorned with feathers and other materials—and performing dances for the benefit of all humanity. Each Katsina represents an aspect of earthly life, such as fertility, healing, the granting of justice, or life-giving rain."[44]

Gerald Lomaventema portrays the Broad-faced Kachina on a belt buckle with triangular inlaid cloud designs on the face. The bodies of the snakes that flank the Kachina carry carved bird tracks. "These are the tracks birds leave in the

OPPOSITE: Gerald Lomaventema, Hopi. On left, sterling silver tufa-cast and overlay belt buckle with Red Mountain turquoise, coral, sugilite, and jet. On right, sterling silver tufa-cast and overlay pendant with 14k gold, Bisbee, and Indian Mountain turquoise. Courtesy of Gene and Mike Waddell.

HOPI CROW MOTHER

Verma Nequatewa depicts the Hopi Crow Mother in her tufa-cast pendant with an 18k gold overlay feather and sunflower on her cloak. Crow Mother appears during the February Powamuya, or Bean Dance, observed on the three Hopi Mesas. At Hotevilla, Nequatewa's village, Crow Mother comes at dawn, walks slowly through the village, singing and distributing corn and bean sprouts to signal an auspicious growing season at Hopi.

Collection of Dr. Gregory and Angie Yan Schaff, Santa Fe.

ground when it rains," he says.[45] The long hair falling from the bottom of the face is another rain symbol. The Broad-faced Kachina, also called the Guard Kachina, keeps order at the Bean Dance and other Kachina dances by reminding observers not to take photographs and to refrain from behavior that interrupts the flow of the ceremony. The Bean Dance takes place in February and is a ceremony to promote fertility in the upcoming growing season. Lomaventema's Water Maiden Kachina is a less common figure. She appears in a rare dance that is held every four years in May at Hopi to bless the planting. On the elaborate headdress, Lomaventema has carved feathers, lightning bolts, and a cloud design. The maiden wears Hopi-style turquoise earrings.

The Sun Kachina bolo tie by Lomaventema won the 2005 Jackie Autry Purchase Award at the Southwest Museum of the American Indian in Los Angeles. Lomaventema shows the figure in the middle of a step, holding a gourd rattle in one hand. Cornstalk designs adorn the tips of the bolo, signifying the life-giving force of the sun to all growing things. Lomaventema also received a fellowship in 2005 from the Southwestern Association for Indian Arts.

Like many contemporary Hopi jewelers, Lomaventema began making jewelry in the traditional Hopi overlay style, taking courses at the Hopi Arts and Crafts Co-op Guild on Second Mesa on the Hopi Reservation in Arizona. Overlay consists of two sheets of silver soldered together. Designs are cut out of the top layer of silver, which is then soldered to a bottom layer of silver. The bottom sheet has been textured or oxidized black so that the designs stand out in relief. The roots of overlay go back to the 1930s and the Museum of Northern Arizona. The founders of the museum, Dr. Harold Colton and Mary Russell Colton, were committed to preserving traditional Hopi art and providing employment opportunities for the Hopi. In 1930, they organized the first Hopi Craftsman Exhibit, which continues as an annual event, to create a venue for artists to sell their work.

Concerned that Hopi jewelry was too similar to its Navajo and Zuni counterparts, the Coltons launched the Hopi Silver Project in 1938 to inspire jewelers to come up with a new style of jewelry based on traditional Hopi designs found on pottery, textiles, and basketry. In the tradition of Juan Lorenzo Hubbell and J. B. Moore, Mary Colton worked with Virgil Hubert, the assistant curator of art at the Museum of Northern Arizona, to collect and reproduce motifs for the silversmiths to use. In her book, *Hopi Silver*, Margaret Nickelson Wright includes a letter from Mary Russell Colton, who writes, "In order to help the Hopi silversmiths to visualize our idea of Hopi design and to show them how to make use of and adopt pottery, basketry, and textile design to various silver techniques already practiced, we have created a number of plates done in opaque water color on gray paper. . . . After we start the idea with our designs, we hope that in a short time the idea will take hold and they will no longer be needed.[46]

After World War II, the Hopi Silvercraft Guild was founded in 1949 to teach jewelry making to returning veterans. Because employment opportunities were limited at the remote Hopi villages in northern Arizona, the crafts served the dual purpose of sustaining cultural art forms and providing an income for the veterans. Fred Kabotie, the illustrious painter, was placed in charge of design, while Paul Saufkie, a respected silversmith, was hired to teach jewelry making and the overlay technique, which evolved out of Colton's project.[47] The G.I. Bill provided funding for the program. The Guild is housed in a modern building on Second Mesa and has been renamed the Hopi Arts and Crafts Co-op Guild. It has continued to be a center for teaching contemporary silversmiths the techniques of overlay, as well as an outlet for Hopi artists to sell their work.

While the techniques of Hopi overlay have been incorporated into contemporary Southwestern Indian jewelry, the popularity of classic Hopi overlay jewelry has waned in

recent years. Roy Talahaftewa, a prominent jeweler from the village of Shungopavi on Second Mesa, says, "The overlay work got to a point where it was not selling well. Jewelers needed to make a change. I wanted to encourage artists to be more innovative and develop a new style of work. Financially, it would help artists support their families better if they had new techniques."[48]

In 2000, Talahaftewa started a series of jewelry workshops at Hopi called "Grandmother's Dream," a tribute to his mother who had died in 1999. (During her lifetime, Evangeline Talahaftewa was named an Arizona Living Treasure for her traditional coiled baskets.) "She was everyone's grandmother," Talahaftewa states, "and she always encouraged me to help the younger artists." Sponsored by the Hopi Pu'tavi Projects, Inc., a nonprofit organization founded in

OPPOSITE: Gerald Lomaventema, Hopi. Sterling silver tufa-cast and overlay bolo tie with 14k gold, Red Mountain turquoise, sugilite, coral, and jet. Courtesy of Southwest Museum of the American Indian, Autry National Center, Los Angeles.

ABOVE: Hopi clan symbols used in silver designs. Seated in the front row are Fred Kabotie (left) and Paul Saufkie (right). Circa 1944–50. Courtesy of Northern Arizona University, Cline Library, Special Collections and Archives.

1999 to make training, education, and business opportunities available to Hopi youth, the workshops included techniques of tufa casting, overlay, hollow form, and lapidary work, as well as practical advice on marketing and business practices. Talahaftewa invited Duane Maktima, a Hopi/Laguna Pueblo jeweler, to address the workshops. Maktima had founded Pueblo V Design Institute in 1998 to help Pueblo artists with the craft and business of jewelry and native arts. Through his workshops, Talahaftewa introduced a new direction in Hopi jewelry that combined tufa casting with overlay and inlay stone work.

Talahaftewa combines overlay and appliqué techniques with inlay and classic stamping on his concha belt entitled *Emergence of New Life*, made in 2000. The inlaid Kachina images at the top of each concha represent different prayers associated with the Hopi cycle of life. In the center of each concha, Talahaftewa has depicted various figures and symbols central to Hopi ceremonial life. Going counterclockwise from the bottom right, the first concha portrays Mother Earth, holding a basket of fruit and an ear of corn, surrounded by solstice symbols, lightning bolts, and stars.

Of the animals portrayed, the bear represents strong leadership and is considered the father and mother of humanity. The eagle, revered by many Native American tribes, is a symbolic forefather of the Hopi. The ubiquitous Kokopelli, or the flute player, keeps Hopi life in harmony. An emblem of fertility, Kokopelli is usually portrayed as a dancer who moves through the villages, spreading the seeds he carries in the hump on his back to germinate the crops.

Many of the dances that inaugurate the ceremonial calendar in January are night dances. On the bottom left concha, Talahaftewa depicts a Kachina spirit coming into the village to attend a dance. To the right is a Cloud Spirit with the zigzag lightning bolt drawn on the body. The stars and moons in the various conchas also signify that the dances are nocturnal.

ABOVE: Roy Talahaftewa, Hopi, in his studio at Shungopavi, Second Mesa, Hopi Reservation, Arizona.

OPPOSITE: Roy Talahaftewa. Sterling silver tufa-cast and overlay concha belt with 14k gold, jet, coral, lapis, fossilized ivory, petrified wood, and white jade. Bottom three conchas set with China Mountain turquoise; bear concha with Number 8 turquoise; and eagle concha with Morenci turquoise. Collection of JoAnn and Bob Balzer.

LIKE OVERLAY, STAMPWORK is a technique of decorating silver. Stamping dates back to First Phase jewelry. Early smiths used a punch, an idea borrowed from Mexican leatherworkers, to decorate the silver with simple holes. The punches soon evolved into dies or stamps, rods of iron with a design on one end used to imprint the silver with a pattern. Many artists use stamps that have been handed down by family members; others make their own stamps to create original patterns. Stamp designs range from geometric patterns found on more traditional jewelry to representational and often whimsical images of flora and fauna, figures, and landscapes. Collectors prize flawless and original stampwork.

Norbert Peshlakai has been acknowledged as a master of stampwork. His work exemplifies the unlimited artistic possibilities within stamping, and he has inspired a generation of contemporary metalsmiths. A silversmith for over thirty years, Peshlakai is the oldest of nine children and a fourth-generation silversmith with Peshlakai ancestors on both sides of his family. His great-great grandmother, Red Woman Peshlakai, was one of J. B. Moore's weavers at Crystal, and his mother is a respected weaver, who has taught his five sisters to weave. Their influence is evident in textile designs that Peshlakai often incorporates into his work.

Peshlakai stumbled into jewelry at Haskell Indian Junior College, where he studied art from 1972 to 1975. Finding himself short one class to complete his art major, he signed up for jewelry but rarely attended class. In order to pass, Peshlakai had to sketch and fabricate six pieces of jewelry. Peshlakai still keeps a notebook of sketches and will do a quick sketch before embarking on a new piece. "I don't want to repeat the same pattern," he says.[49]

In 1977, Peshlakai made his first miniature pot at the suggestion of John Boomer, a well-known Anglo-American wood sculptor and husband of his cousin. The two developed a close relationship that year as Peshlakai helped Boomer build a traditional Navajo hogan. During construction, Peshlakai recalls that Boomer asked if he had brought any silver to work on. "He gave me a space to work in his shop and a block of walnut wood," Peshlakai recalls. "I carved some hollow circles to shape my first silver pot which took me almost one week to complete. That was my first three-inch diameter sterling silver pot with a flare neck. After that, I wanted to do more silver pots so I arranged with John to buy me some silver out of my pay which I used to make thirteen different kinds [of pots]."[50]

Although objects have a long history within Southwestern Indian jewelry, Peshlakai set in motion a new direction in jewelry with his innovative and contemporary miniature sterling silver pots. In 2005, the Heard Museum received a gift from Norman L. Sandfield of approximately

240 silver and gold miniature seed pots, including more than seventy by Peshlakai.[51] The designs on Peshlakai's pots include people, animals, butterflies, dragonflies, and geometric designs. Within the geometric patterns are feathers, textile designs, arrowheads, lightning bolts, swirl designs, and abstract patterns. Included here is a miniature pot Peshlakai has named *Tradition* (from the collection of Norman L. Sandfield). "The design is the old-style tufa-cast buckle," he says. "I remember seeing that buckle on the cover of the 1975 *Arizona Highways* magazine years ago." Rather than casting the design, however, Peshlakai has overlayed the buckle motif onto the pot, texturing the surface with a hammer. Four traditional moustache or corn leaf curves flank the feather motif. Arrowheads are stamped on either side of

the stopper. The stopper is inlaid with coral on one side and Sleeping Beauty turquoise on the other—both traditional stones used in jewelry and both framed by the feather design. While all elements in the pot derive from classic Navajo designs, the overall effect is strikingly modern.

In 1999, Peshlakai developed his own alphabet, using handmade stamps. Each letter of the alphabet is represented by an object: A is an arrowhead; B is a bear; C is a cowboy with tie; D is a drum, and so on. The individual designs are each composed of multiple stamps. For the arrowhead, for example, Peshlakai uses four distinct stamps. Of his alphabet, Peshlakai writes, "I created the alphabet in the fall of 1999. I wanted to do the "ABC" two years earlier and it so happened a friend of mine who taught at Rehoboth

BELOW: Norbert Peshlakai. Sterling silver alphabet concha belt. Collection of Martha H. Struever.

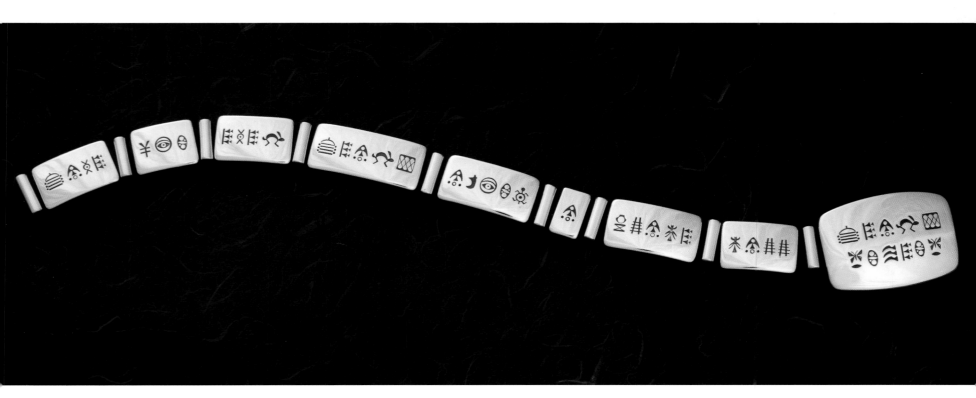

Christian School came to visit me. He saw what I was doing in making an alphabet with my collection of stamps. Later he came back with copies of Egyptian writings and their symbols. That was the start of the development of the letters using stamp pad and engineering paper as my guideline. The year Y2K, I changed the letter "D" instead of using Diamonds as my symbol, I made a new stamp using Drum for the letter D. The letters are approximately ³⁄₁₆ inch horizontal."

"Have you ever heard about a place called Heard Museum" is the message Peshlakai spells out in his concha belt. Each of the forty-two letters is composed of multiple stamps hammered seamlessly together to create a single symbol, a testament to Peshlakai's technical skill and creative imagination.

One of Peshlakai's legacies has been humor. Jewelry can be fun and traditional, serious and ironic at the same

time. Darrell Jumbo, a nephew of Peshlakai's wife Linda, produces jewelry that is both whimsical and thoughtful. In 1991, Jumbo asked Peshlakai to teach him the basics of silversmithing, from soldering and stamping to overlay. Although they spent only a few weeks together, Jumbo picked up the techniques rapidly, adding to skills he had learned years earlier in high-school vocational courses in welding and sheet metal.

As Jumbo began his career in silversmithing, he also worked for a medical supply company from 1994 to 2002, delivering oxygen tanks, wheelchairs, and hospital beds to elderly Navajos all over the reservation. He credits that experience with influencing the subject matter of his work. "You get to know your patients, their dogs and cats, their grandchildren. And then one day they are gone. You don't realize how fragile life is. I wanted to make people smile."[52]

Jumbo's pins reflect his warm sense of humor and his own experience of the universality of mankind gleaned from his experience in the Marine Corps from 1979 to 1983, during which time he traveled to Japan, South Korea, Germany, Sweden, England, and Norway. "People ask me why I make an elephant," he says. "It's not an animal from the Southwest. It is one big world out there, and we can get ideas, just like our materials, from everywhere. I'm going to make penguins next." Dubbed the "Elephant Man" by Norbert Peshlakai in a bit of banter about his last name, Jumbo has adopted the elephant as a hallmark. In another touch of whimsy, Jumbo put a top hat on the elephant to mirror the one he wears to all the Indian markets and entitles the piece *Self Portrait*.

Birds also appear in Jumbo's work perched on comical animals, such as the cat and the goat, entitled *Nobody's Business* and *Listen to Us*, respectively. Jumbo says, "Birds represent peace. I grew up herding sheep for my grandmother. If birds aren't around, they know you're there. But when you see birds riding on the backs of sheep, it feels peaceful."

Like Norbert Peshlakai, Jared Chavez fabricates and textures the silver in his jewelry with unique stamps he has collected and others he has inherited from his grandfather. Chavez's work is characterized by clean, bold lines, abstract designs, and multiple textured patterns on a single piece of jewelry. Open fields of highly polished undecorated silver highlight the meticulous detail of his texturing. He uses guitar wire for the deep lines that form the design on his concha belt entitled *Erosion*. According to Chavez, the belt represents the constant changing and structuring of a person's life. "Every year we change based on our life experience," he says. "The landscape changes from year to year as well, from the erosion of time."[53]

Chavez sketches out the designs for each concha before he places the guitar wire on the silver. In the buckle, he presents his subject with specific references to the landscape—a crescent moon and stars in a night sky above a horizon that encompasses the earth below. The other conchas in the belt carry out his theme in a series of increasingly conceptual designs.

A 2005 graduate of Georgetown University, Chavez majored in studio art with an emphasis on digital art. He did his senior project on printmaking, focusing on Japanese woodblock technology. "I like the graphic work in Japanese woodblock designs and the balance between light and dark. That's what I try to achieve in my jewelry—a balance in design between textured and highly polished surfaces."[54] After graduation, Chavez spent three months at the Revere Academy of Jewelry Arts in San Francisco, taking an intensive program of twenty-two courses, ranging from fabrication to diamond setting to design.

Chavez's real introduction to jewelry, however, came years earlier in the San Felipe Pueblo studio of his father, Richard Chavez, an eminent jeweler and master of design, who taught him the basics of silverwork. In 1994, the younger Chavez entered his first Indian Market in the Youth Division at age 11. Over the years, he has won many awards for his jewelry, including in 2003 the Malcolm and Connie Goodman Fellowship for Native American Artists from the Wheelwright Museum of the American Indian in Santa Fe.

OVERLAY HAS BECOME A popular technique for contemporary jewelers to use because it allows the artist to create intricate designs that embellish both the surface and the underside of jewelry. Kee Yazzie Jr., a Navajo silversmith from Winslow, Arizona, is well-known for his migration motifs that chart the journey of the early Native Americans across the Bering Straits into North America. Growing up in Jeddito near Keams Canyon, he says, "I saw lots of petroglyphs in the cornfields and on canyon walls. I remember my uncle showing me one rock with the spiral design on it and another one with a hand design."[55] Years later, he would incorporate those ancient rock art motifs into his jewelry. Bears, hands, dragonflies, cloud designs, solstice spirals, steps, stars, human figures, arrows, mountain symbols—all are carved out in minute detail. On his bracelet, Yazzie uses overlay to decorate the interior of the bracelet with myriad symbols. On the exterior, he uses an appliqué technique to attach the 14k gold symbols to the stamped silver.

Yazzie gets his designs for jewelry from many places. He is a collector of X-Men comics and a fan of Frank Frazetta, a painter and illustrator, whose work has appeared on comic-book covers from Buck Rogers to Conan the Adventurer. Yazzie has served as a Mormon missionary among the Laotian and Thai communities in Boston and learned the languages of both groups through classes at Brigham Young University in Utah. Following his education and mission work, Yazzie turned to jewelry making in 1993, working on and off with Navajo silversmith Ray Scott for a year. "I worked on design and later did all of his polishing," he says.[56] Yazzie entered his first competition at the Eight Northern Indian Pueblos Arts and Crafts show in 1995, taking second place

OPPOSITE: Kee Yazzie Jr., Navajo. Sterling silver stamped and overlay bracelet and belt buckle with 14k gold petroglyph images. Private collection.

ABOVE: Newspaper Rock, Indian Creek, near the Needles District of Canyonlands National Park in southeast Utah.

OPPOSITE: Kee Yazzie Jr., Navajo. Sterling silver concha belt with Lone Mountain and Bisbee turquoise, and coral. The conchas chart the migration of the Navajos into this world. Center (right to left): petroglyph motifs, solstice designs, coral reef, and migration symbols. Top right: *Avanyu* (water serpent); top left, water design (three wavy lines), stars, bear, and mountains. Bottom (left to right): migration petroglyph motifs, the journey, and cloud design. Courtesy of the artist.

for a bracelet. In 1998 and 1999, Yazzie took workshops in hollowware and reticulation from Duane Maktima as part of Maktima's Pueblo V program.

Inspired by Norbert Peshlakai and Mike Bird-Romero, Yazzie incorporates various techniques in his concha belts, combining overlay with appliqué, texturing, stampwork, and reticulation. Like many contemporary artists, Yazzie varies the design in each concha. This style has become a way for jewelers to express their creativity and illustrate their technical skills. For Yazzie, each concha is part of the story of his ancestors' journey into the present.

Petroglyph fields number in the thousands throughout Arizona, New Mexico, Utah, Colorado, Nevada, and California. Petroglyphs are designs that have been etched into the surface patina, or desert varnish of rocks and cliff walls by prehistoric Native Americans, who left a record of their daily and ceremonial life. While it is impossible to precisely date petroglyphs or to know the meaning of the symbols, many artists have grown up surrounded by fields of primordial rock art and have incorporated the human and zoomorphic motifs into their work.

Arland Ben includes many prehistoric rock art motifs in his distinctive jewelry. One of nine children, Ben was born in Bluff, Utah, into a traditional Navajo family. His father is a medicine man, who imbued the family with a reverence for the natural world. Ben recalls going to Newspaper Rock outside Moab as a child and being overwhelmed by the hundreds of drawings. "Everything we see is an idea that someone had to come up with. The Anasazi were ahead of their time. Art is everywhere."[57] There are over 650 drawings at Newspaper Rock spanning two thousand years and representing the Fremont, Anasazi, Navajo, and Anglo cultures.

Prior to becoming a silversmith when he was twenty-nine, Ben had studied art at Brigham Young University, taking courses in portrait drawing and watercolors, among other subjects. To pay his way through college, he worked as

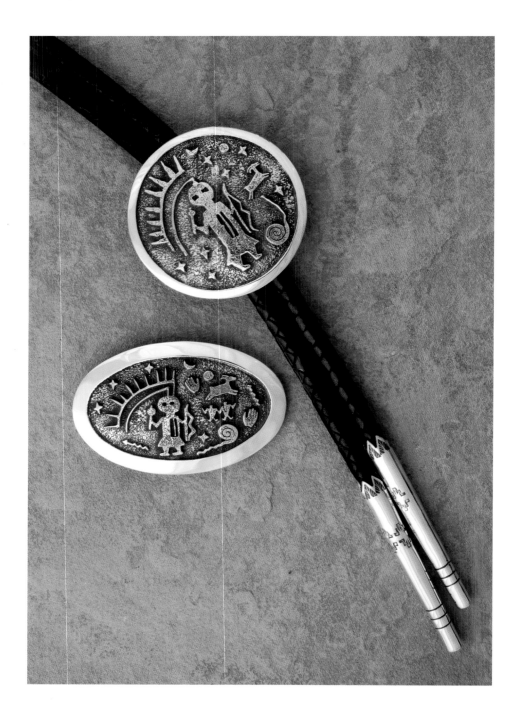

a firefighter. After college he worked in construction, doing stucco and framing, before turning to jewelry at the suggestion of his brother-in-law, Vincent Platero, who taught him the basic techniques of stampwork. Self-taught in overlay and casting, Ben casts both his silver and gold into ingot bars and rolls the metal out to the desired gauge. He alloys his own gold for his overlay motifs that he cuts out by hand, working from sketches he has made.

In the bolo and belt buckle, Ben uses 14k gold and 16k gold overlay designs, respectively. Both the background silver and the gold figures are textured by reticulation, a process of sprinkling minute particles of silver or gold dust on the surface of a piece and then heating it until the granules become part of the surface. The figure in the bolo and buckle is a Yei dancer holding a rattle and a bow and wearing a rainbow headdress. Ben says, "I don't make specific Yei figures or represent actual dances out of respect. This figure could be participating in a summer seasonal dance."[58] Stars, a crescent moon, and the sun surround the dancer. For Ben, the spiral design is an eternity symbol and often has been associated with planting and marking the seasons. The big-horned sheep signify land animals. In the buckle, Ben has added a lightning motif, the hand design, and two people joined together, representing family. The hand motif appears on rocks throughout the Southwest. There have been many interpretations of the hand—that it, perhaps, marks a sacred spot or even a water source. Ben says, "The hand could also be the storyteller's mark, a way of signing the petroglyphs carved into the rock."[59]

An avid collector of historic pieces of jewelry that he finds at trading posts throughout the Navajo Reservation, Ben also prizes fine turquoise and looks for unusual stones. "Turquoise is the life of the Southwest," he says. "Some stones are so beautiful and so far ahead of you that you have to wait for the right design." In the gold bracelet, Ben uses Lander Blue turquoise. The bezels are 18k gold, while the bracelet and

OPPOSITE: Arland F. Ben, Navajo. Sterling silver bolo tie and belt buckle with 14k and 16k gold overlay petroglyph motifs. Courtesy of Packards on the Plaza.

LEFT: Arland F. Ben. 16k and 18k gold bracelet with Lander Blue turquoise and overlay petroglyph motifs. Collection of John and Barbara Chaney.

triangular wire edges, all hand rolled, are 16k gold. On the inside of the bracelet, Ben has stamped a repeating "eye" design. "The gold represents our achievements and what we get done on this earth," he says. "The eye design is a reminder of everything that surrounds us and that lives on after this life."

Petroglyph motifs also characterize the work of Myron Panteah, a Navajo/Zuni silversmith, who works almost exclusively in sterling silver and 14k gold using a combination of cutout, stampwork, overlay, and appliqué techniques. In place of the traditional turquoise and coral, Panteah uses jaspers, agates, dinosaur bone, and more unusual stones, selected for their interest and range of color. "I always liked stones that are earthy in color and that you can find almost anywhere," Panteah says. "I started by picking up stones off the reservation or out of the river, "rez" stones, that I would cut and polish and then set."[60]

A third generation silversmith, Panteah learned by observing his Zuni father and grandmother making jewelry. He was also motivated to make jewelry by the 1970s *Arizona Highways* series on contemporary Indian jewelry his father had collected. "I knew I always wanted to do jewelry," he states. In high school, Panteah began making more traditional Navajo jewelry, though he would not become a full-time silversmith until 1990. After high school, he worked for three years as a furniture maker, running the band saw and cutting out curves in furniture. Later, he worked in the electronics division of General Dynamics in Fort Defiance, making circuit cards for the Phalanx Weapons System. "That job taught me soldering and how to do production work," he recalls. "In my jewelry now, I do all the pre-form work first. I cut out the spirals and water symbols and petroglyph figures and store them. Then I build the silver frames, and so on."

On the weekends, Panteah would travel over two hundred miles from Fort Defiance to Santa Fe to sell his jewelry under the portal at the Palace of the Governors. Encouraged by collectors and other Native American jewelers who were

buying his work, he entered his first Indian Market in 1992, sharing a booth with a friend. By 1995, he had his own booth at Indian Market, the same year he accidentally severed the muscles in his right thumb and forefinger washing a set of new Japanese knives. Unable to do lapidary work because he could not feel the stones to hold them, he switched to making gold and silver work with cutout and appliqué designs. In 1998, Panteah received a fellowship from the Southwestern Association for Indian Arts. He used his grant to take workshops through Duane Maktima's Pueblo V Institute in forging, the marriage of metals technique, anodizing, hydraulic forming, and photography.

Panteah creates his jewelry in steps. He builds the silver frames first; then he uses a fine saw to cut out minute and delicate designs freehand that he solders onto the frame. After the appliqué work, he cuts out further designs on the

OPPOSITE: Myron Panteah, Zuni, Navajo. Sterling silver and 14k gold overlay necklace with petroglyph motifs. Collection of Marcia Docter.

ABOVE: Myron Panteah at Zuni Pueblo, New Mexico.

silver frame. He keeps an index of petroglyph motifs that he has sketched from rock art sites near the Zuni Pueblo where he lives. "I use a lot of water symbols because I am from the Water Edge clan on my Navajo side," he explains.[61] Turtles, dragonflies, cloud designs, frogs—all adorn his necklace, that won a first place ribbon at the 2003 Santa Fe Indian Market. He represents "male rain," the rain that pummels the earth, with lightning bolts that come out of a cloud or spiral design. The softer female rain that nourishes the earth is symbolized by a spiral with a tail.

Spiral motifs abound in Panteah's jewelry. The spiral symbol has multiple layers of meaning within Navajo culture. In the Navajo creation story, the wind gave life to First Man and First Woman and leaves its imprint in the circular pattern on each person's fingertips. The spiral was also the migration path the people followed to reach this world. In the constellations, the spiral became a solstice symbol.

JULIUS KEYONNIE VARIES THE overlay style by using techniques he learned in his career making trophy buckles for rodeos. Rather than oxidizing the bottom sheet of silver, he uses a glossy jewelers' enamel to blacken the silver. With an engraving tool, he embellishes the cutout designs with meticulous filigree patterns—another technique used on rodeo buckles. Keyonnie alloys his own gold, using 14k and 18k depending on the color he wants in his jewelry. In a single piece of jewelry, he may employ several techniques, including engraving, overlay, lapidary work, and stamping.

Among southwestern tribes, rodeos are very popular. They are social occasions that bring people together from remote parts of the reservation. Competitions are fierce among the six events, and the winner is usually awarded a large trophy buckle engraved with the place and date of the rodeo. Such buckles are prized possessions and are often works of art themselves. A calf roper and a team roper on the rodeo circuit, Julius Keyonnie says, "I was born into rodeos. I grew up herding sheep with my brother and learning to rope."[62] Besides competing on the rodeo circuit—in 2005, he won a vintage 1969 GM truck for team roping— Keyonnie had a career making trophy buckles for more than a decade before turning to his own jewelry in his thirties. He credits the late Herbert Taylor, his wife's uncle, with encouraging him to start doing his own designs. In 1996, Keyonnie entered his first Heard Museum Indian Market and his first Santa Fe Indian Market, winning two first place ribbons at the latter. Today, Keyonnie divides his time between training horses, making jewelry, and rodeos.

Reared in traditional ways by his grandparents, Keyonnie incorporates textile designs and Navajo religious motifs in his work. In his bolo tie entitled *Holy Matrimony Bolo*, he represents the union of two people in two spirit figures joined by a ceremonial wedding basket. The turquoise represents the male figure and male rain, while the coral is the female and female rain. The wedding basket design also

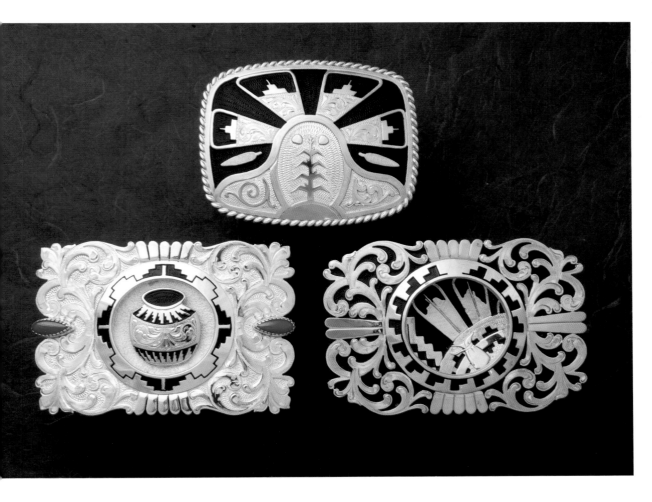

comprises the central medallion in the buckle. The ceremonial basket is one of the few baskets that follows a general design pattern and has symbolic significance. The white center of the basket represents creation and the beginning of life. A rainbow arc divides black stepped terraces into the sacred mountains of the Navajo below the circle and clouds above. In actual baskets, the arc is a series of red bands that can represent several ideas: the marriage of two people, a rainbow, and the life-giving rays of the sun. The opening orients the basket to the east and is a pathway for the spirit of the weaver to leave.

According to Susan McGreevy, a scholar of southwestern basketry, "Wedding baskets are used to serve the special cornmeal mixture during marriage nuptials and also play important roles in other Navajo ceremonies. They hold ritual paraphernalia, serve as an essential part of the payment to the medicine man, and form portions of certain masks. Inverted, they can act as resonance chambers or drums."[63]

As Southwestern Indian metalsmiths move into the twenty-first century, they have expanded their skills to include such nontraditional techniques of manipulating metal as *mokume gane*, or the marriage of metals. Mokume gane is the process of laminating multiple layers of disparate metals, such as copper, silver, gold, and platinum together under intense heat and pressure into a single block. The unfinished metal bar, also called a billet, can then be rolled to a specific thickness. Through forging, hammering, and carving into the layers, the artist creates complex and unusual designs in the metal. Mokume gane, which translates as "wood grain," has its roots in seventeenth-century Japanese sword making in which the amalgamation of the different metals created patterns in the blade of the sword.

Eric Othole, a young Zuni/Cochiti metalsmith, uses the mokume gane technique to create decorative accents in his belt buckle and bolo tie. In both pieces, the base is hammered and textured silver. Othole then overlays a sheet of copper and uses a stencil to cut out the designs with a hand-saw. With the same stencil, he carves out a shallow groove on the copper base to receive the cutouts. The squares and stars on the bolo are mokume gane. On the buckle, Othole uses mokume gane for a flower and the smoke rising from the pueblo chimneys.

To make the mixed metal designs, Othole stacks thirty-two alternating sheets of copper and sterling silver together. He then clamps the sheets tightly together and places the stack in a kiln at 1,300 degrees for ten hours. After the metals are fused, Othole hammers the sheet down to approximately one-eighth of an inch in thickness and uses a small doming stamp to make tiny repoussé bumps on the other side. He then files the bumps down flat, exposing the layers of metal underneath and creating a variegated design.

Of the designs in his bolo and buckle, Othole says, "I grew up going back and forth between Albuquerque and Zuni Pueblo. At Zuni, I always spent a lot of time with my

aunt, Rose Dishta. She made a lot of jewelry in the Zuni style. The flowers are like the needlepoint earrings she made. And the teardrop design around the edge of the buckle reminds me of her jewelry as well."[64] The *vigas*, or wooden support beams in the village homes, are 14k gold, as are the dots around the flowers. Othole has entitled the buckle *Springtime in the Village*. The Zuni Pueblo also inspires the bolo design. The stars remind Othole of the pristine Zuni night sky, remote enough from other communities to be free of light pollution. The step design outlining the center stone references the mountains near Zuni, as well as the kivas within the pueblo. The bolo's center stone is fossilized pinecone.

Tradition meets technology in the hands of Pat Pruitt of Laguna Pueblo and Chiricahua Apache heritage. In place of sterling silver, Pruitt uses stainless steel, and he substitutes

OPPOSITE: Eric Othole, Zuni, Cochiti Pueblo. Sterling silver and copper bolo tie and belt buckle with accents of mokume gane and 14k gold. Buckle, courtesy of the Case Trading Post, Wheelwright Museum of the American Indian, Santa Fe. Bolo tie, collection of Richard and Willa Sisson.

ABOVE: Pat Pruitt, Laguna Pueblo, Chiricahua Apache, Anglo-American. Stainless-steel bracelets. Courtesy of the artist.

hydraulic presses and computer-programmed cutting tools for stamps, files, and hammers. Pruitt's innovative jewelry grows out of a body-piercing business that he started in the 1990s while at Southern Methodist University in Dallas, where he studied mechanical engineering and worked part-time as a machinist. In 1999, Pruitt moved the company back to Laguna Pueblo, where several industrial buildings house his equipment.

In his artist's statement, Pruitt writes: "My work is the creation of aesthetically pleasing objects of adornment for the discerning individual with nontraditional materials and fabrication techniques utilizing evolving technology, equipment, and software."[65] Despite his twenty-first century approach to jewelry, Pruitt has a foundation in traditional silversmithing. When he was fifteen, he apprenticed with Laguna Pueblo silversmith Greg Lewis, learning basic techniques of repoussé and stampwork, which he has translated

into his stainless-steel bracelets. He credits Charlie Bird, another Laguna/Santo Domingo Pueblo jeweler, with expanding his ideas about design and aesthetics.

In 2006, Pruitt won a ribbon at the Heard Museum Indian Market for a concha belt entitled *Wampum Belt*. The individual conchas are round with scalloped edges bearing chiseled straight-line designs in the style of classic belts. There the similarity ends. Made of stainless steel, the conchas have been shaped by a 3-axis CNC machining center. Pruitt has over twenty different cutting tools that he programs to machine the steel with his "hot rod flame motif." In the center of each concha, he has placed a $100 chip from one of the seven Indian Pueblo casinos in the Rio Grande corridor. The back of each concha bears the dead man's hand of aces and eights. Acknowledging the controversy surrounding Indian gaming in the Southwest, Pruitt says, "The big positive is that gaming provides a lot for Indians in terms of jobs and infrastructure at the pueblos. The negative is the addiction and the corruption of large money."[66] With his command of technology and social sensibility, Pruitt represents the new breed of Southwestern Indian metalsmiths who use their jewelry, as a painter does the canvas, to make personal and political statements.

MORE THAN ONE HUNDRED AND FIFTY years have passed since Atsidi Sani became the first documented Navajo silversmith to inaugurate a new art form that remains unparalleled today in its quality and creative expression. The commonality among the five generations of jewelers, whose work spans the twentieth century and reaches into the twenty-first century, is a deep attachment to heritage and a respect for those who came before. All of the jewelers and silversmiths presented in this chapter view their work through the lens of history and have been students of process and technique, at the same time they are moving the field of metalwork ahead with individual imagination.

OPPOSITE: Pat Pruitt, Laguna Pueblo, Chiricahua Apache, Anglo-American. Stainless-steel concha belt with casino chips. Courtesy of the artist.

CHAPTER 2

LAPiDARY ART

The history of Southwestern Indian jewelry has been the story of turquoise, a semiprecious stone that is indigenous to the Southwest and has been mined there for two thousand years. Turquoise ranges in color from the yellow greens of Orvil Jack to the sky blue of Sleeping Beauty to the deepest indigo of the rare Lander Blue turquoise. Turquoise may be laced with matrix or flawless in color. Its hardness may denote gemstone quality, or it may be soft and porous. The high desert of the Southwest is the perfect environment for turquoise, which is found at higher elevations in semi-arid rocky and hilly landscapes. A hydrated phosphate of copper and aluminum, turquoise is formed over centuries by groundwater percolating through igneous rock, leaving behind trace elements of the minerals that harden into turquoise in fissures and pockets of the host rock. Turquoise with a higher copper content yields a bluer stone, while a greener stone contains more iron.[1]

Turquoise is a sacred stone to all of the Southwestern Indian tribes, emblematic of the sky and revered for its healing and protective qualities. Turquoise is central to the religious, ceremonial, and social organization of southwestern

Delicate Arch in Arches National Park, southern Utah.

BEADWORK

Jimmy "Ca'Win" Calabaza weaves together handmade beads of Kingman turquoise on sinew in this necklace. He cuts, shapes, and polishes each bead from the rough turquoise before drilling and stringing them together. Calabaza is one of many outstanding jewelers at Santo Domingo Pueblo, known for its beadwork and mosaic jewelry.

Courtesy of the artist.

tribes. To administer their ceremonial calendar, Rio Grande Pueblo tribes divide their population into two groups—the Winter People and the Summer People, also known as the Turquoise People and the Squash People. Each group has its own kiva, a center for secular clan business, as well as for private religious ceremonies and preparations before dances. For the Corn Dances, Pueblo women wear tablita headdresses painted turquoise with cutout cloud designs to summon rain. In *Diné bahanè–The Navajo Creation Story*, Paul Zolbrod recounts that First Man and First Woman created the sun from rock crystal, placing turquoise around the perimeter.[2] Mount Taylor, one of the four sacred mountains circumscribing the Navajo homeland, is *Tsoodzil*, which translates to Blue Bead Mountain and is known as Turquoise Mountain. Turquoise is also one of the four principal colors used by Navajo medicine men in their sandpaintings.[3]

Chaco Canyon, which lies in the northwest corner of New Mexico and was the foremost center of the Ancestral Puebloan cultures from approximately 850 to 1250, was a hub for the trade and production of turquoise. Pueblo Bonito, one of the largest structures at Chaco Canyon, included an estimated six hundred rooms and spread over three acres. In 1896, Richard Wetherill, a rancher and archaeologist by avocation, and George H. Pepper, curator of anthropology at the American Museum of Natural History in New York City, began a three-year excavation of Pueblo Bonito, uncovering turquoise in virtually every room. Frederick and Talbot Hyde, New York philanthropists and collectors, funded the Hyde Exploring Expedition and arranged for many of the artifacts to be sent to the American Museum of Natural History, only to be moved by Pepper later to the fledgling Museum of the American Indian–Heye Foundation in 1909.[4] (George Gustav Heye's collection of close to one million Native American artifacts from North and South America are today housed in three locations: the George Gustav Heye Center of the National Museum of the American Indian in New York City;

the National Museum of the American Indian on the Smithsonian Mall in Washington, D.C.; and the Cultural Resources Center in Suitland, Maryland.)

Archaeologists have identified much of the turquoise found at Pueblo Bonito as Cerrillos turquoise. The Cerrillos Mining District lies approximately twenty miles south of Santa Fe and 125 miles east of Chaco Canyon and was named Cerrillos by the Spanish to reflect the "little hills" that dotted the landscape. Geological evidence has shown that mining has taken place there since approximately 500. One of the largest mines at Cerrillos is Mount Chalchihuitl, a Nahuatl name which means blue stone and was used by the Aztecs to signify both turquoise and jade in the prehistoric Southwest. Such a name also suggests that the turquoise trade extended to Mexico long before the arrival of the Spanish under Hernán Cortés in 1519. Over the centuries, the Cerrillos mines changed hands several times—from Indian tribes to

Spanish colonists and eventually to American mining companies. By the end of the nineteenth century, the Tiffany mine in the Cerrillos region owned by the American Turquoise Company had generated over two million dollars' worth of turquoise. In 1978, Mount Chalchihuitl was enrolled on the New Mexico State Register of Cultural Properties.

In 1967, New Mexico made turquoise the official state stone in recognition of its central role in the cultural and economic history of the state. Until the early twentieth century, New Mexico was the largest producer of turquoise in the United States, the bulk of the stones coming from the Cerrillos mines. By the first decade of the twentieth century, Nevada had surpassed New Mexico in turquoise production, though New Mexico would remain the "nation's top center for the cutting and crafting of the stone," according to Susan Arritt in her essay, "Exploring the Miracle of Turquoise."[5] By the middle of the twentieth century, most of the great

ABOVE LEFT: Turquoise kiva at Santo Domingo Pueblo, New Mexico, circa 1910. Courtesy of Palace of the Governors.

ABOVE RIGHT: Pueblo Bonito, Chaco Canyon, New Mexico, circa 1954. Photograph by Harold D. Walter. Courtesy of Palace of the Governors.

99

turquoise mines of the American West had closed, many of them depleted over the years, others abandoned because of the economics of mining. Arritt says, "Some blame strict occupational safety regulations. Others point to the $50,000 to $100,000 cash bonds that must be paid in advance to ensure that land and vegetation are reclaimed."[6]

In 1993, Joe and Kate Lowry and their son Joe Dan Lowry opened the Turquoise Museum in Albuquerque, New Mexico. The museum features an enormous private collection of turquoise gathered together decades earlier by Kate Lowry's father, J. C. Zachary, Jr. Experts on the turquoise trade, Joe Lowry and Joe Dan Lowry write, "Since the 1980s, China has become the largest source, accounting for as much as half of today's worldwide turquoise trade. . . . Chinese turquoise is more affordable than American turquoise because the supply is abundant, labor costs are

lower, and there are fewer environmental restrictions governing mining in China. . . . Major deposits are found in the Hubei Province north of Xian."[7] Unlike mines in the American Southwest, Chinese turquoise is not identified by mine. Rather, all of the turquoise mined in all its variations of color and hardness is simply called Chinese turquoise. Despite the dominance of China in the global turquoise market, artists and collectors alike have preferred turquoise from the mines of the Southwest, paying a premium for gem-quality stones that have become increasingly rare and are often sold by traders to the best jewelers. It is not uncommon for partnerships to occur between stone dealers and jewelers with the dealer essentially financing the artist by providing high-quality stones for a given piece.

In the twenty-first century, only a handful of American turquoise mines have been operational. These include the Carico Lake mine in Lander County, Nevada; the Sleeping Beauty mine in Globe, Arizona; and the Kingman mine, also in Arizona, which reopened in 2004 for production. For mines that have not been depleted, some mining has continued on a smaller scale and for a very specific audience. The Lone Mountain mine in Nevada is one such example, reopening in 2000 after seventeen years. Gene Waddell, one of the partners in the mine, has been brokering and selling turquoise to jewelers for more than three decades. An acknowledged

ΠATURAL TURQUOiSE

"As a child I always had an interest in pretty rocks and plain ones too," says Cheryl Marie Yestewa, a Hopi/Navajo. Well known for her hand-carved and polished beads from natural gem-quality turquoise, she says, "I strive for simplicity, elegance, and timeless style."[8] A self-taught artist, Yestewa has been making jewelry since 1974. While her last Indian Market was in 1980—she has been a busy mother of nine children—her work has been avidly sought after by collectors and is in the permanent collection of the National Museum of the American Indian, Smithsonian Institution, in Washington, D.C., and the Heard Museum in Phoenix, Arizona. She used Indian Mountain turquoise with 14k gold for the single-strand necklace and Fox turquoise and 14k gold for the multiple-strand necklace. The hand-shaped flat nugget necklace is Lone Mountain turquoise with 14k gold.

Collection of Chris and Howard Klein.

expert on turquoise, Waddell grew up in the Indian arts and jewelry business started by his parents in 1938. His father, B. C. Waddell, owned the West Y Trading Post in Gallup, New Mexico, in the 1940s until it burned down in 1950 and the family returned to Arizona. B. C. Waddell had also once owned the Fox Turquoise mine in Nevada. A copper miner during World War II at the Castle Dome mine in Yuma County, Arizona, the senior Waddell one day noticed turquoise on the ground at one of the mining sites and began gathering and selling it. Gene Waddell says, "My dad sold Castle Dome turquoise to C. G. Wallace at Zuni Pueblo, who in turn sold it to Leekya Deyuse for his carvings."[9]

As part of their business, the Waddells brokered and sold high-quality turquoise to Native American jewelers, focusing on mines that were still producing in the 1950s and 1960s, including Bisbee, Blue Gem, Castle Dome, Kingman, Lone Mountain, Morenci, and #8. Gene Waddell joined the business after college and began selling turquoise to jewelers throughout the Southwest. During his years on the road, he established close relationships with many jewelers whom he would later represent through the Waddell Trading Company that he and his wife Ann founded in 1973. In 2006, Waddell opened a gallery in Scottsdale, Arizona, representing many award-winning contemporary jewelers and Native American artists. Of the dearth of American turquoise in the current marketplace, Waddell says, "A lot of the jewelers are buying old pieces just to harvest the stones. The silverwork may be mediocre, but if the stones are good, they will pop them out to reuse them in their own work. Collectors want great American turquoise."

Even for mines that are currently operational, the yield of high-grade turquoise has been quite limited. Waddell estimates that the Lone Mountain mine has only produced two to three hundred pounds of gem-quality turquoise over the life of the mine. "When the mine was producing in the 1980s," Waddell says, "we might mine as much as 300 pounds of turquoise in a month, but of that, maybe only three to five pounds would be gem quality. Charles Loloma bought half of what we produced in those days."[10]

Lone Mountain turquoise, prized for its hardness and rich color, is popular among contemporary jewelers. Raymond Yazzie, a Navajo jeweler from Gallup, New Mexico, uses Lone Mountain nuggets in his necklace with 18k gold spacers and beads inlaid with different cuts of turquoise. A master lapidary, highly respected for his ability to cut stones in different shapes, Yazzie credits Joe Tanner and his brother Lee Yazzie for getting him started in jewelry. Yazzie says, "I

LEFT: Raymond and Colina Yazzie in front of Yazzie's Indian Art Gallery, Gallup, New Mexico.

OPPOSITE: Raymond C. Yazzie, Navajo. Necklace, Lone Mountain nugget turquoise; bracelet, Lone Mountain turquoise, cabochon cuts, 18k gold. Collection of Chris and Howard Klein.

belt appeared on the back cover of the August 1974 issue of *Arizona Highways* along with two bracelets by Lee Yazzie, putting the two brothers on the southwestern jewelry map.

In 2004 Raymond Yazzie made a bracelet entitled *Life's Beginning* with a rare piece of fossil Lone Mountain turquoise that he bought from Joe Tanner. Fossil turquoise forms in hollows and dimples in the host rock once occupied by fossil plants. In describing the bracelet, Yazzie writes, "Life is a miracle and nature is as well," referring to the millennia required to produce such a stone within the earth. The bracelet is an interpretation of birth and is remarkable because of the size of the fossil turquoise that forms the mother's body. Yazzie fabricated the bracelet from 18k gold sheets and used a mosaic-style inlay technique, winning ribbons for the bracelet at the 2004 Heard Museum Indian Market, the Gallup Inter-Tribal Indian Ceremonial, and the Santa Fe Indian Market.

Like many contemporary jewelers, Yazzie builds his jewelry around a theme. *Blessings* is the title he has given to a bracelet he made in 2002 based on his admiration for Hopi artist Dan Namingha's abstract paintings of Kachina masks. The base for the bracelet is a rare Water Web Kingman turquoise, and the central design is the Maiden Kachina. On either side are two more abstract Kachina masks. He says, "I have cut, shaped, and polished approximately 700 stones in making the bracelet. Some were not good enough quality for me to set. Approximately 485 of the stones became part of my bracelet."[12] Almost every stone has a unique size and shape, adding to the drama of the bracelet.

In 1994, Raymond and his wife Colina opened Yazzie's Indian Art Gallery in Gallup, New Mexico. Like many jewelers in the Gallup area, Yazzie worked for other people before starting his own business. Today, Yazzie mentors younger jewelers and has been part of a growing community of artists who share ideas and encourage each other in their designs and techniques.

ABOVE: Raymond C. Yazzie, Navajo. 18k gold bracelet with Lone Mountain fossil turquoise and coral. Collection of Hiroumi Imai.

OPPOSITE: Raymond C. Yazzie. 18k gold bracelet with Water Web Kingman turquoise, Orvil Jack turquoise, Fox turquoise, and Utah jade turquoise. Private collection.

was brought in, asked to work with Joe Tanner when I was between ten and eleven years old. Joe Tanner . . . always worked with my family. . . . He took us in and he provided jobs for the family."[11] Initially hired to clean the lapidary sticks for his brother Lee, the younger Yazzie soon apprenticed with Lee. He learned to cut cabochons, gemstones that are cut and polished in a domed shape, as opposed to faceted. When he was fourteen, Raymond Yazzie won the Best of Show at the 1973 Gallup Inter-Tribal Indian Ceremonial in Gallup, New Mexico. He designed and inlaid a silver concha belt made by Hopi jeweler Manuel Hoyungwa. The concha

If turquoise has been the centerpiece of Southwestern Indian jewelry, shells have been the foundation. Like turquoise, shells have been used in jewelry since prehistoric times. The Hohokam Indians were a cultural group (circa 300 B.C. to 1450 A.D.), who migrated into Arizona from Mexico and settled in southern Arizona along the Gila, Salt, and Santa Cruz rivers. They traded shells from the Gulf of California to the Anasazi in the Four Corners area. The shells included the *conus*, *glycymeris*, and *spondylus* species. In their own jewelry, the Hohokam made bracelets from the round glycymeris shells, carving designs into the shells. They collected more exotic shells for trade, such as abalone, on their annual expeditions to the Pacific Ocean.

In their turn, the Anasazi decorated the shells with *mosaic*, combining turquoise, jet, shell, and other materials in geometric grids of color. In mosaic, stones and shells are sliced into small, uniform pieces that are affixed to a base. The rough materials are then ground down to a flat, even surface. After the grinding, the mosaic is sanded and polished to a high sheen. The Anasazi used shell and cottonwood for a base and either mesquite gum or piñon pitch for an adhesive.[13]

Like turquoise, shell has symbolic significance in Southwestern Indian cultures. In Navajo culture, White-Shell Woman is a deity who appears both as the sister of Changing Woman and, at times, as Changing Woman herself. She dwells at Blanca Peak, one of the four sacred mountains of the Navajo. After First Man and First Woman made the sun, they made the moon from mica, around which they placed white shells. Over the centuries, the combination of turquoise on shell took on ceremonial significance, representing the coming together of opposites—the sky and the earth, male and female—symbolizing growth and propagation on multiple levels. At Santo Domingo Pueblo, men wear dance shells inlaid with turquoise and jet as part of their traditional dress for the Corn Dance. The dance shell is a physical symbol of their prayers for rain and a fruitful harvest.

ABOVE: Hohokam glycymeris shell bracelets, circa 700 to 1300. Photograph by Arthur Vokes. Courtesy of Arizona State Museum, University of Arizona.

RIGHT: Angie Reano Owen, Santo Domingo Pueblo, selling jewelry under the portal of the Palace of the Governors, Santa Fe Plaza, circa mid-1950s Courtesy of The Rainbow Man.

TOP: Angie Reano Owen. Mosaic tab choker necklace with Sleeping Beauty turquoise and spiny oyster. **BOTTOM:** Reverse side with abalone shell. Collection of Melinda and Bernard Ewell.

Angie Reano Owen, renowned for her role in reviving the tradition of mosaic jewelry at Santo Domingo Pueblo in the early 1970s, recalls some of her first challenges in making mosaic: "My father [Joe I. Reano] scraped chimney soot and mixed it with water and added a little to the glue to get the right color. If there was too much soot, the glue turned to rubber. If there wasn't enough, the glue turned gray when I started to grind the stones."[14] Owen's first pieces of jewelry were mosaic-on-cottonwood earrings and dance shells which she sold at pueblo feast days. Museums began ordering her jewelry, giving her the confidence to experiment with more elaborate pendants and necklaces.[15]

Like many Santo Domingo Pueblo jewelers, Owen began her career by selling her family's jewelry under the portal on the Santa Fe plaza when she was twelve years old in the late 1950s. She soon learned what styles were popular among the tourists. In the 1960s, most Santo Domingo people were making *heishi* necklaces to meet the market demand. Heishi means shell in the Santo Domingo language. The process of making heishi is very labor intensive. Jewelers start with the raw shell from which they cut strips. From the strips they cut square tabs, which are then drilled and strung tightly together on fine wire. The final step is to grind the tabs down into round beads. "It wasn't profitable," Owen recalls. "We were only getting $1.50 a strand. I talked with my father, and he suggested that I start gluing."

Owen's mother, Clara Lovato Reano, had made mosaic jewelry during the Depression, using the backs of car batteries and 78 rpm records for a foundation in the absence of shells. After World War II, though, mosaic slowly died out, as bead-making and heishi necklaces became more popular. In the late 1960s, Owen met Oscar Branson, an avid collector and author of several popular monographs on Indian jewelry making and turquoise. "Oscar is the one who told me about the Hohokam people making bracelets out of shells," she recalls. "He is the person who inspired me to make my

first mosaic bracelet from a glycymeris shell. He also told me where I could get epoxy."[16] After much experimentation, in 1970, Owen became the first person at Santo Domingo Pueblo to apply mosaic to a glycymeris shell in the style of her ancestors. In 1974, she made her first mosaic bangle bracelet on a green-snail shell.

Owen's signature bracelet style is a cuff bracelet made from a tiger cowrie shell. Her mosaic patterns range from diamond-cut designs to the popular herringbone pattern. To highlight her designs, she colors the epoxy black. Within the last decade, Owen has introduced a new style of bracelet inlaid with mosaic on all sides. In place of shell, she crafts a base of cottonwood, overlaying the mosaic from the inside to the outside. Since 2000, Owen has been mentoring Rena Owen, her daughter-in-law, who is her assistant and is crafting mosaic jewelry under her own name.

OPPOSITE: Angie Reano Owen, Santo Domingo Pueblo. Mosaic cuff bracelet, nugget necklace, and mosaic pendant with Villa Grove turquoise, coral, mother-of-pearl, lapis, malachite, jet, and pearls. Private collection.

LEFT: Angie Reano Owen. Mosaic bracelet on cottonwood base with Sleeping Beauty turquoise and spiny oyster. Collection of Melinda and Bernard Ewell.

RIGHT: Charlene Sanchez Reano, San Felipe Pueblo, and Frank Reano, Santo Domingo Pueblo. Reversible mosaic-on-shell necklace with purple and orange spiny oyster, mother-of-pearl, and abalone. Collection of Marcia Docter.

OPPOSITE, LEFT: Charlene Sanchez Reano in her studio, San Felipe Pueblo, New Mexico.

OPPOSITE, RIGHT, TOP: Charlene Sanchez Reano and Frank Reano. Reversible mosaic tab necklace with orange spiny oyster, abalone, mother-of-pearl, black lip oyster shell, melon shell, and green jade. Private collection.

BOTTOM: Reverse side with orange spiny oyster, mother-of-pearl, black lip oyster shell, and green jade. Private collection.

Charlene Sanchez Reano of San Felipe Pueblo is another distinguished mosaic jeweler, well known for her "sandwich" necklaces of graduated pendants of shell with mosaic designs. She combines purple spiny oyster and orange spiny oyster with mother-of-pearl to create her geometric design. The first step is to cut the blanks out of shell. The blanks are the foundation upon which the mosaic is placed. She then glues on the various materials to the base in their rough form. The final step is to grind the materials flush with the base shell and then polish each pendant separately before they are strung on the necklace.

Sanchez Reano, the sister-in-law of Owen, began making jewelry at age eighteen, learning initially from her in-laws at Santo Domingo Pueblo—Rose Reano, a sister-in-law, and Clara Lovato Reano, her mother-in-law. She studied business and art at New Mexico Highlands University for a year before going to work for Kabana, Inc., a jewelry produc-

tion company in Albuquerque, New Mexico, where she created her own style of inlay in gold and silver for two years. In the early 1980s, she and her husband Frank Reano branched out on their own, studying mosaic with Owen for about a year. Like many couples who collaborate in jewelry making, there is a division of labor. Sanchez Reano designs the jewelry and cuts and glues the mosaic to the shell, while Frank Reano does the grinding, sanding, and buffing.

Noted for her multifaceted mosaic, Sanchez Reano varies the patterns and the colors of her double-sided necklaces. She uses orange spiny oyster for the herringbone design, which is primarily orange with accents of gray and black. On the reverse side, the color palette is predominantly black with accents of orange, and the pattern is more random, creating a distinctly different look. The single mosaic pendant is a popular earring style. When clustered together, the multiple pendants produce a dramatic and unique necklace. Sanchez Reano has won many awards for her jewelry over the years, including the Best of Division at the 2005 Santa Fe Indian Market and the Judge's Choice Award at the 2006 Heard Museum Indian Market.

In the hands of Charlie Bird, of Laguna Pueblo and Santo Domingo Pueblo heritage, mosaic has been a canvas for his abstract designs in stone and shell. Bird frames his mosaics in silver, using simple color schemes to highlight his geometric designs. "You can do the same pattern in a different color and the overall effect is completely new," he says.[17] Bird draws inspiration for his designs from many sources, combining several influences in a single piece. An avid sportsman and a former firefighter, Bird has spent a lot of time in the mountains of New Mexico, and he has mirrored the changing colors of that topography in the subtle earth tones in his bolo ties. He combines such exotic materials as Cocobolo wood with light and dark fossilized ivory, using the iridescence of mother-of-pearl to mimic light reflections on rock. In another bolo with a single checkerboard design, he has used ebony as a border. "A friend once gave me some piano keys," he recalls, "and I kept thinking of the Paul McCartney song, *Ebony and Ivory*, that he and Stevie Wonder performed. That got me started on using ebony as a material."

While popular culture is part of Bird's background, he states that the checkerboard design in his bolos was inspired by Mimbres pottery (550 to 1150).[18] Isolated in a long valley in southern New Mexico, the Mimbres people developed a highly sophisticated tradition of painted pottery, decorating their black and white vessels with abstract and figurative designs. Bird has spent time studying and sketching Mimbres pottery designs at Western New Mexico University Museum in Silver City, which houses one of the largest permanent collections of Mimbres pottery in the world. "A lot of the pottery has the black and white checkerboard designs, as well as multiple fine straight lines that are left unpainted and appear white on the surface of the pottery," Bird says. "The abstract designs are just amazing." Bird's minimalist palette sets off his intricate mosaic in a way that is thoroughly modern and timeless.

WHEN THE FIRST ANASAZI artisan created a mosaic of turquoise on shell over one thousand years ago, he or she unwittingly inaugurated a tradition of inlay in Southwestern Indian jewelry. It would take another nine centuries for inlay to become a standard technique, and that would happen in the twentieth century with the introduction of silver as a foundation onto which jewelers could place their designs in stone. In the twenty-first century, inlay stands out as the most identifiable characteristic of Southwestern Indian jewelry. The design possibilities are myriad, ranging from abstract compositions to figurative scenes. While turquoise and coral remain the bedrock of Indian jewelry, contemporary artists use stones from around the world.

Inlay falls into two basic categories: *flat inlay* and *raised* or *stacked inlay*. In both cases, pre-cut stones are glued

OPPOSITE: Charlie Bird, Laguna Pueblo, Santo Domingo Pueblo. Bolo ties, mosaic on sterling silver. Left to right: Cocobolo wood, fossilized ivory, mother-of-pearl; light and dark fossilized ivory, mother-of-pearl; jet, mother-of-pearl; ebony side panels, mother-of-pearl, and jet. Courtesy of Case Trading Post, Wheelwright Museum of the American Indian, Santa Fe.

STONE-ON-STONE INLAY

Jimmie Harrison, a Navajo jeweler, made these two *Yeibichai* bracelets in 2007. Yeibichais are the masked dancers who represent the *Yeis*, or Navajo Holy People, in the Night Chant, a nine-day winter healing ceremony. Harrison uses a stone-on-stone inlay, placing his abstract designs directly into the jet base. The middle figure in the larger bracelet is a male Yeibichai with a stylized headdress and earrings. He is flanked by a female dancer on the left and a sun face on the right. In the smaller bracelet, a female Yei is in the center and on the side, so designated by the red dot at the bottom of each figure. "I was taught that the red dot with silver means that the woman can bear children. The red is her blood," Harrison says.[19] Harrison uses thin slices of jet to separate the colors of the geometric designs on either side of the figures. The stones include coral, Sleeping Beauty and Chinese turquoise, white and yellow shell, lapis and denim lapis, rhodonite, and orange spiny oyster. One of the first Navajo silversmiths to develop a contemporary inlay style, Harrison learned inlay initially by watching Jesse Monongya work. From 1980 to 1981, Harrison did inlay for Jesse's father, Preston Monongye. Harrison has been a full-time jeweler since 1981 and has won the Best of Show award at the 1981 Museum of Northern Arizona's All Navajo Show in Flagstaff and Best in Design in Contemporary Jewelry at the 1988 Eight Northern Indian Pueblos Arts and Crafts Show, among many awards.

Courtesy of the artist and Yazzie's Indian Art Gallery.

into a shallow channel or trough. In *flat inlay*, the stones are ground down to become flush with the surface. *Channel inlay* is a variation of flat inlay in which stones are set in pre-constructed compartments of silver, as opposed to a single groove, making the silver a design element. *Mosaic* is an *overlay* technique in which stones are glued into thin lines grooved into the base metal to further secure the inlay. In the Santo Domingo Pueblo style of mosaic, rough stones or shells, as opposed to finished cuts, are glued on to the surface of shell or cottonwood and then ground down to an even plane. *Etched inlay* refers to designs that are imposed upon stones, once they are set.

The second category of inlay is the *raised* or *stacked inlay*, and refers to a style in which stones extend beyond the metal to create a three-dimensional or sculptural effect. A more recent innovation has been *stone-on-stone inlay*, in which stones are embedded in other stones as part of the design. It is not uncommon for contemporary jewelers to be versatile at several types of inlay and to integrate a variety of techniques in a given piece.

The Zuni Pueblo has long been recognized as a center for inlay, producing artists who have portrayed the flora and fauna of the Southwest in cameos of technical and artistic virtuosity. Jake Livingston has become well known for his realistic representation of animals and birds of the Southwest. In 1976, he won the Best of Show at the Gallup Inter-Tribal Indian Ceremonial for a reversible concha belt with birds inlaid on both sides of each concha. Born Jacob Haloo, Jr., to a Zuni father (Jacob Haloo, Sr.) and a Navajo mother (Lola P. Haloo), Livingston is fluent in Zuni and Navajo. He began making jewelry when he was ten years old, learning inlay from his father, who was a respected Zuni artist. (He changed his name legally to Livingston in 1969, taking the name of his mother's uncle.) As a young boy, Livingston lived with his Navajo grandparents in the summer, caring for his grandfather's sheep, cattle, and

SANDPAINTINGS

Sandpaintings are one part of Navajo healing ceremonies, also called chantways. The purpose of a sandpainting is to restore balance and harmony and therefore health to an individual. A medicine man creates a painting with colored dry sand on the floor of the hogan. "The sandpainting is a symbolic representation of some portion of Navajo mythology. The patient is seated on the sandpainting after it is completed and parts of it are placed on his body. By identifying in this way with the deities invoked, he gains power from them. The evil, which has caused the sickness, is absorbed by the sand and is then ceremonially buried. The sandpainting is created and destroyed between sunrise and sunset of one day."[21] This sandpainting from the Beauty Way Chant was made by Fred Stevens in 1969. A Rainbow Yei surrounds it.

Photograph by Arthur Taylor. Courtesy of Palace of the Governors.

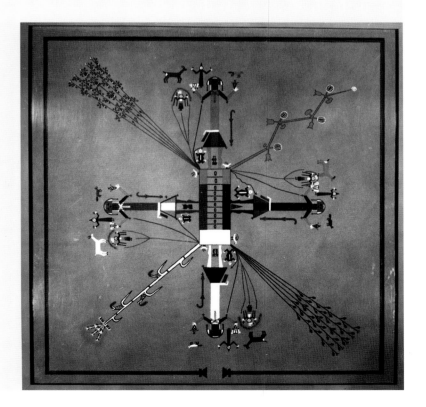

horses, and learning ranching, which would become his livelihood. After serving four years in the marines and spending two years in Vietnam, where he received three Purple Hearts, Livingston returned to Arizona and studied jewelry with Kenneth Begay at Navajo Community College in Tsaile, Arizona, in 1972. "He taught us the basic techniques—how to make our own tools like chisels and how to do Navajo-style work," Livingston recalls.[20]

In 1977, Livingston constructed a necklace with an ingenious design that highlighted his talent in lapidary work. He fabricated beads with four sides and inlaid different birds on each side. There are nine beads and thirty-six birds in the necklace, making the necklace a miniature gallery of birds of the Southwest. Livingston based his designs on

photographs of actual birds, which he sketched in advance. He placed the pattern on the silver to cut out the various sections to be inlaid. He fabricated the beads and the necklace first and then cut out the stones that were used for his mosaic inlay. Each bird is accompanied by the flora and fauna of its natural habitat. Livingston's wife, Irene Owens Livingston, helped inlay the flower and leaf designs with the smaller stones that he cut. "I taught her how to inlay. She helps me a lot, and we sign our pieces with both our initials. It's always teamwork." In the final step, Livingston etches the details onto each scene with a carving chisel or a dremel.

In choosing birds for his subject matter, Livingston pays tribute to the place of birds within Zuni culture. Bird migrations mark the changing seasons and influence the

OPPOSITE: Jake H. Livingston, Navajo, Zuni. 14k gold necklace with nine four-sided reversible beads inlaid with thirty-six distinct bird designs. Stones include turquoise, coral, jet, serpentine, lapis, mother-of-pearl, and abalone. Collection of Thomas J. and Edna J. Brimhall.

LEFT: Jake H. Livingston. 14k gold bracelet and ring with Yei figure and inlaid with Kingman turquoise, coral, lapis, jet, and mother-of-pearl. The reversible centerpiece has a bluebird on one side and a sun face on the other. Collection of Thomas J. and Edna J. Brimhall.

cine men in their healing ceremonies. They are painted and decorated with the feathers of birds that carry prayers to the gods. Within the Zuni social organization, there are the Eagle, Turkey, Sandhill Crane, and Roadrunner clans, among others. And then there is simply the plethora of birds that inhabit the Southwest and fascinate observers with their beauty and colorful plumage.

Livingston has also drawn upon his Navajo heritage in his jewelry. In the bracelet and ring made with Kingman turquoise, he depicted the Rainbow Yei figure, a guardian holy person associated with healing and often drawn around the perimeter of a sandpainting for protection. Livingston inlaid one side of the rotating medallion with the sun face of his Zuni clan. On the other side of the medallion is a bluebird. The bracelet earned Livingston the coveted Artist of the Year award in 1988 from the Indian Arts and Crafts Association.

Shells are the material of choice for Dale Edaakie, who creates another type of mosaic inlay in his fanciful holiday pins. The son of Dennis and Nancy Edaakie, Dale Edaakie studied painting at Haskell Indian Junior College from 1979 to 1981. "I wanted to be a still-life artist and a muralist," he says.[22] Although Edaakie began making jewelry at age twenty-three, learning techniques from his parents, he worked initially as an art and photography teacher at San Simon School on the Tohono O'odham Reservation in Arizona, where he moved with his wife and family in 1981. In 1992, the family returned to Zuni Pueblo, and in 1996, Edaakie made the decision to devote himself full-time to jewelry and to carve out a niche as a wildlife artist. In 1997, He entered his first show at the Museum of Northern Arizona's Zuni Marketplace, winning Best of Show and Best of Division awards for a wildlife concha belt, the first of many awards.

With his skills as a painter, Edaakie has created an imaginative menagerie of animals, primarily from shell. Edaakie inlays directly on a sheet of silver that has been soldered to a heavier gauge silver backing. He scores the

ceremonial calendar. Their feathers are attached to carved fetishes and they adorn prayer sticks in symbolic combinations. Prayer sticks are used throughout Southwestern Indian cultures as petitions for rain, a good harvest, and a healthy life. The Zuni plant prayer sticks in the earth over a twenty-one day period as part of their winter solstice ceremony. Prayer sticks are part of the paraphernalia of Navajo medi-

design on the top sheet of silver with a sharp nail to create shallow troughs into which he glues the various shells for his design. He then grinds the materials down until they are flush with the silver. At that point, he uses a dremel to etch details into the various materials. In the turkey pin, Edaakie uses coral for the feet and the beak, and white mother-of-pearl for the neck; the eye is made from lapis. The breast feathers are abalone, and the tail feathers are a combination of brown pen shell, as well as black, gold, and white mother-of-pearl. After the grinding, Edaakie adds fine details to the feathers, neck, and body of the turkey, creating the illusion of a fine art painting. In the witch pin, Edaakie lets more of the silver show in the spiral designs on the skirt. The broom and handle are silver with etched designs. On the white mother-of-pearl blouse, he inlays the Kokopelli figure, a fertility symbol, in black pen shell, adding the accent of a turquoise necklace. The face is pink mussel shell. As with the turkey, Edaakie achieves much of the detail in the rabbit pin with the dremel, adding detail to the eggs in the basket and to the tail, ears, and feet of the rabbit. For the Halloween pumpkin, he inlays the orange spiny oyster with black jet to create a three-dimensional effect.

Gomeo Zacharias Bobelu is another Zuni jeweler, who employs the etched mosaic technique in his figurative pendants. With his own spin, Bobelu crafts pieces after the style of Zuni jewelry made during the C. G. Wallace era. "I love the use of turquoise, shells, fossilized ivory, ironwood, and other natural stones to create color schemes from the 1900s," Bobelu says.[23] In 2007, Bobelu received a Goodman Fellowship from the Wheelwright Museum of the American Indian in Santa Fe for emerging artists. With a background in graphic design and a passion for photography, Bobelu says, "I would like my art to be considered painterly."

While Bobelu acknowledges that there is a "taboo" at Zuni Pueblo about carving human figures, he began making them in 2005 as a way to heal himself after experiencing his brother's death. *Singing Boy* is the title he gives to the dancer on the left, dressed in moccasins of apple coral with a mother-of-pearl body. The necklace and rattle are made from Chinese turquoise. The two female figures are a tribute to his grandmother and are portrayed in ceremonial Zuni dress. The central figure wears a traditional tablita headdress of Sleeping Beauty turquoise with an abalone dragonfly attached, and she carries a white feather, a cloud symbol. Her shawl is red spiny oyster, black pen shell, and Kingman turquoise—colors that signify life, death, and the sky.

The smaller female figure is entitled *Guadalupita*. The face, hands, and moccasins are made from fossilized ivory. Within the shawl of Kingman turquoise, Bobelu has inlaid abalone shell. The fringe of her dress is Chinese turquoise.

BOTTOM: Gomeo Z. Bobelu, Zuni. Sterling silver figurative pendants inlaid with etched mosaic. Left to right: *Singing Boy*, a tablita dancer, and *Guadalupita*. Courtesy of Case Trading Post, Wheelwright Museum of the American Indian, Santa Fe.

In the mid-1970s, Charles Loloma made some of his first "height" bracelets, introducing the *stacked* or *sculptural* inlay style into Southwestern Indian jewelry. By placing large stones perpendicular to the base, he shifted the emphasis away from a flat design to a three-dimensional design. This was a ground-breaking innovation in jewelry that would influence ensuing generations of jewelers. Loloma also experimented with colors in his jewelry, at times using just an accent of turquoise to bring out the drama of other stones. In a 1976 essay, he said, "I still use the silver and turquoise that is Indian jewelry but I've added my own things to it. If you take the Kachina doll cult, and understand the color schemes and all, and hold one of my pieces up to a doll, they will fit together very well."[24]

Loloma fervently believed that artists should draw on their individual cultures for inspiration, stating that "Southwestern people are probably the greatest designers in the world."[25] By his example, Loloma ushered in the contemporary era of jewelry, freeing jewelers to experiment with materials and designs with increasingly sophisticated inlay techniques.

While Loloma's impact on contemporary Southwestern Indian jewelry has been profound, his legacy has been especially notable in the striking jewelry of Verma Nequatewa, his niece. In 1966, Loloma invited Nequatewa to become his apprentice at his studio in Hotevilla, initiating a relationship that would last for the next twenty-three years. For eight years, from 1969 to 1977, Nequatewa and her son Bryson lived in the studio with Loloma, before they moved into a house across the road that he had built for them. Nequatewa recalls the rigor of their daily schedule from 8:00 AM to 5:00 PM: "Charles always emphasized that jewelry is a vocation. You must be committed and disciplined and treat it like a real job."[26] Of Loloma's aesthetic sensibility, she says, "He taught me his color sense, how simple something can be, that just the addition of one color can make the whole

piece come alive. I could see his designs in my head and would know where to place a stone. We were on the same wavelength. He would hand me something, and I would finish it." Loloma also emphasized the importance of using the best stones available. "Charles never had limits on materials," Nequatewa recalls. "He had to have the best materials."

The master-apprentice relationship was a two-way street, and Nequatewa also shared her ideas about the shapes she thought women would wear, putting her own designs and color combinations into the mix of their jewelry. Loloma had pioneered the use of gold in American Indian jewelry in the early 1950s. Now he used gold as often as he used silver, creating a new audience for contemporary Southwestern Indian jewelry among eastern collectors. As Loloma's fame grew, so did his commitments and his travel schedule. From 1978 to 1980 and again from 1983 to 1988, Sherian Honhongva, Nequatewa's sister, also worked in the studio making jewelry.

OPPOSITE: Charles Loloma, Hopi. Sterling silver and gold height bracelet with ironwood, turquoise, coral, fossilized ivory, and lapis; circa 1975. Courtesy of Wheelwright Museum of the American Indian, Santa Fe.

ABOVE: Verma Nequatewa, outside her home on Third Mesa, Hopi Reservation, Arizona.

RIGHT: Verma Nequatewa, Hopi. 18k gold bracelet with ironwood, vermillion, ebony, abalone, red and peach coral, and Lone Mountain clear and spiderweb turquoise. Collection of Dottie and Steve Diamant, Santa Fe.

OPPOSITE, LEFT: Verma Nequatewa. Sterling silver Hopi Maiden bolo tie with 18k gold, coral, sugilite, ebony, and turquoise. Collection of Donald and Noël Neely.

OPPOSITE, MIDDLE: Verma Nequatewa. 18k gold figurative bolo tie set with Mediterranean coral, Lone Mountain turquoise, sugilite, and lapis. Collection of Donald and Noël Neely.

OPPOSITE, RIGHT: Verma Nequatewa. Sterling silver Butterfly Maiden bolo tie with inlay of fossilized ivory, ebony, turquoise, lapis, coral, sugilite, and gold. Collection of Donald and Noël Neely.

In 1988, the Loloma studio closed, two years after a near-fatal accident rendered Loloma incapable of making jewelry. The next year the two sisters began to exhibit their own jewelry under the name of *Sonwai,* which translates to "beautiful." Loloma had given the name to Nequatewa and had encouraged her to sell her own jewelry under that name. In 1993, when Nequatewa and Honhongva decided to work independently of each other, Nequatewa kept the name of *Sonwai,* which she uses to sign her jewelry.[27]

In 1988, Nequatewa built her own studio across the road from the one she had shared with Loloma for twenty years. Her bracelet entitled *Mesas* is inspired by the rock formations she sees from her workbench. She also gets design ideas from a higher vantage point when she and her husband, Robert Rhodes, pilot their small airplane across the Hopi landscape. "We use our plane to fly around Hopi and places like Canyon de Chelly to look at the rock formations," she says. "The stones on the mesas are how our inlay designs came about. It's really nice from the plane. It's a birds-eye view."[28] Fabricated in 18k gold, the bracelet includes ironwood, ebony, abalone, red and peach coral, clear and spiderweb Lone Mountain turquoise, and vermillion (a red granite from Canada). Nequatewa cuts and polishes each stone before she sets them into the trough. "The gems tell me how to put them together," she says. "Lapis will make turquoise sing, but ivory next to turquoise will kill the color. It's like a painting, knowing which colors complement each other."

Since Loloma's death in 1991, Nequatewa has successfully faced the challenge of carrying on his legacy and of establishing her own artistic identity in the history of Southwestern Indian jewelry. Loloma reached beyond the American Southwest to an international audience, demonstrating that jewelry rooted in one's culture could have universal appeal. Nequatewa has expanded that legacy, moving jewelry into the realm of fine art. Faithful to Loloma's mandate that "artists should create from their roots," Nequatewa

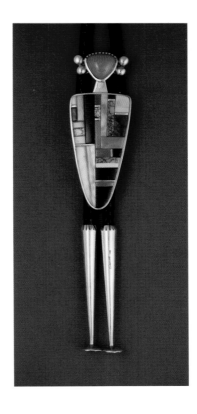  

incorporates many motifs from her Hopi culture in her work. Her bolo ties range from abstract figures to stylized interpretations of a Hopi maiden with the classic butterfly hairstyle. Their bodies are the frame for Nequatewa's artistic vision. "People like colors, especially turquoise and coral," she says, "but the design always dictates the materials." Having independently demonstrated her skill as a colorist and designer over the last sixteen years, Nequatewa has become the standard-bearer of sculptural inlay for the new generation of contemporary Southwestern Indian jewelers.

Like Nequatewa, Ken Romero crafts jewelry from multiple individually cut and polished stones that he combines in three-dimensional patterns. He has created a variation of the raised inlay technique that he terms Pueblo Design

Inlay©. He places multiple stones of different sizes at various levels to mirror the architecture of the New Mexican pueblos. Romero's bracelet, *First Snow at Taos*, represents his vision of the Pueblo after a snowstorm. "The colors move from the dark brown of adobe to all white, and then the sun comes out. It's always a nice day at Taos," he says.[29] Turquoise and coral accents, symbolic of the sky and earth, set off the fossilized walrus stones. In 2007, the Poeh Museum in Pojoaque, New Mexico, acquired the bracelet for its permanent collection.

Romero offers another visual interpretation of Taos Pueblo in his two rings. *Ode to Taos Pueblo*, crafted in coral with a feather design carved into the base, was designed to look like an aerial view of the pueblo with all the colors that play on the adobe architecture throughout the day. The monochromatic fossilized walrus ring depicts both sides of Taos Pueblo. Romero denotes the Rio Pueblo River that runs through Taos Pueblo with a slender slice of turquoise. The round opal set in the distance symbolizes Blue Lake, the headwaters of the Rio Pueblo.

Of Taos Pueblo heritage on his father's side and Laguna Pueblo heritage on his mother's side, Romero received degrees from the Institute of American Indian Arts and the California College of the Arts. After college, he taught art at the Bernalillo County Juvenile Detention Center in Albuquerque, New Mexico, for five years. He began his jewelry career at age twenty-nine. Acknowledging the influence of Charles Loloma, Romero says, "Since I am also a painter, I use colors to tell my story." He titles his red coral and black jade bolo ties *Twin Warriors*, explaining that those are masculine colors in his lexicon. The step design at the top of each figure suggests the Taos Pueblo. Romero has also added his hallmark below the headdress. "My hallmark is stamped into each piece of jewelry. The story and meaning behind my logo are twofold: High in the mountains there is a pass with a beautiful open aspen meadow. In this pass, a deer trail

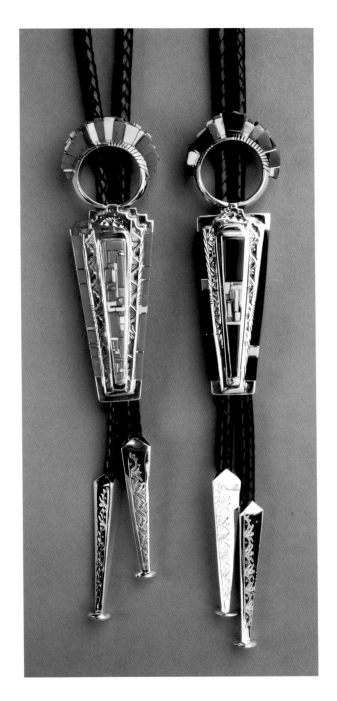

OPPOSITE, TOP LEFT: Ken Romero, Laguna Pueblo, Taos Pueblo. 18k gold ring set with Corsican coral, Sleeping Beauty and New Lander turquoise, lapis, and fossilized walrus. Collection of Donald and Noël Neely.

OPPOSITE, BOTTOM LEFT: Ken Romero. 14k gold ring inlaid with fossilized walrus, Sleeping Beauty and New Lander turquoise, and Mintabi opal. Collection of Donald and Noël Neely.

OPPOSITE, RIGHT: Ken Romero. Sterling silver sculptural inlaid bracelet with 589 stones, fossilized walrus tusk, turquoise, coral, black jade, and lapis. Courtesy of Poeh Museum Permanent Collection.

LEFT: Ken Romero. Sterling silver bolo ties with Corsican coral, Sleeping Beauty turquoise, and black jade. Left, collection of Jean Birger. Right, collection of Donald and Noël Neely.

winds through and over the mountain. My logo is a mountain, with a dot signifying where the pass is. This symbolizes my name, meaning 'Where the deer feed, rest, and go through the aspen meadow.' Second, in the dark night sky, there are three stars in a row that are Orion's belt. I have added one more. The four stars honor the memory and spirits of my mother and father, my son, and my sister. One more star to the far right is stamped to honor those not forgotten."

Don Supplee, of Hopi heritage on his mother's side and French on his father's, presents another vision of pueblo architecture in his 18k gold bracelet inlaid with Burnham turquoise from Nevada. "The village of Walpi on the bracelet is based on a photograph that Jerry Jacka took that was on the cover of the April 1979 issue of *Arizona Highways* magazine," he says. "It took me two years to collect the stones so they would match."[30] The ancient village

of Walpi, located at First Mesa on the Hopi Reservation, is one of the oldest continuously inhabited villages in North America. Walpi is home to a handful of people and can only be visited by permission and with a guide.

Using the lost-wax technique, Supplee carves the entire bracelet first in wax, including the section that will hold his lapidary work, using a diamond drill for the intricate details. Lost wax is a method of casting in which a model is carved from wax and then coated with a liquid clay or plaster called the *investment*. When the covering hardens, the piece is heated in a kiln to melt the wax. The object is then placed in a crucible within a casting machine and centrifugal force is used to force molten metal into the mold through a sprue hole, filling the space left by the melted wax. After cooling, the object can then be polished or textured. Supplee uses a needle to texture the gold, which is called *royal yellow*. "I alloy a lot of my gold, and I make my own sheet metal and wire," he says. "I also order gold and I just love the soft, warm color of *royal yellow*."

Supplee began making jewelry in 1991, when he was twenty-six years old, following eleven years of working as a chef. "I was looking for something new to do, because I was burned out with the food business," he recounts. "My brother, Charles Supplee, volunteered to help me, and I started working with him, doing some polishing and soldering chains. After a while, Gene Waddell hired me at an hourly rate." Charles Supplee had studied with Pierre Touraine, a renowned French jeweler, who moved to Scottsdale, Arizona.[31] In Arizona, Touraine became interested in Native American jewelry and established an apprenticeship program with selected jewelers. He introduced them to diamond and gemstone setting and other techniques required to fabricate fine jewelry.

Although Don Supplee did not study directly with Touraine, he learned many of Touraine's concepts from his brother, Charles Supplee. "Pierre Touraine emphasized three-dimensional work, jewelry that was very sculptural," Don

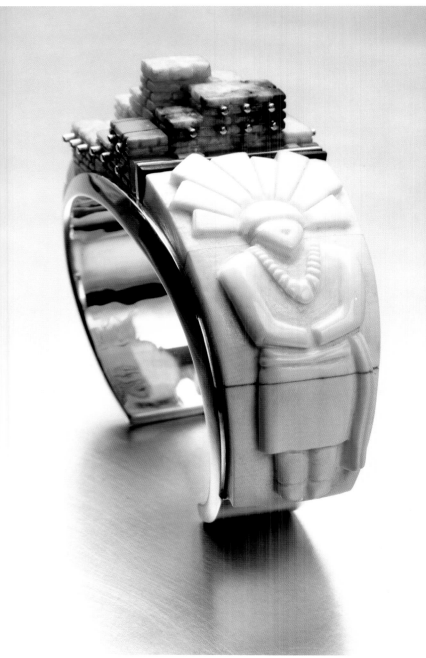

says. "Start with a big idea and then scale it back. I like to create designs in relief in my jewelry. They are little sculptures." In another Hopi village bracelet, which he has fabricated, as opposed to cast, Supplee carves an oversized Hopi maiden from fossilized walrus tusk on one side of the bracelet. On the other side is a bear with an inset of lapidary work that is a tribute to Charles Loloma.

Pierre Touraine encouraged the jewelers he mentored—including Charles Loloma, Harvey Begay, and Charles Supplee—to learn diamond and gemstone setting. The addition of diamonds to Indian jewelry was a new idea in the 1970s, and it was one that resonated for Harvey Begay, who studied with Touraine for eighteen months from 1979 to 1981. Although Begay had grown up surrounded by the jewelry of his father, Kenneth Begay, and had apprenticed with him and even worked for a brief time at the White Hogan, he did not think of jewelry as a career. Instead, he went into aviation, earning a degree in aeronautics from Arizona State University and joining the U.S. Navy as a flight officer from 1961 to 1965. Following the service, he was a test pilot for McDonnell Douglas in St. Louis until 1970.

By 1970, with the warplane industry in a temporary slump and at the urging of his father, Begay returned to the Southwest, taking a jewelry course from the senior Begay at Navajo Community College. By 1972, after briefly working with the Navajo tribal government in Window Rock, Begay decided to become a full-time jeweler. At Touraine's suggestion, Begay signed up for a diamond course at the Gemological Institute of America in 1980.

Begay uses the lost-wax technique to cast his gold bracelet with diamonds. "I made this bracelet around 1986," he says. "In the rough, the Indian Mountain turquoise was about the size of a small fist. I cut from the best end of the rough and shaped the stone, keeping as much of the material as I could. I then began drawing sketches until one jumped out at me. I wanted to use diamonds around the

turquoise. The lightning motif was the last touch. I carved the bracelet in wax and textured the surface in the wax form, using a small round burr."

While more and more Native American jewelers have been taking courses at the Gemological Institute of America in Carlsbad, California, the use of diamonds and precious gemstones is still somewhat limited in Southwestern Indian jewelry. Eddie Two Moons Chavez is one artist who is reversing that trend in his fine art jewelry. In 1982, Chavez graduated from the Gemological Institute of America, and in 1984 he became a Certified Gemologist Appraiser. A Chiricahua

OPPOSITE: Don Supplee, Hopi, French. Both sides of 18k and 14k gold fabricated bracelet with fossilized walrus ivory, coral, and turquoise. Collection of Gene and Mike Waddell.

ABOVE: Harvey A. Begay, Navajo. 14k gold cast bracelet set with Indian Mountain turquoise and diamonds. Private collection.

EUROPEAN ELEGANCE

Charles Supplee was only twenty-two when Pierre Touraine spotted his jewelry in a store in Scottsdale, Arizona, in 1982 and invited him to become an apprentice. Supplee recalls the importance of working with Touraine. "He introduced a European influence into southwestern jewelry, a more refined look. He had a flare and a style that was very new at the time."[32] For Supplee, the European influence translates into elegant lines and modern color combinations, such as sugilite with turquoise (left) and sugilite with coral (right). Supplee also adds a sylized mask to his 18k gold bracelet. Adept at lost-wax casting, tufa casting, fabrication, and diamond setting, Supplee creates graceful jewelry that exemplifies his philosophy that beauty often resides in simple well-executed designs.

Courtesy of the Faust Gallery.

Apache artist from Albuquerque, New Mexico, Chavez has been a jeweler since 1969. From 1975 to 1989, he designed and fabricated fine jewelry for Mindlin Jewelers in Albuquerque before going out on his own. In 2000, he returned to creating jewelry based on Native American subjects, drawing on his Apache heritage for themes. He says, "My name is Two Moons, which represents two worlds, the one we live in, the other a spiritual world."[33] Music is also a source of inspiration for Chavez, who was a music major in college and divides his time between music and jewelry. He is a student of traditional Apache songs and a singer. Several times a year, he is invited to sing with spiritual leaders at Apache ceremonies, which further provides him with themes that inform his jewelry. He also plays electric bass guitar for the highly successful music group, Thunderhand Joe and the Medicine Show. He tours with the group ten weeks of the year, playing at a number of casinos throughout the Southwest, among other venues. Of his dual career, he says simply, "I have always been a jeweler and a musician."[34]

For all of his jewelry, Chavez sketches designs in advance. He is adept at all forms of lapidary work, gemstone setting, fabricating, and casting. He develops his jewelry around subjects stemming from his Apache culture. In his pendant, *Twin Dancer*, Chavez combines Sleeping Beauty turquoise with deep red pyrope garnets from the San Carlos Apache Reservation. "This pendant depicts the dual purpose of dances and ceremony," he says. "The Crown Dancer is present to make sure that the creator has blessed our people and listened to our prayers."

Child of the Water is the name Chavez gives to the other pendant, which is tufa cast in 18k yellow gold and set with diamonds and thirty carats of druzy quartz. *Druzy*, also spelled *drusy*, refers to an aggregate of crystals that forms inside the quartz or host rock. In the Apache creation story, *Child of the Water* is responsible for making sure the human race continues to exist and for insuring that humans do not infringe

on the rights of other living beings. Chavez depicts the two roles of *Child of the Water* with his line of diamonds that dissects the druzy quartz. The garnet drop unites the two halves. Through his jewelry based on Apache themes, Chavez hopes to counteract the view of Apaches that has been promulgated by movies and the media. "The Apache tradition is one of courage, pride, and gentleness," he says. "People don't see that view of Apache culture in the movies."

ABOVE: Eddie Two Moons Chavez, Chiricahua Apache. Gold pendants (on left) set with druzy quartz, diamonds, and a chrome pyrope garnet; and (on right) set with Sleeping Beauty turquoise, diamonds, and chrome pyrope garnets. Courtesy of the artist.

LIKE SCULPTURAL INLAY, the variations within flat inlay are diverse. Carl and Irene Clark have been acknowledged as masters of *micro-fine intarsia inlay*, a technique they introduced into Southwestern Indian jewelry in the late 1970s. During the 1970s, Indian jewelry was at its height in popularity, and the Clarks wanted to carve out a niche for themselves that would make their jewelry distinct. In 1976, they lived in Phoenix, Arizona. "We worked long hours, raised our family of four children and made time to go to the public

library to do research on jewelry, art, and fashion," Carl says.[35] Among the many jewelers they studied was Fortunato Pio Castellani, an Italian jeweler who founded his studio in Rome in 1814. A master jeweler, Castellani was fascinated by history and the jewelry of the ancient Greeks and Romans. Through his own research, Castellani revived the technique of granulation, in which small particles of gold were applied to an object's surface for decoration. The Etruscans had used the granulation technique in their jewelry from the ninth to the fourth century B.C. Castellani was also a master of micro mosaic, combining hundreds of tesserae, or minute tiles of glass, silver, and gold, into elaborate figurative mosaics. His painted scenes resonated with the Clarks, who had been crafting their micro-fine inlay jewelry for four years when they discovered Castellani's work. Though Castellani had worked more than a century earlier, the Clarks felt a kinship with a fellow artist who was exploring the same techniques they were developing on their own. Carl Clark also studied Castellani's technique of blending colors, and would introduce his own version of color blending into inlay in 1986.

Although they are both from large Navajo families with rug weavers in them, neither Carl nor Irene had jewelers in their immediate families. With a background in drafting and mechanical engineering, Carl took a job as manager of a jewelry production shop in Winslow, Arizona, when he was twenty-one years old. Within weeks, he began to experiment with jewelry on his own, based on what he observed from the other silversmiths. The next year, he taught Irene the basics of silversmithing. Initially, they made Navajo-style jewelry, while Carl refined his skills at casting, reticulation, granulation, repoussé, overlay, and inlay. Proficient at all aspects of making jewelry, Carl and Irene share the tasks of their intricate lapidary work.

The Clarks draw on their Navajo heritage for their subject matter. "We use our Navajo traditional way to make our jewelry," Carl says. "We use the 'Beauty Way' in the sense

tthat beauty is before you, behind you, all around you. You walk in beauty."[36] The Beauty Way is a philosophy for living a life of balance and harmony and striving for beauty and order in every activity, no matter how large or small. The Clarks have become well known for their jewelry of protection that incorporates figures from Navajo sandpaintings. A consistent figure in their work is the Rainbow Yei that is drawn around the circumference of a sandpainting to protect the deities within. The headdress of the Rainbow Yei is composed of prayer sticks and feathers. An eagle and an otter, two guardian figures, are depicted in the bracelet (see page 132), which contains over 7,000 stones. The lapidary work in the bolo illustrates color blending. In color blending, Carl cuts the stones so that the shades of turquoise gradually bleed into the coral.

Their medallion of *Mother Earth/Father Sky* is another example of their technical mastery of lapidary work. There are close to 3,000 stones in the piece. Associated with three important Navajo healing ceremonies—the Shooting Way, the Mountain Way, and the Blessing Way—*Mother Earth and Father Sky* are powerful images that tell the story of creation. Mother Earth's body includes symbols of the emergence and the four sacred plants of southwestern tribes—corn, beans, squash, and tobacco. Father Sky's body encompasses the constellations, sun, and moon. The horns are symbols of power. In the sun, they hold male lightning and male rain. The horns on the moon hold female lightning and soft rain. The medallion was originally conceived by their son, Carl Clark, Jr., who had become a promising jeweler in his own right. When he died unexpectedly in 2004, the Clark's found his notes on the design of the piece, which they have followed to honor his memory and his artistic vision.

If the Clarks have become renowned for their microfine inlay, Jesse Monongya has been the paragon of figurative inlay, creating intricate scenes of Monument Valley and the Navajo night sky in jewelry that has garnered many awards

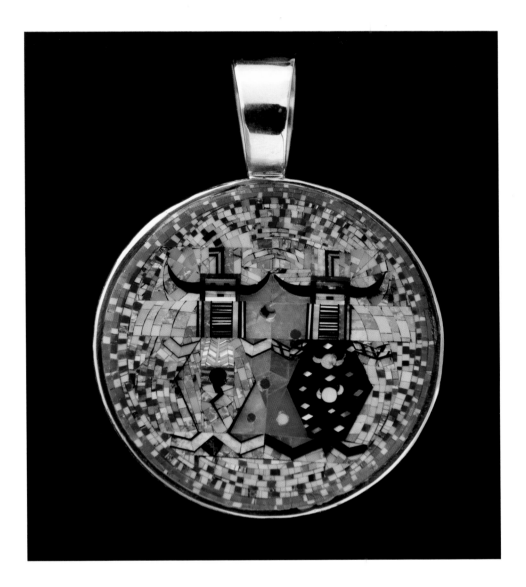

since 1977. His career has been well documented by Lois Sherr Dubin in her book, *Jesse Monongya—Opal Bears and Lapis Skies*, published in 2002. Abandoned as a child near the Grand Canyon with three of his siblings, Monongya grew up in the Two Grey Hills region of the Navajo Reservation with his

ABOVE: Carl Clark and Irene Clark. Gold tufa-cast medallion *Mother Earth, Father Sky*. Collection of Dr. Gregory and Angie Yan Schaaf, Santa Fe.

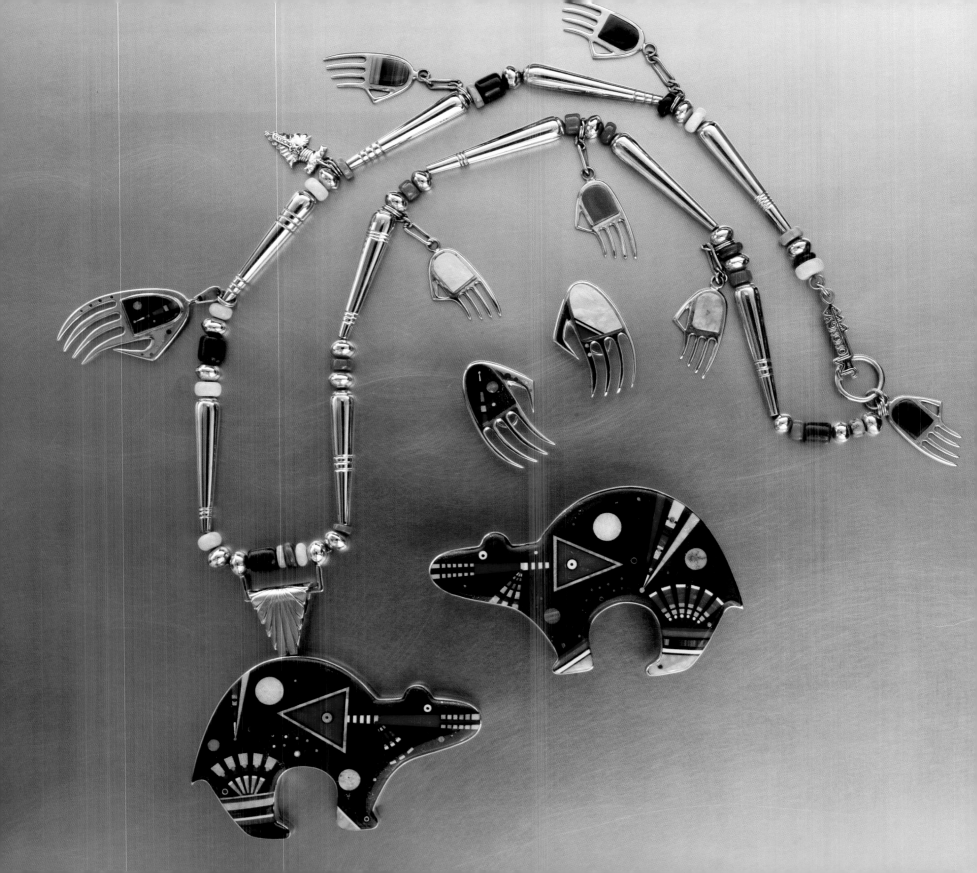

adoptive grandparents, Lucille and Allen Mailman. Known as Grandmother Yellow and Grandfather Mailman, they changed the children's surname to Lee.[37] From his grandmother, a revered medicine woman, the young Jesse Lee developed a knowledge of Navajo traditions and religion, as well as a respect for the land that would later inform his jewelry.

In 1975, after serving with the Marines, Monongya learned that his father was Preston Monongye. Already a highly respected jeweler in the Indian art world, Monongye was living in Arizona when Jesse met him for the first time.[38] The two agreed that Monongya would become an apprentice to his father. In 1977, Monongya made his first bear pendant, while he was still working for his father. A bear, the ultimate symbol of power and strength to the Navajos, had appeared in a dream, reminding Monongya of a real encounter he and his grandfather had had years earlier with a bear. Monongya believed they had escaped harm because his grandfather had offered quiet prayers in Navajo and asked permission for safe passage. By 1979, Monongya was among the jewelers included in the April 1979 issue of *Arizona Highways* along with Preston Monongye, Charles Loloma, James Little, Larry Golsh, and Richard Chavez. Monongya says, "That issue [entitled "The New Look in Indian Jewelry"] was the turning point in Indian jewelry."[39] For Monongya, the full-page photograph of his bear pendants established the bear as a hallmark piece.

In 1992, Monongya won the Best of Jewelry Award at the Santa Fe Indian Market for a lapis bear set with earrings, a necklace, buckle, and a bolo tie. The reversible bear pendant represents day and night. The lapis side is the night sky with a full moon, stars, planets, and a comet. The arrowhead at the end of the heartline is an emblem of the life force of the bear. The coral side is the day sky with an inlaid sun face and the first rays of sunlight. The bear paw earrings and satellites on the necklace are inlaid with miniature constellations, further accenting the theme of day and night.

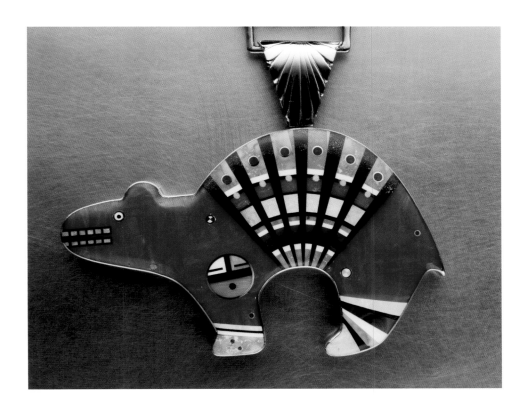

With his bears, Monongya popularized the use of opals in Southwestern Indian jewelry, using his lapidary skills to capture the iridescence of the fragile stones. He also demonstrated the versatility of lapis, substituting it at times for Acoma jet in his night sky scenes. "Lapis has its own stars and flecks in the stone, and I just add to that," he says. He also refined the technique of stone-on-stone inlay, crafting his designs within a coral or lapis base. He expanded inlay imagery to include constellations, shooting stars, comets, and sunbursts—all natural phenomena he had witnessed firsthand growing up in the rural area of Two Grey Hills. Throughout his career, Monongya has created worlds within worlds, embedding the tiniest sunspots, stars, moons, and comets in his jewelry.

OPPOSITE: Jesse Lee Monongya, Navajo, Hopi. 14k gold bear set: necklace, buckle, and earrings inlaid with coral, lapis, opal, malachite, Birdseye turquoise, and dolomite. Bolo tie not shown. Collection of Mr. and Mrs. N. Smith.

ABOVE: Jesse Lee Monongya. Bear pendant (reverse side). Collection of Mr. and Mrs. N. Smith.

Monongya has often combined several ideas in a single piece. His Bowerbird necklace, for example, grew out of an interest in Pueblo pottery bird motifs that he discussed with Susan Peterson, a scholar of Pueblo pottery. Peterson referred to the tropical birds often found on historic Pueblo pottery as "the ancient birds." Monongya was also inspired by the bowerbird, a small- to medium-size bird found in Australia and New Guinea.[40] The male bowerbird attracts the female by building an elaborate nest, or bower, decorating it with hundreds of brightly colored objects, such as shells, stones, berries, feathers, and pieces of colored glass. The male spends hours arranging the objects in such a way that his bower will stand out above those of his competitors.

Monongya combines the colorful plumage of the birds painted on Pueblo pottery with the story of the bowerbird, which holds a diamond ready to be placed in the nest. The reverse side of the pendant is the bower already decorated with dozens of colored diamonds.

Within the body of the bird, Monongya includes an image of Mitten Butte in Monument Valley, another signature motif in his work. "The very first time I ever laid my eyes on Mitten Butte, I said, 'There has to be a creator,'" he says. "Someone left the rock formation that way so we would always be fascinated by it. I've been there at all times of the day, and sometimes before sunrise, you can almost see the dinosaurs going through behind the rocks." Monongya's challenge in designing the image was to scale the enormous rock formation down to an inch in size and still have room to depict the road into Monument Valley in the foreground.

In 2007, Monongya created a new design—a thunderstorm over Monument Valley—in an 18k red gold buckle framed by cabochon cuts of Candelaria, Lander Blue, and Lone Mountain turquoise. Beneath the Big Dipper, a brilliant full moon illuminates the monsoon waters that flood the landscape. The opal tops of the butte reflect the moon's radiance and an array of shooting stars that soar over Venus in the distance. On the desert floor is a yucca plant, and behind the thunderstorm is a rainbow of color. Monongya says, "Before a storm, the sky begins to change color. My grandmother could read the colors and tell if a storm was three days away, two days away, or one day away. She would say the Water Dog is coming."[41]

The turtle is another popular motif for Monongya. "My grandmother was a medicine woman and always said we are like turtles," he says. "As a baby, you are crawling. At the end of your life, you come home crawling." Like the bear pendants, Monongya fabricates reversible turtles, inlaying the belly of the turtle with the day and night skies. The back of the turtle is inlaid with diamonds and precious stones. On the collar for the pendant, Monongya has placed a hand and a lightning symbol, tributes to his grandmother, explaining, "For certain cures, she would paint a lightning motif from her hand to her heart in corn pollen. This reminds me of her gift of vision."

Turtles are also a popular motif for Benson Manygoats, a Navajo jeweler who worked for Ray Tracey for fourteen years before opening his own studio in 2002. Tracey—a Navajo jeweler, designer, and actor—founded Tracey Ltd. in Gallup, New Mexico, in the 1980s to produce inlaid jewelry that he designed and sold nationally through galleries and museum stores. He has employed only Native American silversmiths and lapidary artists and has been instrumental in providing a training ground for younger silversmiths to

OPPOSITE, LEFT: Jesse Lee Monongya, Navajo, Hopi. 18k gold belt buckle set with cabochon cuts of Candelaria turquoise (top), Lone Mountain turquoise (bottom), and Lander Blue turquoise (sides). The bright green of the yucca plant is gaspeite. Private collection.

OPPOSITE, RIGHT: Monument Valley, with Mitten Butte on the right, circa 1935. Photograph by T. Harmon Parkhurst. Courtesy of Palace of the Governors.

TOP, LEFT: Jesse Lee Monongya. 18k gold Bowerbird necklace with coral, Sleeping Beauty turquoise, opals, lapis, and diamonds. Collection of Mr. and Mrs. N. Smith.

BOTTOM, LEFT: Jesse Lee Monongya. 18k gold Bowerbird necklace (reverse side) set with colored diamonds. Collection of Mr. and Mrs. N. Smith.

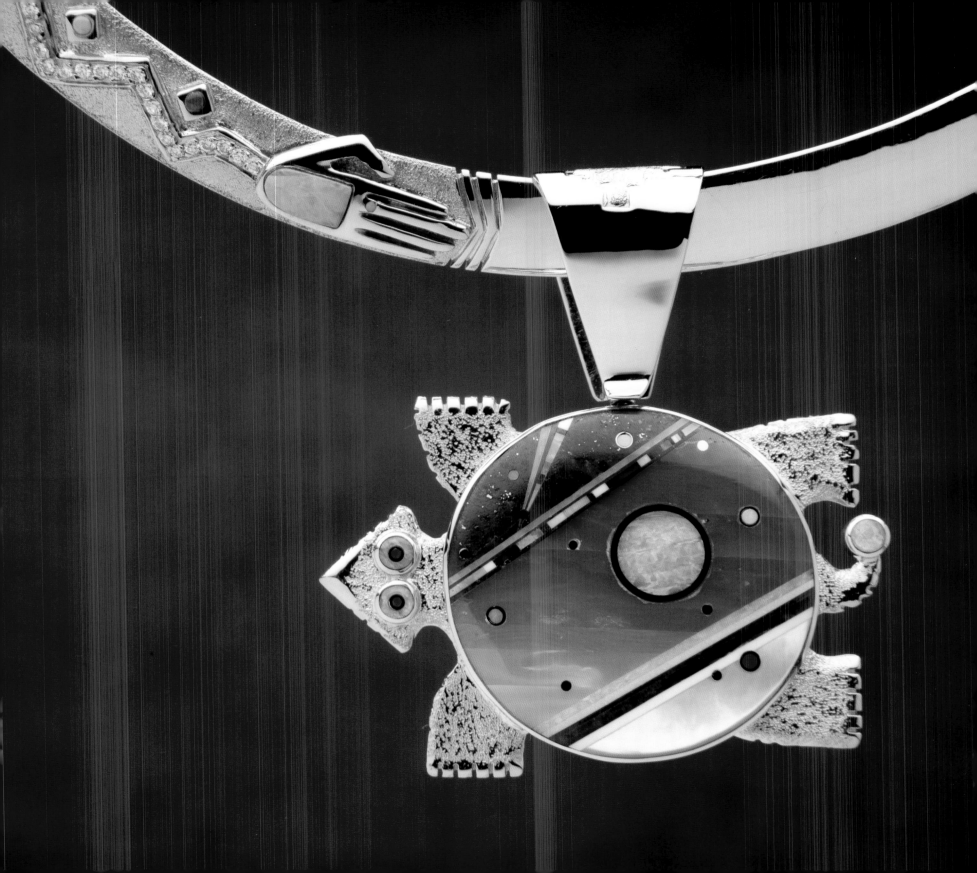

OPPOSITE: Jesse Lee Monongya, Navajo, Hopi. 14k gold turtle necklace with coral, turquoise, lapis, opals, and diamonds. Collection of Marcia Docter.

RIGHT: Benson Manygoats, Navajo. 14k gold turtle necklace with inlay and satellites and inlaid beads. Collection of Mr. and Mrs. N. Smith.

learn their skills. Manygoats applied for a job with Tracey after graduating from high school. "Ray showed me the basics of inlay," Manygoats recalls. "I made a bracelet in his style, and he hired me."[42] With a natural talent for inlay, Manygoats eventually took over as the inlay manager, overseeing the work of thirty jewelers and maintaining the quality control of each piece. Like many jewelry production shops in Gallup, there was a division of labor. "Ray would design a piece and give it to a silversmith," Manygoats says. "I would do the inlay, and then the piece would go to a polisher. Everyone had a job."[43] Manygoats also did the inlay work for many of the larger one-of-a-kind pieces that Tracy designed. Over the years, Manygoats has taught his five brothers how to make jewelry, one of whom works for Ray Tracey.

Manygoats combines flat with raised inlay in his turtle bolo and necklace. He cuts, shapes, and polishes the symmetrical pieces of coral for the body of the turtle in the *corn row* style of inlay. On the bolo, he demonstrates his versatility with lapidary work, inlaying the body, feet, and head of the turtle with different patterns (see page 229). He also adds inlaid spacers to the bolo and continues the turtle theme with miniature turtles on the tips. On the necklace, he adds a hand satellite. In the center of the hand and the oval disk on the necklace is Manygoat's logo, a diamond. "My birthstone is diamond. I love diamonds and the diamond shape."

Diamonds are also part of Manygoat's ladybug bracelet, in which he combines channel inlay for the Australian opals and raised inlay for the coral and chrysoprase cabochons on the side. Chrysoprase is a gemstone form of chalcedony (quartz) and usually has an apple green color. For the small coral squares, Manygoats uses a stone-on-stone inlay, embedding the coral in the opal. His diamond-logo signature appears in the center of the rectangle satellite on the side of the bracelet. With a touch of whimsy, he adds an inlaid ladybug to the bracelet, saying, "I was having lunch with my wife one day at Sonic, and a little ladybug just flew in and landed on her arm. It just struck me, and I decided to do a ladybug." Manygoats entered his first Indian Market in Santa Fe in 2003. Since that time, he has won multiple awards for his jewelry at competitions throughout the Southwest.

Alvin and Bryon Yellowhorse are two of the new generation of jewelers, who have distinguished themselves with their imaginative inlay. Born into the entrepreneurial Yellowhorse family, their studio is part of the Yellowhorse Village located on the border of Arizona and New Mexico at Interstate 40. Their father, Frank Yellowhorse, began his trading career by selling rugs at his parents' roadside stand on the old Route 66. "During the 1960s, my dad got into the service-station business, selling jewelry along with gas," Alvin says.

OPPOSITE: Benson Manygoats, Navajo. 14k gold bracelet with Australian opals, coral, turquoise, Acoma jet, lapis, chrysoprase, and diamonds. Courtesy of the artist.

BELOW: Alvin and Bryon Yellowhorse in front of a petroglyph rock near Lupton, Arizona.

"He had a silversmith who would come to demonstrate to the tourists. My dad would draw up a pattern, and the silversmith would make the jewelry."[44] A trading post soon replaced the roadside stand, and other buildings were added over the years, including numerous signs along the roadside to attract tourists to pull off the highway to see a Navajo trading post.

Alvin Yellowhorse's first job after high school in 1987 was with Ray Tracey. "Ray Tracey was hiring anyone without experience," he says. "All my friends were working there, and the pay was good. Ray Tracey is the one who really taught me inlay. I owe him all the credit."[45] In 1989, Alvin started a small jewelry business with his father, where he was put in charge of supervising and designing the jewelry. "I was the manager," he says. "I gave out the stones to the jewelers. We had about twenty people working for us. We stamped all the jewelry with Frank Yellowhorse for the stamp." In 1991, Alvin went to work in Gallup at Bilagaanas, a wholesale jewelry manufacturing business, where, he says, "The artists were allowed to use their own stamps." However, since Alvin did the inlay, not the silverwork, it was the silversmith who stamped his name on the piece. In his next move, Alvin writes, "In my search for better designs, I traded my inlaying knowledge for diamond setting and goldsmithing experience with Thane Deleon in Scottsdale, Arizona, who

OPPOSITE: Alvin Yellowhorse, Navajo. Gold fabricated bracelets with multicolored inlay of stones and opals. The bracelet (right) illustrates the wavy inlay style in which stones are cut in curved shapes. Courtesy of the artist.

LEFT: Alvin Yellowhorse. Sterling silver necklace with inlay of Monument Valley in center medallion. Petroglyph motifs are depicted on the right panel. Courtesy of the artist.

143

taught me everything I needed to know to continue on my own."[46] Alvin worked with Deleon the next four years and entered his first Santa Fe Indian Market in 1999.

Fascinated with the rock art of the Anasazi, Alvin Yellowhorse has a digital library of over 300 photographs of petroglyphs he has taken from sites all over the Southwest. He has often incorporated motifs from a petroglyph field near his home into his jewelry. One of his favorite designs is the *Three Day Journey,* which he uses in his necklace. The wavy turquoise lines represent the journey, while the moon and the sunburst signify time. The square box has been interpreted as an eternity symbol or a solstice symbol. In the center medallion, he depicts a Navajo sheepherder in Monument Valley. In his bracelets, Yellowhorse combines figurative scenes like Monument Valley with abstract geometric patterns. Recently, he has refined a technique he calls wavy cornrow inlay that he uses in his bracelet and bolo. "My designs come from Navajo, Zuni, Hopi, and Pueblo cultures," he says. "I mix it all together to make contemporary jewelry."

During the years when Alvin was making jewelry, Bryon was in the Navy, from 1990 to 1994. After his military service, Bryon took up jewelry for the first time at age twenty-two, initially learning from his mother, Elsie Yellowhorse. He helped her make the jewelry she sold to outlets in Gallup, New Mexico. After a year, she bought him a lapidary machine for his birthday, and he joined Alvin in making his own style of jewelry. "When I got the machine, I practiced and practiced," he says. "I had to be perfect."[47] Like Alvin, Bryon became skilled at figurative and geometric inlay. He has been recognized for his textile patterns based on Navajo eyedazzler weavings. "I did my first weaving bracelet in 1999, because I wanted the challenge of doing it," he says. "I start in the middle and do an entire half and then I go back and match the design on the other side." With remarkable precision, he replicates in stone the diagonal chevron motifs of Navajo eyedazzler weavings.

TOP RIGHT: Richard I. Chavez, San Felipe Pueblo. Sterling silver bracelet with Siberian green jade, Black Wyoming jade, coral, and turquoise. Collection of Martha H. Struever.

BOTTOM RIGHT: Richard I. Chavez. Sterling silver belt buckle with fossilized walrus ivory, coral, turquoise, and 14k gold. Collection of Martha H. Struever.

OPPOSITE: Richard Chavez. 14k gold bolo tie with Black Wyoming jade, red and pink coral, and turquoise. Collection of Donald and Noël Neely.

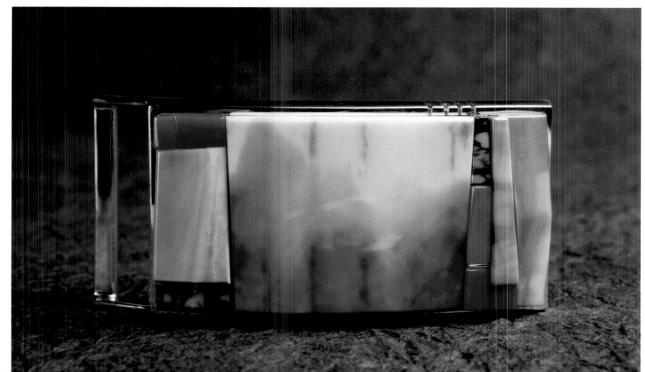

RICHARD CHAVEZ was twenty-nine years old and had only been making jewelry for three years, when he was included in the 1979 issue of *Arizona Highways* entitled "The New Look in Indian Jewelry." In stark contrast to the other jewelers in that issue, Chavez's jewelry was minimalist with no more than three to four colors in a given piece, and his shapes reflected the purity and simplicity of Scandinavian design. Chavez planned to be an architect and studied architecture and also worked as an architectural draftsman for Harvey Hoshour, who had worked for the German architect Mies van der Rohe. One of the principle architects of the Bauhaus School of Architecture founded in Germany after World War I, Mies's well-known motto was "less is more." He prized simplicity, clean lines, and minimal structure to complement open space—design principles that Chavez learned through his association with Hoshour.

In 1973, Chavez learned to make heishi and turquoise necklaces from his grandfather, which he sold locally for extra income. The labor involved in making the necklaces quickly became counterproductive because of competition from mass-produced necklaces imported from the Philippines. In 1975, Chavez taught himself silverwork by reading *Indian Silversmithing* by W. Ben Hunt.[48] His innovative jewelry earned him multiple awards and one of the first fellowships from the Southwestern Association for Indian Arts in 1982, only the second year the association had awarded fellowships.

Over the three decades of his career, Chavez has introduced a painterly style into Southwestern Indian jewelry. A skillful lapidary artist, he has used irregular cuts of stone to create a cubist pattern in the Siberian green jade bracelet. With the simple addition of three stones—Chinese turquoise, coral, and Black Wyoming jade—Chavez highlights the depth of the jade and creates the illusion of multiple planes, even though the stones are all flush with each other. In his belt buckle, Chavez has carefully selected different hues of

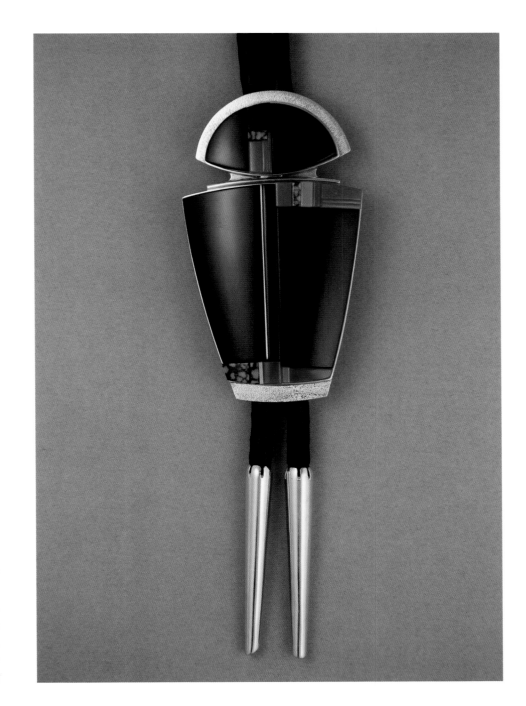

fossilized walrus ivory against which he places accents of coral and Chinese turquoise to create an abstract composition. Also called ancient ivory, fossilized walrus ivory has been buried anywhere from 100 to 2,500 years. The color depends upon the length of time it has been in the ground and the color of the surrounding soil. "The fossilized ivory can even be black at times," Chavez says. "I get my pieces from a gentleman who comes down from Alaska for each Indian Market."[49]

While Chavez does not use any specific cultural references from his San Felipe heritage, he does create figurative shapes as a background for his minimalist compositions, such as his bolo made from Black Wyoming jade, coral, and turquoise and set in 14k white gold. He is well known for his black and red color combinations, evocative of the summer sunset over Black Mesa near his home at San Felipe Pueblo. Of his work over the years and the acclaim he has received, he says, "I enjoy creating new designs and exploring the limitless potential of stones. Because my collectors are so appreciative and supportive of my work, I continue to redefine what I do, always striving to expand upon my previous creations."

Raymond Sequaptewa, Sr., is another painterly jeweler, who sees art in the humblest of objects that he may discover on his walks on the Hopi Reservation. He says, "For me, the creative process is about ideas. It's the idea or thought that goes into my artwork that matters more than expensive materials."[50] He often finds his subject in the materials themselves, doing minimal carving to reveal a shape. His journey to jewelry began in an unlikely way at Hopi, working as a janitor at a shop/gallery where jewelry was made. "I would get to work early and look at the tools. Pretty soon, I got some odd jobs of polishing, sanding, and soldering. I worked there for seven or eight years," he says. During the 1970s, Sequaptewa moved to Second Mesa to work at the Hopi Arts and Crafts Co-op Guild, where he made

Hopi overlay jewelry. "I started building my own studio at Hotevilla, one wall at a time. It took about four years," he recalls. However, before Sequaptewa could complete his studio, he fell ill and was given two years to live. His recovery changed his life and the way that he perceived the world. It also changed his jewelry. "I would take long walks to clear my head and suddenly the universe seemed to open up to me," he says. "I saw art in found objects, like old radios, ironwood, leather, or a deer antler. I started putting them together into jewelry."

Of his buckles, Sequaptewa says, "The top buckle is called *A Simple Life*. Sometimes living a simple life will make you a happier person." The turquoise on the left of the three stones is Fox turquoise that Sequaptewa took out of an old necklace. He left the drill hole exposed to show its origin in another piece of jewelry. On top of the buckle is a horizontal bar that Sequaptewa calls a "magic wand." It is constructed from walrus ivory and heishi beads, also taken from another necklace. "The wand represents humbleness, peace, and happiness, and trying to get a better life," he explains. The middle buckle is an abstract design of night and day with the lapis and high grade Chinese turquoise symbolizing the night sky filled with stars. On the bottom half, Sequaptewa uses different colors of fossilized walrus ivory to suggest the changing light of the day. The coral accent is early morning light, while the Nevada green turquoise marks the transition from twilight to evening.

In the third buckle, Sequaptewa has cast the water serpent and placed it on another cast piece. The double triangle motif and the colors on the bottom suggest the kilts that Hopi men wear at ceremonial dances. The round turquoise bead on top represents the sun. Of the stones on the bottom, the pink stone is a local rock that Sequaptewa found and cut and polished for the piece. Half human and half serpent, the water serpent is a shamanic figure, considered to be a mediator between the spirit world and the material world.

OPPOSITE: Raymond Sequaptewa, Sr., Hopi. Three belt buckles inlaid with stones and found objects. Courtesy of Case Trading Post, Wheelwright Museum of the American Indian, Santa Fe.

RIGHT: Michael Garcia, Pascua Yaqui. Sterling silver necklace, bracelet, and earrings set with black jade and Morenci turquoise. Courtesy of the artist.

OPPOSITE: Michael Garcia. Sterling silver dragonfly pins, clockwise (from top left) Orvil Jack turquoise on wing tips with New Lander turquoise; Demali and Orvil Jack turquoise; Orvil Jack turquoise; and Kingman turquoise and coral. Courtesy of the artist.

Minimalism also characterizes the jewelry of Michael Garcia, who combines black jade with Morenci turquoise in his elegant Pueblo Maiden set that won a blue ribbon at the 2007 Santa Fe Indian Market. Known for his beveled contemporary inlay and his asymmetrical accents of color, Garcia says, "I like to offset the dominant color with another color to bring the stones to life. With turquoise, you have to chase the color. I look at the stone and see where the valleys are."[51]

A member of the Pascua Yaqui tribe and a third-generation jeweler, Garcia started making jewelry at age fourteen by doing basic chores for two uncles, who did piece-work for traders. He learned to buff, polish, stamp, and cut out bezels. By the time he was twenty, in 1973, Garcia had mastered the basics and was making his own jewelry. Inspired by Charles Loloma's jewelry that he saw in the 1976 *Arizona Highways* magazine, he tried his hand at contemporary jewelry. "When I first saw Loloma's work, I said, 'I've got to try this,' but I couldn't give it away. People thought my jewelry was too new, too contemporary. The trend in the early 1970s was for traditional Hopi, Navajo, or Zuni jewelry. There wasn't a big art show market back then. Now you can go to a show almost every weekend of the year, but then we had no outlets to sell our jewelry." By the late 1970s, imported imitation Indian jewelry had also flooded the market and Garcia couldn't make a living, so he stopped making jewelry from 1978 to 1991. Instead, with a business degree from the University of New Mexico, he opened up two offset printing companies, one at Nambe Pueblo, the tribe of his wife, and the other in Santa Fe. He also acquired his Tewa name, NaNa Ping, which became his hallmark. "When I moved to Nambe, my wife's grandfather told me that I had to have a Tewa name, if I was going to live with the Tewa people," he says. "He was an elder, so he gave me the name, NaNa Ping, which means Aspen Mountain."

Since 1991, Garcia has won many awards for his jewelry, including the 1997 Arlene Feddes Fellowship for Excellence

in American Indian Art from the Southwestern Association for Indian Arts, and the 1999 Best of Show at the Eight Northern Indian Pueblos show. He has also developed a national following for his unique dragonfly pins inlaid with unusual stones. He says, "The dragonfly is a symbol of everlasting life, and I wanted to give it the respect it deserves. When the Millennium came in 2000, I saw people trying to turn the dragonfly into a novelty like the Kokopelli figure or the howling coyote. I tried to reverse that trend with an unusual design and unique stones."[52] A committed advocate for the arts, Garcia has been on the board of directors of the Southwestern Association for Indian Arts.

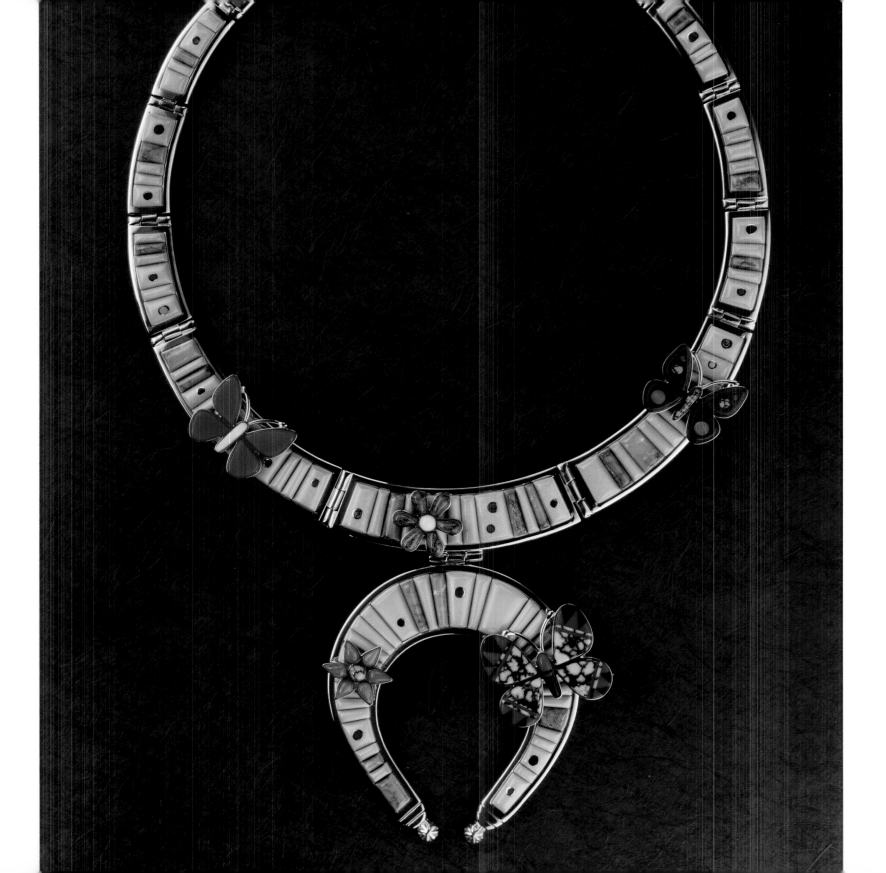

Michael Garcia's son and daughter-in-law, Michael and Causandra Dukepoo, are among the younger generation of innovative designers and skilled lapidary artists. Michael, who uses his mother's Hopi name, initially learned jewelry techniques from Garcia. He says, "I started getting a real appreciation for jewelry, when I became his apprentice. I saw how hard he was working to meet deadlines, and I asked if I could help."[53] That was in 1991, when Dukepoo was twenty years old. Dukepoo studied painting at the Institute of American Indian Arts in 1996, and he took courses in anthropology and Southwest studies at the University of New Mexico in Taos, where he and his wife live. Causandra Dukepoo grew up at Taos Pueblo, working at her family's Taos Indian Horse Ranch as a trail guide and horse trainer. She also attended the University of New Mexico at Taos. The couple married in 1997, and Michael began to pass on his knowledge of jewelry to Causandra. In 2001 they entered their first Indian Market.

Equally skilled at lapidary and metalwork, Michael and Causandra share the labor in making their larger pieces, such as the domino belt made from obsidian and inlaid with coral, sodalite, and lapis. Causandra says, "We had to cut each obsidian concha and grind it down and polish it to get the mirror finish. Then we inlay the other stones into the obsidian." Each concha is constructed with an opening for the leather to go through the stone. The reverse side of the belt carries another pattern called *Life Line*. For *Fluttering Butterflies*, a double-sided inlaid necklace, Causandra starts with rough sketches to sort out the colors she will use for each side. She uses a mosaic inlay technique, and cuts and polishes each stone before placing it in a silver frame (see page 154–155).

Butterflies–New Beginnings is the title of Ernest Benally's necklace that won the 2006 Southwest Indian Art Award of Excellence, sponsored by the Arizona State Museum in Tucson, Arizona. "This was the first big piece I did after my father passed," he says. "I knew I had to keep working, but it was very hard. My wife Veronica suggested the butterflies, because they represent transformation. They start in a cocoon and are born into another life."[54] Butterflies are a popular motif in Southwestern Indian jewelry for their symbolism, as well as their beauty. Their symmetry reflects the Navajo principle of *hózhó*, or balance and harmony. Benally fabricates the choker in 18k gold and inlays the channels with a corn roll inlay of Sleeping Beauty and Morenci turquoise, sugilite, coral, and China Mountain turquoise. Within the turquoise, Benally inserts small dots of color to suggest other flowers in the background. He inlays the large butterfly on the naja with China Mountain turquoise and sugilite.

Benally's first exposure to jewelry came in 1975, when he was sixteen years old and he and his sister, Rita Benally-Quezada, took summer jobs at Gilbert Ortega's Jewelry Company in Gallup, New Mexico. He says, "I didn't know anything about jewelry. At that time, the inlayers didn't glue their stones into bracelets or rings. They would bring them to me, and I would be responsible for drying off each stone and gluing it in exactly as they had designed the piece." The following summer, Benally returned to work for Ortega's again, this time polishing the jewelry. When Ortega's closed its Gallup shop and moved to Scottsdale in the late 1970s, Benally and his sister went to work at Sunburst Handcraft, another manufacturing company in Gallup. Over the next decade at Sunburst, Benally spent seven years at lapidary work and three years at silversmithing. He recalls, "There were fifteen inlayers at Sunburst and twenty silversmiths. Each had a specific job." In 1990, Benally decided to make and sell his own jewelry, although it would be ten years before he would enter his first Indian Market in 2000. Like many contemporary jewelers, Benally has chosen to sell his jewelry at Indian markets around the country, because of the exposure he receives. He typically travels to ten shows a year. Of his many awards, including the Best of Jewelry at

OPPOSITE: Ernest Benally, Navajo. 18k gold necklace with Sleeping Beauty, Morenci, and China Mountain turquoise. Other stones include coral, sugilite, and lapis. Courtesy of the artist.

LEFT: Michael Dukepoo, Hopi, Laguna Pueblo, Pascua Yaqui, and Causandra Dukepoo, Taos Pueblo. Sterling silver concha belt inlaid with obsidian, coral, lapis, and sodalite. Courtesy of the artists.

OPPOSITE: Causandra Dukepoo, Taos Pueblo. Right: Sterling silver butterfly necklace with multi-stone inlay, including lapis, turquoise, coral, and sugilite. Left, reverse side. Courtesy of the artist.

the 2001 Santa Fe Indian Market, he prizes his Best of Show at the 2002 Gallup Inter-Tribal Indian Ceremonial, saying, "I always wanted to win in my hometown."

Melanie Kirk-Lente and Michael Lente of Isleta Pueblo, New Mexico, also add a butterfly motif to their double-strand necklace of hand-rolled opal and sugilite beads. Opals are exceedingly fragile and require patient and precise lapidary skills, making them valued by artists and collectors alike. Known for her exceptional ability to shape opal beads, Kirk-Lente says, "I love opal. It is a very temperamental stone. You have to be patient and be in a calm, peaceful state of mind. I can only work a few hours at a time on opals."[55] She drills and shapes each stone by hand from the rough stone, acknowledging that over half of the stone may be lost because opals tend to shatter or fracture. The satellites on the necklace reflect the couple's deep commitment to their Isleta culture. "The butterfly and the hummingbird are the spring and summer spirits," Kirk-Lente explains. "The hummingbird also honors my grandfather, because his Isleta name translates to hummingbird. The sun face medallions are also spirit medallions. On the reverse are blossoms, which symbolize the awakening of the mind, body, and spirit." Small bears, symbols for strength and protection, are a signature in all of their major necklaces. The charm bracelet attached to the necklace as an extender also has a Corn Maiden charm, a Mesa Kachina inlaid with sugilite and opal, and a triangle with a motif from a man's traditional dancing kilt.

Kirk-Lente began making jewelry at age twelve under the tutelage of her father, Andy Lee Kirk, who died in 2001 and who instructed Lente as well. In 1995, the young couple attended the Gemological Institute of America, completing the Graduate Jeweler Program in 1996. Skilled in all aspects of jewelry making, Kirk-Lente says, "My father was a huge influence. He is the reason I'm a jeweler today. He always encouraged me to be free and to explore." He also instilled in her the concept that Native American jewelry could change

and still be part of a tradition. "The greatest challenge is to combine contemporary design with traditional values," she says. "We try hard to create jewelry that has balance and fluidity—a basic flowing design that reflects harmony and the continuity of life." To their bracelet inlaid with opals, sugilite, and diamonds, Kirk-Lente adds a repeating pottery motif taken from the pottery of her grandparents. Of their collaboration, Kirk-Lente says, "We both help at every stage of every piece. I tend to do the design and carving, while Mike does the metalwork and all of the casting for lost-wax pieces. We both do inlay, and Mike does the diamond setting."

OPPOSITE: Melanie Kirk-Lente and Michael Lente, Isleta Pueblo. Gold necklace with double-strand of hand-rolled opal and sugilite beads, inlaid satellites, and charm bracelet extender. Courtesy of the artists.

ABOVE: Melanie Kirk-Lente and Michael Lente. 14k gold bracelet with sugilite, opals, and diamonds. Courtesy of the artists.

A RECENT TREND IN contemporary jewelry has been for artists to vary the designs within the individual conchas on a belt. Traditionally, conchas in a single belt bore the same pattern. If stones were used, the stones were matched as well as possible and cut to the same size. The buckle of a concha belt could have a different shape—rectangular rather than oval or circular—and the design might vary a bit. Today, concha belts are characterized more often than not by their diversity of design. Vernon Haskie demonstrates his superb lapidary skills and inventive design sense in his concha belt in which each of the nine conchas bears a unique pattern. Renowned for his multilayered inlay style, Haskie combines channel and sculptural inlay techniques with cabochon and other cuts to create innovative and artful jewelry. He achieves a harmony among the disparate parts of his belt by seamlessly matching the coral in each concha and keeping

the ratio of coral to silver evenly balanced. Since entering his first Santa Fe Indian Market in 1998, Haskie has taken top honors for his jewelry, received a fellowship from the Southwestern Association for Indian Arts, and been awarded Best of Show at the 2000 and 2007 Heard Museum Indian Markets in Phoenix, Arizona.

Haskie comes to his geometric shapes and their patterned variations armed with a background in math and science. He earned a degree in biology from the University of New Mexico in 1996 and has taught math and science at Diné College (formerly Navajo Community College) in Tsaile, Arizona. As a child, Haskie grew up watching his parents make jewelry for wholesalers—his mother did inlay, and his father was a silversmith. He soon experimented on his own at age nine, learning to make jewelry by trial and error. In between his academic studies, teaching, military service, and raising a family, Haskie made jewelry on the side to earn some extra income. Lacking the confidence he felt necessary to pursue a full-time career in jewelry, Haskie had a Blessing Way Ceremony performed for him in 1996. "Many doors were opened after the ceremony," he recounts. "My self-doubt began to fade, and I became more confident." [56] By 1998, he was ready to take the leap into jewelry at the urging of his artist friend Teddy Draper, Jr. "I was working for the telephone company at the time and got assigned to the local route in Chinle. After work, I would stop off and visit with Ted. He encouraged me to leave the telephone company and become a full-time jeweler."

Haskie draws upon his Navajo heritage in creating a horned toad bolo from coral and 22k gold. A ubiquitous inhabitant of the Southwest terrain, the horned toad plays a role in coyote tales and is often portrayed in sandpaintings. Barre Toelken, the eminent folklorist, writes, "the small lizard is equated with power, longevity, healing properties. . . ." [57] For Haskie, "The horned toad is called grandfather and is a symbol of protection for the Navajo." To

OPPOSITE: Vernon Haskie, Navajo. Sterling silver concha belt with coral inlay. Courtesy of the artist.

BELOW: Vernon Haskie in his cornfield with the Lukachukai Cliffs in the background. Lukachukai, Arizona.

OPPOSITE: Vernon Haskie, Navajo. 18k gold bolo tie inlaid with coral. Courtesy of the artist.

LEFT: Vernon Haskie. 18k gold bracelet with coral inlay. Collection of Deborah Allender.

simulate the rugged back of the horned toad, Haskie does an unusual raised cut of coral that he mirrors in the jagged gold edge of the body. He sprinkles cuts of gold throughout the coral and places a Navajo arrowhead on top of the head, another symbol of protection.

Haskie's coral bracelet is a contemporary interpretation of a classic Navajo style. He says, "I try to achieve symmetry and balance and a feeling of something flowing from one direction to another like a rainbow." Haskie highlights the coral cabochons by setting them on a recessed textured gold surface that is framed by the high polish of his channel inlay design. Haskie says, "A lot of artists are trying to modify traditional forms. They are able to do that because of the technology we have available today." With all of the twenty-first century high-tech options at his fingertips, Haskie's ultimate goal is to produce jewelry that embodies the principle of *hóhzó*.

As artists have mastered the lapidary skills to cut stones in any number of ways, they have expanded their ability to tell stories in stone. Diamond drills allow jewelers to inlay infinitesimal cuts of stone in other stones, painting masterful scenes of their world. The stones themselves are diverse, and come from all over the world. It is the artist's choice to match the materials to the subject, whether it is the flora and fauna of the Southwest, Yei figures, Corn Maidens, petroglyphs, or sacred landscapes. Phil Loretto, who is a Jemez and Cochiti Pueblo Indian, is one jeweler for whom every stone has a symbolic reference. An inveterate collector of old stones, he has amassed a collection of turquoise that was mined prior to 1940, black jade from temples in South America, and Afghanistan lapis that was smuggled out during World War II, for his thematic pieces of jewelry that illustrate both his lapidary artistry and his unique creativity.

A 1969 graduate of the Santa Fe Institute of American Indian Arts, Loretto initially planned to go into architecture and studied briefly with Paolo Soleri at Arizona State Uni-

versity. He would later earn a degree in art with an emphasis on Southwest studies in 1976 from Fort Lewis College in Durango, Colorado. A poet, activist, and track and cross-country star, Loretto found an expression for his political views in painting. In 1974, when he was twenty-three years old, he began making jewelry, learning basic silversmithing techniques from his Navajo father-in-law, Chee Keams. In 1979, Loretto was one of a handful of contemporary jewelers to be included in the *Arizona Highways Collector Edition*, "The New Look in Indian Jewelry." Throughout his career, Loretto has explored both the historical events of the day and the mythic underpinnings of tribal cultures in his art.

No Bricks in the Wall is the title Loretto gives his bracelet that represents the fall of the Berlin Wall. He inlays an aurora borealis of colors in the large ivory stone on top of the bracelet to signify all the colors of the human race, saying, "I wanted to express explosions of color in the sky to say that all nations and all peoples of the world were ecstatic when the wall fell."[58] Underneath the ivory centerpiece are the eyes of the world watching. Of the balloon with the crown shape, Loretto says, "There are two meanings here. As a child, I read that many people made all kinds of efforts to escape and get over the wall, and some of them were by balloon. The balloon is to honor their courage. The crown shape symbolizes Russia's influence in East Berlin through its dome-style architecture." Next to the balloon is another inlaid stone of black jade with blue Brazilian opals showing through. Loretto explains, "There are always blue skies even in the darkest hour. You can't hide from the truth. The opals symbolize hope." A further detail is the small green stone that represents an awning over a café entrance, where, Loretto says, citizens planned their escape.

Loretto's bracelet entitled *East and West* was a special commission for private collectors. Using nature as an emblem of marriage, Loretto uses Bisbee turquoise and seafoam turquoise to represent clouds. The opal accent is a sundog

or tiny rainbow. Sundogs are an optical burst of light caused by the refraction of sunlight shining through ice crystals in clouds. He says, "The bracelet explores how the creator brings water to the pueblo and how the water flows through the landscape, just as couples have to intertwine their paths in order to live together. The two bands of inlay are reflections of two lives running parallel."

Loretto's necklace, *Creation's Blessing*, is an exuberant tribute to life, to the union of man and woman, as well as the marriage of heaven and earth. On the left is the male, and on the right is the female. The male wears a bowguard, a lightning symbol on his arm, and an ankle cuff. He is dressed in a dance kilt complete with tassels, Zuni-style leggings, and lapis moccasins. The female wears deer leggings of opal and red leather moccasins of coral with opal deerskin soles. She wears a turquoise bracelet and a coral necklace. Both the man and the woman hold turquoise seeds. Off the foot of the male is a diamond, symbolizing the planet of Venus. Of the headdress, Loretto says, "When the earth, moon, and sun make love, there is an eclipse. The opals on top of the headdress represent eagle prayer plumes. The head is both the sun and the moon." The body is Blue Gem turquoise that was mined in 1910. All of the other turquoise is Bisbee. The opals are from Brazil and Australia. The male horn on the left of the Navajo-style headdress is a fossilized opal. With a touch of humor, Loretto has a second title for the necklace: *He Who Kicks Stars*.

FOR OVER A THOUSAND YEARS, turquoise and shell have been the foundation of Southwestern Indian jewelry. Turquoise has continued to be the centerpiece of contemporary jewelry for its beauty and layers of religious and ceremonial significance. The red earth colors that complement turquoise so beautifully come from the spiny oyster shell and from coral. Although coral and turquoise are considered a traditional combination, coral wasn't routinely imported into the Southwest until the 1930s and would not become widely used in jewelry until the 1950s.[59] Good-quality coral is prized by jewelers and collectors alike, as it has become more and more difficult to obtain from the over-fished waters of the Mediterranean, the Japanese Sea, and the South Pacific.

The other stones and materials that have been associated with contemporary Southwestern Indian jewelry have been fairly recent arrivals as well. Kenneth Begay introduced ironwood into jewelry in the 1950s. Loloma would popularize lapis lazuli and fossilized ivory in the late 1960s and early 1970s. By the mid-1970s, Loloma was working more in gold, inaugurating a new direction in Southwestern Indian jewelry. Through the mentorship of Pierre Touraine, jewelers began attending the Gemological Institute of America in the 1970s and early 1980s to learn diamond and gemstone setting, adding precious stones to their cache of materials. Although sugilite, a popular purple stone, was discovered in 1944 by Japanese geologist Kenichi Sugi (for whom the mineral is named), it was not mined in any significant quantity until 1979 in the Southern Kalahari Desert of South Africa. By 1981, Native American jewelers were incorporating sugilite into their inlay, the same year that Yazzie Johnson and Gail Bird combined pearls with coral for the first time. Richard Chavez has introduced various colors of jade into contemporary jewelry, while Jesse Monongya has demonstrated the artistic possibilities of opals. More recently, jewelers have been including the rich apple greens of gaspeite and chrysoprase in their jewelry.

South America, Australia, the Mediterranean, China, Afghanistan, Alaska, South Africa, and the American West have been sources for the stones in Southwestern Indian jewelry. Just as the Hohokam and Ancestral Pueblo peoples journeyed to the Pacific and to ancient mines to procure the shells and turquoise for their jewelry, today's artists reach into remote corners of the planet for the stones they will craft into tomorrow's traditions.

OPPOSITE: Phillip C. Loretto, Jemez Pueblo, Cochiti Pueblo. Multi-stone inlay necklace with satellites. Collection of Marilyn Grossman.

CHAPTER 3

OBJECTS AND SCULPTURAL JEWELRY

n February 1880, the Santa Fe Railway arrived in Santa Fe. Two months later, tracks connected Santa Fe with Albuquerque, New Mexico. By 1883, tracks had been laid all the way to the West Coast, making it possible for Americans to travel from New York to California with stops throughout the Southwest.[1] The arrival of the railroad ushered in the tourist era in the Southwest, as easterners could now venture into the new territory in relative security and comfort. In tandem with railroad travel came the Harvey Houses— well-appointed restaurants and hotels along the route where travelers could count on a respectable meal and decent dining service rendered by young, pretty Harvey House girls in their formal uniforms. Tourists could also get a glimpse into the life and art of the Native American cultures of the Southwest and buy souvenirs of their adventures from the vendors who lined the tracks.

Fred Harvey, an imaginative entrepreneur and English immigrant, had started a restaurant and hotel chain in 1876 in Topeka, Kansas. In 1887, Herman Schweizer, a sixteen-year-old German immigrant, began working for Harvey at his restaurant in Coolidge, New Mexico, buying crafts from

Bluffs near Lupton, Arizona.

local Native Americans to sell to the tourists.[3] Schweizer acquired the art through his friendships with artists and traders on the reservation, including Juan Lorenzo Hubbell at Ganado, Arizona. Schweizer advanced quickly to become the manager and principal buyer for the Fred Harvey Company by 1899. Years later, in 1944, John Adair would write about Schweizer's influence on Southwestern Indian jewelry: "The commercialization of the craft [silverwork] began in 1899 when the Fred Harvey Company first started to order silver made up expressly for white consumption. Before that time, the Fred Harvey Company had bought pawned Navajo silver from the traders. It had proved to be too heavy for sale to the tourists, who wanted lighter jewelry which they could wear in the East. In 1899, Mr. Herman Schweizer, who for many years has been in charge of the Harvey Company's curio department, asked a turquoise-mine owner in Nevada to cut stones into flat, square, and oblong shapes for Indian use. Schweizer took these stones and some silver to a trading post at Thoreau, New Mexico. He asked the trader there to have Navajo smiths make jewelry lighter in weight than that which they made for their own use. This method of "farming out" to the trading posts silver and turquoise, which had been polished and cut to the right size and shape, proved to be a very satisfactory method of obtaining jewelry for the tourist trade."[4]

The railroad, the Fred Harvey Company, and the reservation traders formed a perfect symbiotic relationship. The Fred Harvey Company promoted travel to the West and provided food, lodging, and authentic artifacts. The Santa Fe Railway benefited from the business, as did the traders and silversmiths who now had a market for their work. Much as traders Juan Lorenzo Hubbell and C. N. Cotton had collaborated with Navajo weavers to come up with designs that would resonate with an eastern audience, Schweizer streamlined the production of jewelry to meet the burgeoning tourist demand. He commissioned Navajo silversmiths through the traders to make lightweight jewelry that was more wearable. The traders in turn recommended that the silversmiths

STAMPWORK

Daniel Sunshine Reeves, a Navajo, is well known for his intricate stampwork on an array of unique objects. In 1997, he won the Best of Show at the Santa Fe Indian Market for a sterling silver tea set, and in 1998, he won the Best of Jewelry award for a sterling silver train. He fabricated this second train in 2004 using more than 200 ounces of silver. He used approximately thirty different stamps to create the different designs. Inspired by the Russian jeweler, Peter Carl Fabergé, whose work he has studied, Reeves says, "I wanted to make something challenging, and I wanted to show that you can do something else besides jewelry as a silversmith."[2] In his repertory of objects, Reeves has made over three hundred sterling silver yo-yos. He is also known for his lamps, bowls, candlestick holders, boxes, and small pots in addition to more traditional Southwest Indian jewelry. One of twelve children, Reeves began making jewelry by watching his older brothers work with silver. He worked alongside several brothers, making earrings for a wholesale jewelry manufacturer in Albuquerque. In 1990, Reeves entered his first Indian Market. The blondest of his siblings, he got the nickname of "Sunshine" as a child.

Courtesy of Richardson Trading Company.

viduals and museums around the country, further stimulating a national appreciation for Southwestern Indian art.

By the 1920s, the Fred Harvey Company had expanded its offerings to include guided tours by car to various pueblos that were located along the corridor of the railroad, where tourists could meet artists and experience pueblo culture firsthand. The automobile would also signal the beginning of the end of the railroad monopoly on travel. This eventually diffused the domination of the Fred Harvey Company. In 1922, the Gallup Inter-Tribal Indian Ceremonial was founded to "improve the national and world markets for the profusion of American Indian arts and crafts."[6] The Santa Fe Indian Market also started in 1922 as a way to preserve and perpetuate the traditional arts of the Southwest, creating a new venue for artists and collectors alike.

Prior to the 1920s, silversmiths were making objects to meet the growing tourist demand for mementos. In the early decades of silverwork following Bosque Redondo, silversmiths fabricated tobacco canteens for soldiers and made bridles for their horses. They made buttons for their bandolier bags and for their clothing. In her book, *Navajo Spoons: Indian Artistry and the Souvenir Trade*, Cindra Kline documents that Navajo silversmiths were also making spoons as early as the 1880s.[7] By the beginning of the twentieth century, the tourist era had generated a new market for objects like spoons, forks, boxes, bowls, ashtrays, and letter openers.[8] "The merging of Victorian tastes with travel in the West, made possible by the extension of the railroad across the country, was well met by Navajo silversmiths in the 1880s and 1890s. These two decades saw the refinement of tools and techniques, the availability of high-quality silver, and the production of masterworks in both silver jewelry and utilitarian items. The result was to lift the souvenir spoon to a level of artistry equal with the best Navajo-made silverwork of the period."[9]

In May 2003, the Wheelwright Museum of the American Indian in Santa Fe mounted an exhibition entitled

ABOVE: Harvey car at Tesuque Pueblo, New Mexico, circa 1926. Photograph by T. Harmon Parkhurst. Courtesy of Palace of the Governors.

OPPOSITE: Sterling silver spoons commissioned by the Wheelwright Museum of the American Indian. Horizontal spoons (top): truck spoon by Clarence Lee; (bottom) by Mike Bird-Romero. Vertical (from left to right): L. Eugene Nelson, Norbert Peshlakai, Darrell Jumbo, Kee Yazzie Jr., Cippy CrazyHorse, Darryl Begay, Liz Wallace (a pair), and Perry Shorty. Courtesy of Wheelwright Museum of the American Indian, Santa Fe.

decorate the silver with motifs, such as arrows and swastikas, that appeared "Indian" and would attract the new buyer. "From 1905 to 1906, sixty thousand swastikas in various forms, some made by Indians and others not, were sold to tourists in New Mexico as genuine Indian articles."[5]

The market notwithstanding, Schweizer was also a serious student of Southwestern Indian culture. In 1902, the year after Fred Harvey died, Harvey's daughter and son-in-law, Minnie Harvey and J. F. Huckel, created the Fred Harvey Indian Department, a collection of museum-quality ethnographic material that they housed in the newly opened Alvarado Hotel in Albuquerque. The museum within the hotel was yet another attraction for railroad tourists. Soon, Native American artists were hired to demonstrate their crafts. Over the next four decades, Schweizer would buy and sell important collections of ethnographic material to indi-

A *Stirring Story–Navajo and Pueblo Spoons* that highlighted the silverwork Cindra Kline discussed in her book. Contemporary jewelers were hired to make spoons in their own style, which were included in the exhibition.

In 2006, Edison Cummings made history by winning the Best of Jewelry classification at both the Heard Museum Indian Market and the Santa Fe Indian Market for non-jewelry items—a sterling silver purse and a sterling silver coffee pot, respectively. "I wanted to surprise everyone," he says. "I wanted to find a design that would combine a contemporary look with the traditional repoussé work of Navajo jewelry. The design on the purse is a daisy, and it took me over a month to complete."[10] Nearly a century after the tourist era introduced objects into the repertory of Southwestern Indian silversmiths, Cummings is one of a group of talented contemporary artists who are becoming as distinguished for their objects as they are for their jewelry.

Cummings initially started out studying painting and sculpture at the Institute of American Indian Arts in Santa Fe,

OPPOSITE: Edison Cummings, Navajo. Sterling silver purse with repoussé design. Private collection.

BELOW LEFT: Edison Cummings. Sterling silver teapot. Courtesy of Packards on the Plaza.

BELOW RIGHT: Edison Cummings in the plaza at the 2007 Santa Fe Indian Market.

RIGHT: Edison Cummings, Navajo. Sterling silver flatware. Courtesy of Packards on the Plaza.

graduating in 1984. In 1986, following two years on a basketball scholarship at the College of Ganado in Ganado, Arizona, Cummings enrolled at Arizona State University in Tempe to pursue a secondary teaching credential in art education. That same year, he took up bull riding, winning several regional finals over the nine years of his career before an accident forced him to quit. "Bull riding is the number one sport on the reservation," he says. "Rodeos provide a chance for everyone to get together." At Arizona State University, Cummings also studied jewelry and metalwork with David Pimentel, a renowned artist in his own right. In 1991, Cummings began looking for a job as a silversmith. He recalls, "I had heard about the White Hogan. I just walked in and introduced myself to Jon Bonnell. I got the job cold." During his tenure at the White Hogan from 1991 to 1996, Cummings developed new designs in collaboration with Bonnell. He also made objects from existing templates, some designed by Kenneth Begay. He made flatware and objects such as a chalice and altar plate for a church in Mexico. For such projects, Cummings would sketch out eight or nine large drawings to scale before beginning a piece.

In 1996, Cummings entered his first Heard Museum Indian Market and he made his first teapot, winning Best of Class and Best of Division. Cummings estimates that a teapot takes him approximately 120 hours to make. To "stretch" the silver into the shape he wants, he heats the metal and then hammers it as it is cooling. After each hammering, he anneals the metal to make it soft again, often going through the process of annealing and hammering at least twenty times. He crafts the teapot in sections, first stamping the base and the lid. He then fabricates the spout and the handle. The bottom is made in two sections. Modern in design and pristine in execution, Cummings's work evokes the classic simplicity of First Phase jewelry.

Teapots have become a popular object for contemporary artists to make because of their design opportunities

FLATWARE

Myron Panteah employs a cutout technique for his imaginative flatware, incorporating images from petroglyph fields near his home at Zuni Pueblo. With a handsaw, he cuts out miniature figures related to his water and bear clans, including dragonflies, turtles, and bear paw motifs. He solders the 14k gold accents onto the silver base before he does the cutouts.

Collection of Ellen and Bill Taubman.

JEWELRY PURSE

Mike Bird-Romero was one of the first contemporary silversmiths to fabricate purses in the mid-1990s. He used Persian turquoise to complete the stamped floral and leaf motif. An interlocking garland frames the center design.

Private Collection.

and technical challenges. Amelia Joe-Chandler crafts her sterling silver teapot in the shape of a Navajo hogan with a wooden tree handle. The hogan is the traditional home of the Navajos and the center for religious ceremonies and special occasions. A round dwelling with the entrance facing east to meet the rising sun, the hogan has eight sides. It is constructed with four poles representing the four directions and the four sacred mountains of the Navajo. The domed ceiling represents the sky above; the floor is the earth. "I grew up in the *Hooghan* way," Joe-Chandler says. "My father is a medicine man and a sandpainter. Hogans are part of my everyday thinking and will always be part of my work."[11] One of eleven children, Joe-Chandler learned sandpainting from her parents, which helped support her through her college education and strengthened her knowledge of Navajo traditions and philosophy. She also learned basic jewelry-making techniques from her parents. In 1987, she earned a degree in art education from New Mexico State University and taught art at the elementary, middle, and high school levels. In 1996, she and her husband moved to Indiana, where she later received a graduate degree in art education from Indiana University with an emphasis in metalsmithing and jewelry design. A full-time metalsmith since 1997, Joe-Chandler was named the 2006 Artist of the Year by the Indian Arts and Crafts Association. She has recently returned to teaching art education in Cortez, Colorado. "We are losing our traditional ways," she says. "I want to teach Native American kids how to respect the job of being an artist. I also want to help children understand their culture."

An accomplished metalsmith and designer, Joe-Chandler has been inspired by her Navajo culture in all of her work. Her ring holder is both a pendant necklace and a sculpture and is entitled *Living Between Mother Earth and Father Sky*. A ring designed in the shape of a hogan fits into the bottom half of the pendant. Inside, Joe-Chandler has fabricated miniature pieces of furniture. For her sandstone inlay, she gathers rocks from the Navajo Reservation and grinds and sifts them into minute particles that she then separates by color. The sky is a chip inlay of Sleeping Beauty turquoise that surrounds Mount Hesperus, the sacred mountain of the North, also known as Jet Mountain. Cornstalks and sage bushes signify the southwestern landscape. The dead juniper tree is a somber reminder of the drought that has plagued the Southwest.

In her most ambitious project to date, Joe-Chandler has made a chess set, using Navajo figures to represent the different chess pieces. "I've always enjoyed the game of chess since my fourth-grade teacher introduced the game to us," she recounts. "I remember thinking how fun it would be to change the pieces to represent familiar items for myself and my classmates. I'm a little late to share it with my fourth-grade classmates, but at least I have accomplished one of the goals I set as a child." On the circular base of the chess board, Joe-Chandler creates a sandpainting of the current Navajo Reservation surrounded by the four sacred mountains designated by their colors: To the East is Blanca Peak (white); the South is Mount Taylor (blue); to the West are the San Francisco Peaks (yellow); and in the North lies Mount Hesperus (black). Using the lost-wax technique and 2,014 grams of sterling silver, Joe-Chandler spent four months creating the chess set.

The king and queen are represented by a Navajo man and woman dressed as they would be for a traditional dance or ceremony, replete with jewelry and moccasins, a hat for the male and a shawl for the female. The man wears a protective ketoh, and the woman has her hair done in a traditional hair style. The bishop is a medicine man. He is depicted wrapped inside his blanket and dressed to work. The knight is represented by a horse, an indispensable animal for the Navajos. The rook is a hogan. "This hogan is actually called *hooghan nímaz* (a round home)," Joe-Chandler explains. "It represents a female home and is considered a sacred place where all ceremonies take place. Prayer meetings, healing ceremonies, and initiations take place in the hogan. There is one door that faces toward the east and a small hole on top where the stove pipe sticks out. There is a corn symbol below the hogan that is also considered sacred. Corn is used to feed the people and the corn pollen is used in prayers." The pawn is a sheep,

BELOW: Amelia Joe-Chandler, Navajo. Sterling silver teapot with wood. Courtesy of the artist.

ABOVE: Amelia Joe-Chandler, Navajo. Chess set. Collection of Jan McVey.

OPPOSITE: Amelia Joe-Chandler. Sterling silver ring holder with sandstone and chip inlay of Sleeping Beauty turquoise. Ring with Blue Gem turquoise. Courtesy of the artist.

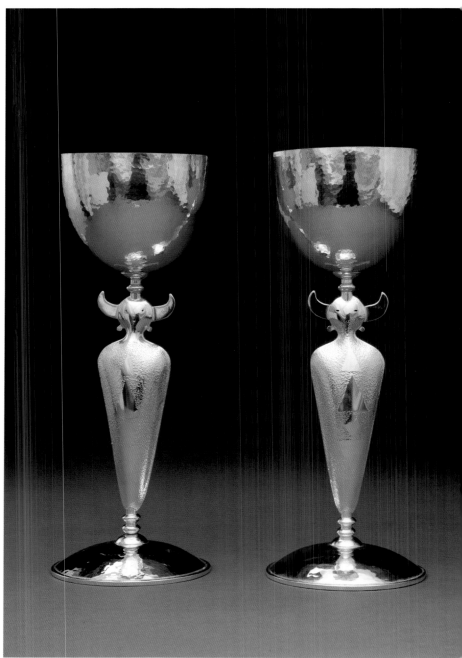

perhaps the most important animal to the Navajos, raised for its wool and for its meat. With the exception of the pawn, all the pieces are solid sterling silver.

Linda Lou Metoxen also uses motifs from her Navajo heritage in designing her sterling silver teapot and goblets. A trademark style of hers is the stylized Yei figure, which she has used as a handle in the teapot and for the base of her goblets. "My mother is a rug weaver," she says. "When I was a child, she did a lot of weavings with Yei figures in them and she always explained their significance as deities to me."[12] Metoxen's mother also inspired her to pursue her education. "My mom was a single mother and raised three children," Metoxen states. "We didn't have any electricity or running water. To make money, she raised sheep and did the shearing, carding, spinning, and dyeing of the wool to weave her rugs. She encouraged us to go to school and learn to speak English. My mother never spoke English and still doesn't."

In 1987, Metoxen graduated from the Institute of American Indian Arts with a degree in sculpture. Through a tribal scholarship she attended the University of Wisconsin and received a bachelor's degree in 1993 and a master's degree in fine arts in 1996, both in sculpture. By then, her interests had moved to jewelry, but there was no room in that program, so she continued her studies in sculpture with an emphasis on metalwork. Known for her hand-hammered sculptural pieces, Metoxen combines a variety of techniques in her work. She uses a hydraulic press to form the Yei figures from dies that she has fabricated. For the body of the teapot and the bowl shape of the goblets, she employs a hollow-form technique of raising the metal from a single sheet of silver. The handle of her teapot is a stylized Navajo sun figure with a 14k gold feather and horns, a traditional emblem of power. Among her many awards, Metoxen won the Best of Division at the 2000 and 2001 Santa Fe Indian Markets for a teapot/coffee service entitled *Deer Hunter* and a serving dish with ladle, respectively.

OPPOSITE, LEFT: Linda Lou Metoxen, Navajo. Sterling silver teapot with Yei figure on handle. Courtesy of the artist.

OPPOSITE, RIGHT: Linda Lou Metoxen. Sterling silver goblets with Yei motif. Courtesy of the artist.

ABOVE: Linda Lou Metoxen in her booth at the 2007 Santa Fe Indian Market.

VESSELS, BOXES, AND MINIATURE POTS have been among the objects that have challenged silversmiths and attracted collectors since the early 1900s. Among contemporary metalsmiths, Thomas Curtis, Sr., and his daughter, Jennifer Curtis, are well-known for their classic stampwork on beautifully hand-hammered vessels. When Thomas Curtis started making vessels in 1978, he had already been a full-time silversmith for over a decade. Reared in a traditional way in the remote area of Dilkon on the Navajo Reservation, Curtis grew up observing his two grandfathers make jewelry, picking up techniques and making jewelry on his own at age twelve. By the time he was thirteen, he was also participating in rodeos and would have a dual career as a silversmith and rodeo rider over the next twenty-eight years. "When I grew up in Dilkon, there were only dirt roads," he says. "We traveled with a wagon and horses. We rode horses to herd the sheep and haul wood. It was the Diné way of life."[13] Similarly, Curtis learned the traditional methods of silversmithing. From his uncle who repaired the wagons, Curtis learned blacksmithing techniques that he later used to make his own tools and stamps. By the time he was twenty-four, Curtis was a full-time silversmith, doing periodic bench work in production shops in Phoenix, Holbrook, and Winslow, Arizona.

As early as 1958, Curtis was making tobacco canteens, using techniques he would later incorporate into his vessels in the late 1970s. In 1985, he won Best of Show at the Museum of Northern Arizona's annual Navajo Festival of Arts and Culture for a concha belt. In 1987, he won Best of Classification at the Santa Fe Indian Market for a stamped vase, one of dozens of awards he has won over his long career.

Jennifer Curtis learned to make jewelry from her father when she was barely ten years old. "I got to play with the scrap silver," she says. "As an older child, I did buffing, polishing, and some filing for my father."[14] After high school, Curtis attended Mesa Community College in Phoenix and received an associates degree in computer-aided design drafting from the Miller Institute in Phoenix. Following her studies, she worked in the electronics division of Motorola in Scottsdale for several years before deciding to become a full-time jeweler in 1991. Like many Native American silversmiths, she has worked for production companies. From 1997 to 2000, she designed and made jewelry for Peyote Bird in Santa Fe. She entered her first Santa Fe Indian Market in 1994, winning a blue ribbon for a squash blossom necklace. At her first Heard Museum Indian Market in 2004, she won top awards for a stamped pot.

Both father and daughter are known for their precise and meticulous deep stampwork. The senior Curtis says, "I work from the center of the silver to the edge. I envision the design before I start." Jennifer shapes her miniature pots on a stump in her studio. She combines traditional designs with contemporary motifs, saying, "Both of my grandmothers are weavers, and I sometimes put rug patterns in my work." Thomas Curtis makes all of their stamps. Both excel at freehand stamping without the aid of templates or rulers, layering their objects with perfect repeating designs.

When Jared Chavez went off to Georgetown University in 2001, he did not realize that he would be the only full-blooded Native American in the freshman class. Nor did he fully appreciate until later that the entire Native American enrollment at Georgetown was less than one percent of the student body. Going from the tiny village of San Felipe Pueblo to Washington, D.C., would be a culture shock for anyone, which Chavez decided to document in his *Commemoration Box*. Fabricated in the shape of the National Museum of the American Indian that opened on the Smithsonian Mall in Washington, D.C., on September 21, 2004, the box is divided into panels upon which Chavez records his experiences and personal growth each year. For his senior project, Chavez made carved wooden panels overlaid with woodblock prints that inspired him to try the same concept in sterling silver.

OPPOSITE: Thomas Curtis, Sr., Navajo, and Jennifer Curtis, Navajo. Sterling silver stamped vessels. Two pots with lids by Thomas Curtis, Sr.; (center) two pots by Jennifer Curtis. Courtesy of Packards on the Plaza.

TOP and **BOTTOM:** Jared J. Chavez, San Felipe Pueblo, Navajo, Hopi/Tewa. Sterling silver *Commemoration* box. Photograph by Ernest Amoroso. Courtesy of National Museum of the American Indian, Smithsonian Institution.

"Vessels appeal to me," he says. "Curves are also important. I wanted to shape the box to represent a life path, that there are twists and turns along the way."[15] Chavez used a series of fabrication techniques, including hammering guitar wire into the silver for all the curves.

The story begins in his freshman year. "I went into this year fresh out of the Santa Fe Indian School. I had traveled a great deal, met people of all walks of life, and I felt I was prepared, but when it all came down to it I couldn't have been less aware of what I was going into."[16] Chavez shapes the first panel of the box to reflect his feeling that the world is closing in on him. The flames signal turmoil, while the lightning and rain reflect his feelings. In the background is San Felipe Pueblo on one side and Georgetown on the other. The central figure is split down the middle with another lightning bolt, representing Chavez's division of feelings.

As Chavez goes through his college career, things start to look up, which is expressed in the outward curve of the box. He meets friends and depicts the apartment he shares with them. Throughout the panels is a path that crosses back and forth between his ties to his pueblo, always represented in the background, and his increasing sense of well-being in his new world. Along the way, Chavez also includes images such as a small butterfly in the corner of the panel of his sophomore year. "This butterfly represents my first and only niece born into my family and one of her given Indian names in Keres means butterfly," he says. "It was an exciting time for my family."

In the last panel, Chavez includes an image of the Golden Gate Bridge in the foreground of the San Francisco skyline to signify his future studies at the Revere Academy of Jewelry Design. He also has the road leading him back to San Felipe Pueblo. "You can see the road leading me back to my culture," he says. "I illustrated this with a pueblo design and my kiva in the background with the surrounding mountains. While my culture has always been a part of me during these past four years, there have been certain aspects that I have not been able to participate in while in school, and this symbolizes a return to practice those aspects." The lid is constructed to look like an abstract eye, looking toward the future. The box is in the permanent collection of the National Museum of the American Indian in Washington, D.C.

ABOVE: Jared J. Chavez (foreground) and Richard I. Chavez in their studio, San Felipe Pueblo, New Mexico.

SEED POT

Navajo silversmith Darrell Jumbo entitles his miniature pot *Nizho'ni ni de'e'*—*It was Beautiful*. "I was living in Arizona when 9/11 happened," he says. "The newscast would always end with a shot of the Twin Towers at sunset. It was so beautiful." For a short time, Jumbo lived in New Jersey, where the emotional impact of 9/11 inspired him to begin work on the commemorative sculpture a year later. On one side, the Twin Towers soar above the landscape. When the top is inverted, the towers disappear and become a seed pot. Jumbo says, "I wanted to create something to honor the people who died. The flower designs mark our innocence. The opal on the side of the stand represents the firemen. The Sleeping Beauty turquoise at the base is Mother Earth. This was my way of saying to the people in the East that they are not alone." Jumbo fashioned the base with four sides and placed four opals on the top, signifying the four directions and four sacred mountains of the Navajo People. The first in a series of four commemorative pieces that Jumbo plans to make, he donated *Nizho'ni ni de'e'* to the Montclair Art Museum.

Courtesy of Montclair Art Museum, Montclair, New Jersey.

In 2006, the Eiteljorg Museum of American Indians and Western Art in Indianapolis purchased a three-dimensional truck from Clarence and Russell Lee. Entitled *Mr. Yazzie Goes to Town*, the sterling silver truck is a signature piece for the father and son team, who have been collaborating on their popular storytelling jewelry and metalwork for more than two decades. There are over two dozen pieces of silver that are soldered together to make the truck, which has turquoise headlights and coral taillights. Nationally recognized for his storytelling jewelry and his portrayal of rural scenes from reservation life, the senior Lee has drawn on his own background for his subject matter. He learned silversmithing from his father, Tom Lee, who owned the trading post at Twin Lakes, New Mexico, and had learned to make jewelry to supplement the family income. A World War II veteran and prisoner of war for four years, Tom Lee became New Mexico's first Native American State Senator in 1971, and his wife Emma, Clarence Lee's mother, made the first Navajo Nation flag.

In elementary and high school, Clarence Lee excelled at drawing and painting and took courses in metal sculpture as well. After high school, he traveled with his parents to various arts and crafts shows across the Southwest to help sell their jewelry. He also started making traditional-style jewelry at age nineteen. By accident, he cut out a piece of silver one day in the shape of a dog and made it into a ring. Suddenly all of his talent in drawing had a new outlet, and he began crafting jewelry based on his childhood memories of summers spent with his great-grandmother in the mountains. Clarence has added whimsical cowboys, cowgirls, children, dancers, sheep, cattle, water barrels, windmills, wood stoves, and hogans to dozens of his award-winning designs. He attends twenty-five to thirty national and regional art shows each year, where his popular jewelry has always been in high demand.

Russell Lee grew up in the family jewelry business going to shows with his father from the time he was four

TOP and BOTTOM:
Clarence Lee, Navajo, and
Russell Lee, Navajo. *Mr.
Yazzie Goes to Town*, sterling
silver with turquoise, front
view. Rear view with coral.
Courtesy of Eiteljorg Museum
of American Indians and
Western Art, Indianapolis.

years old. "When Russell was about ten or so he wanted a toy he saw at the mall," Clarence recalls. "I told him you have to earn it by selling something first. From there Russell was encouraged to try his hand as a silversmith."[17] An invaluable asset to Clarence, Russell has learned all aspects of jewelry making and does everything from design cutting to buffing to maintaining the large inventory necessary for their shows. He has also fabricated jewelry under his own hallmark. When he was twelve, Russell began entering regional competitions, winning many awards, including the Judges' Choice award at the 1998 Heard Museum Indian Market. In their latest collaboration, Clarence and Russell have made a nativity scene replete with the three wise men, a shepherd, angel, and many charming animals.

ABOVE: Clarence Lee, Navajo, and Russell Lee, Navajo. Sterling silver, copper, and brass nativity scene with turquoise, coral, and lapis. Courtesy of the artists.

In 1990, Duane Maktima received the Distinguished Alumni award from the College of Fine Arts at Northern Arizona University. A master metalsmith, Maktima graduated from Northern Arizona University in 1982 after several bumps in the road of his academic career. He had originally enrolled in 1971, hoping to go into forestry. His father was a business administrator for the forest service and Maktima liked the field. However, the program was already filled and Maktima entered a general arts program instead. In 1975, he accepted a two-year art internship at the Museum of Northern Arizona to study with Jacob Brookins, who had also been his art professor at Northern Arizona University. From Brookins, Maktima furthered his skills in silversmithing and learned new techniques in metalwork and sculpture. He also had time to explore the vast Native American art collection of the museum, which spurred his interest in learning more about his Hopi and Laguna Pueblo ancestry. Upon completing his internship, Maktima moved to his mother's pueblo of Laguna and lived there among his extended family for three years, participating fully in the ceremonial and religious life of the pueblo—something he had not had a chance to do growing up in Holbrook, Arizona. In 1980, he returned to NAU to complete his degree.

"I was in that generation of artists trying to break the mold from the traditional jewelry that was still popular in the 1970s," Maktima says.[18] Working with Joe Cornett, a new professor, Maktima discovered a whole new world of metalsmithing. "Cornett had studied with the Finnish master jeweler, Heikki Seppa," he says. "Seppa was a professor at the School of Fine Arts at Washington University in St. Louis and had started breaking ground in the 1970s by applying industrial technology to jewelry."[19] One of the techniques Cornett taught was hollow-forming, a technique that Maktima would use to make an elegant oversized canteen decorated with Pueblo symbols. The New York City branch of Fortunoff's, a fine jewelry store, featured the canteen in a display of hollowware in 1986. Maktima has also explored hydraulic forming, a technique he would use to make the goblets that won Best of Class at the 2001 Santa Fe Indian Market. "The hydraulic press is the latest tool for metalsmiths to use," he states. The base of the goblets is fabricated and inlaid with pearls, quartz, and agates.

During his studies at Northern Arizona University, Maktima also became friends with a docent at the Museum of Northern Arizona, who was from Denmark. "She had an extensive collection of exquisite contemporary jewelry from Germany and Scandinavia," he says. "She liked my work and would make suggestions to me." Through their friendship, Maktima developed an appreciation for the clean lines of Scandinavian design, an aesthetic that has informed his jewelry for twenty-five years. He also refined his own technique within hollow form of leaving cavities for inlay where two pieces of metal were joined. "With hollow form, the jewelry is lightweight and wearable, at the same time it has a three-dimensional or sculptural presence," He states. In 1998, Maktima made a reversible concha belt. Within each concha, he suspended a medallion inlaid with different stones on each side and engineered so that each satellite turns, creating multiple combinations of designs.

Maktima's most lasting achievement, perhaps, has been his commitment to mentoring younger artists. In 1998, he founded Pueblo V Design Institute as an educational and networking forum for emerging artists, in which they could learn about new techniques, new stones, and the ins and outs of doing business. "No one was helping the Pueblo people to advance their craft," he says. Initially, Maktima offered workshops in basic jewelry techniques. Over a three-year period, he brought in local and nationally acclaimed jewelers to teach classes as disparate as patinas to making findings for earrings and pins.

Besides creating a community among the artists, Maktima was also an advocate for contemporary jewelry to

the museum and collecting world. In selecting Pueblo V as the name of his organization, Maktima had gone full circle back to his early days at the Museum of Northern Arizona. "Pueblo V is an anthropological term. It means 'after European contact,'" he says. Although Pueblo V eventually dissolved, it was an important catalyst for bringing together experienced and emerging artists, creating a dialogue about design and techniques that had not previously existed in the field of Southwestern Indian jewelry.

Cheyenne Harris also graduated from Northern Arizona University with a degree in jewelry and metalsmithing in 1987. Like Maktima, she studied with Joe Cornett, learning

ABOVE: Duane Maktima in front of the kiva and Mission church at Pecos Ruins, Pecos National Historic Park, New Mexico. The Pueblo of Pecos was founded in approximately 1300 A.D. and abandoned by the mid-nineteenth century.

OPPOSITE: Duane Maktima, Laguna Pueblo, Hopi. Sterling silver canteen and goblets with gold accents and stone inlay. The stones in the base of the goblets are pearls, quartz, and agates. Collection of Sam and Judy Kovler.

ABOVE: Duane Maktima. Sterling silver and gold concha belt with reversible inlaid medallions in each concha. Collection of Sam and Judy Kovler.

RiGHT: Cheyenne Harris, Navajo, Northern Cheyenne. Sterling silver and gold bead necklace. Courtesy of Wright's Indian Art, Albuquerque, New Mexico.

OPPOSiTE: Cheyenne Harris. 14k gold bracelet with Morenci turquoise and diamond. Courtesy of the Faust Gallery.

192

hollow-form techniques that she would later incorporate into her modern jewelry. Through Cornett, she was able to take a workshop with Heikki Seppa, applying the minimalism of Scandinavian design to her own Navajo aesthetic. Harris is Navajo on her mother's side and Northern Cheyenne on her father's. She says, "I grew up Navajo in Rough Rock and Shiprock, New Mexico. My father is from Lame Deer, and I used to go to Montana in the summer to spend time with his family."[20] A fourth-generation jeweler, Harris grew up around jewelry, learning from her mother, who had taken courses in jewelry in the early 1960s at Arizona State University and later studied with Kenneth Begay at Navajo Community College in 1968. Of other jewelers in her family, Harris says, "My great grandfather was Harry Yazzie. He would take the sheep out in the morning and go back to silversmithing during the day. He made all of his own stamps."

After her graduation from Northern Arizona University, Harris taught at the Institute of American Indian Arts for a year. She took graduate courses in architecture and interior design at Arizona State University. Later she enrolled in the graduate metalsmithing program at the University of Massachusetts in North Dartmouth. A candidate for a Master of Fine Arts degree, she had completed all of her coursework when she was hit by a car in a hit-and-run accident and forced to abandon her studies in 1993.

When Harris enrolled at the University of Massachusetts, she spent a lot of her free time visiting the museums in the Boston area, particularly the Museum of Fine Arts. "They had a good collection of eighteenth and nineteenth century French and English silverwork," she recalls. That experience inspired Harris to make flatware. Since her college days, she has been showing her jewelry and winning regional competitions The recipient of a fellowship from the Southwestern Association for Indian Arts in 1994 and three grants from the prestigious Haystack Mountain School of Crafts in Deer Isle, Maine, Harris has exhibited her jewelry

and objects nationally in numerous invitational and juried shows. In 2002, her work was included in the Museum of Arts & Design exhibition, *Changing Hands: Art Without Reservation*, in New York City.

For her 14k gold bracelet with Morenci turquoise and a diamond, Harris hammers out the individual gold sheets and solders them together in a sculptural hollow form. She uses a 1903 stone mason's hammer, which she found in an antique store, to texture the gold and to further hammer out the shape of the bracelet. She finishes the bracelet with gold wire on the edges and flat gold on the ends. Of the rich color of the bracelet, she explains, "After the process of annealing and hammering several times, gold changes color." In her

necklace, she combines classic silver beads with her signature hollow beads embellished with random gold designs. Both the bracelet and the necklace illustrate Harris's artistry and technical mastery of metals.

WHEN CHARLES LOLOMA made his first height bracelet in the mid-1970s, he unconsciously introduced the sculptural jewelry movement. Jewelry would begin to move away from the smooth surface of mosaic and channel inlay to the raised inlay style that would be firmly established by the beginning of the 1980s. The raised inlay style has been called a *cobblestone* inlay, a *pillow* inlay, and a *sculptural* inlay style—all denoting the three-dimensional quality of the

BELOW: Lyndon B. Tsosie, Navajo. Sterling silver tufa-cast concha belt inlaid with Kingman, Lone Mountain, and Morenci turquoise, fossilized ivory, coral, lapis, African ebony wood, and Cocobolo wood. Private collection.

stones rising above the surface of the metal. Loloma also introduced another concept that would pave the way for artists to experiment with form, as Marti Streuver notes, "He was always concerned with the appearance of a piece as it was being worn."[21] Loloma himself had written in 1976 that "Even the littlest people can wear some of my big jewelry. In one case a very small girl is enjoying a ring that is three inches above her fingers. There is no reason for anything to project out that far, but there is no limit and no rules in what will work for a person, especially now that men are wearing jewelry."[22] Experimentation and exploration have been the hallmarks of the sculptural jewelry movement, as artists push the limits on functionality, shape, and form, combining such disparate materials as quartz with diamonds, or turquoise with colored glass.

The legacy of Loloma has been evident in the work of many contemporary jewelers, including Lyndon Tsosie, a Navajo from Gallup, New Mexico, who blends traditional silverwork with sculptural inlay in his concha belt. "Loloma has been a great inspiration to all of us," Tsosie says. "This is my first concha belt in twelve years, and I wanted to do it in the cobblestone inlay style as a tribute to Loloma."[24] Combining traditional tufa casting with innovative lapidary work, Tsosie inlays a different design on each concha with asymmetrical cuts of semiprecious stones. Stylized female figures alternate with abstract patterns evocative of the southwestern landscape. The small silver balls that adorn each figure signify the passage of time and generations. Tsosie sketches out his designs in advance, drawing to scale the patterns he will use for his lapidary work.

Like many Navajo silversmiths, Tsosie had his first introduction to jewelry making in high school "Tommy Jackson, a prominent Navajo jeweler, was our instructor at Tohatchi, and he taught us the basics," Tsosie recalls. Following graduation, Tsosie worked for a jewelry manufacturing company in Gallup. "I needed a job. There were forty-five Navajos

SCULPTURAL JEWELRY

Ken Romero's *The Maiden's Gift to Her Lover, The Long-Haired Dancer* won the Best of Jewelry award at the 2003 Heard Museum Indian Market. The hair pick is inlaid with pink coral in the hairstyle of a maiden. It can be removed from the sculpture and worn separately. She is dressed in a manta with a leather shawl. Romero says, "I think of this piece as a painterly sculpture."[23]

Courtesy of the artist.

working there," he says. "Everyone had a specific function. There were stampers, stone setters, buffers, etc. I did nothing but stampwork for six months."

In 1989, Tsosie began making his own jewelry. "I bought forty sheets of pre-cut silver from Indian Jewelers Supply Company in Gallup, made twenty pairs of stamped earrings and sold them to a retail store." Over the next few years, Tsosie supported himself and his family by making stamped bracelets and earrings that he sold in Albuquerque and Gallup. In 1994, he traded in a stereo system to buy a lapidary machine and began teaching himself stonecutting.

A turning point in his career came in 1995, when he met Teddy Draper, Jr., a distinguished Navajo painter, teacher, and silversmith, who would mentor Tsosie for five years in art, jewelry making, and the core beliefs of Navajo culture. Tsosie says, "He brought me back to my culture. We talked about who the Navajos were and where they came from. We talked about all the early leaders and their courage." Well-known for his pastel landscapes of Canyon DeChelly and other sacred Navajo landmarks, Draper incorporates the concept of hózhó, or balance and harmony, in his work. Tsosie says, "He taught me that jewelry was about life, not just about making jewelry."

In reconnecting with his heritage, Tsosie has become well known for his boxes that reflect a personal experience or tell a story related to Navajo cultural beliefs. His hogan box is a tribute to his grandmother and his mother. "My grandmother lived alone in a hogan until she was 93 or 94," he says. "She didn't have much. She was very humble. When she died, she had a soul filled with love that I tried to represent by the river of opals inlaid on the inside of the box. My mother was born in that rock hogan and had modest beginnings also. She was able to leave and become a physician's assistant. The box is to honor both of them, their beauty and their strength." Inlaid with sugilite, opals, turquoise, lapis lazuli, and coral, the box is tufa-cast in gold and silver.

ABOVE: Lyndon B. Tsosie, Navajo, in front of his ancestral hogan, north of Gallup, New Mexico.

OPPOSITE: Lyndon B. Tsosie. Sterling silver and gold box in shape of hogan, inlaid with sugilite, turquoise, coral, lapis, and opals. Courtesy of Urban Spirit Gallery (formerly Indians on Columbus).

RIGHT: Lyndon B. Tsosie. Interior view of hogan box. Courtesy of Urban Spirit Gallery (formerly Indians on Columbus).

Today, Tsosie has established himself as an imaginative designer and talented lapidary artist. He has won many awards at the Santa Fe and Heard Museum Indian Markets since he entered both for the first time in 1996. He is also the owner of The House of Lyndon, an art gallery for his work and that of other artists in Gallup. Tsosie says, "Beauty is essential to Navajo people. We don't have a word for God, but we see beauty all around us. That's what I try to create."

For Eugene Nelson, Loloma's influence freed him to think differently about design and to apply his background in math and science to the challenge of creating a three-dimensional object based on a two-dimensional design. "The phrase 'form follows function' is widely used in architectural design," Nelson states. "Likewise, in jewelry making, the jewelry has a 'function' in that it is to be worn. There are physical boundaries and limitations to consider as you design and make jewelry. However, the 'function' should not limit the uniqueness of the design."[25] Nelson's jewelry is exceptionally distinctive, sculptural, futuristic, and conceptual. He assigns titles to his series, such as the *Melt-Down Series* and the *Galaxy Series*, although sometimes the titles don't become obvious until he has completed a series. He fabricates his bolo with a soldered sheet-and-wire construction, which highlights the use of lines, angles, surface textures, and the shadowing effects of oxidation.

Born in Utah, Nelson moved to Shiprock, New Mexico, with his nine siblings when he was in elementary school. His parents, Tom and Virginia Nelson, had made the decision that the senior Nelson would leave his government position, and they would become Southern Baptist missionaries. As early as junior high school, Nelson exhibited a talent for architecture and mechanical drawing, which he pursued through high school and later at the Southwestern Indian Polytechnic Institute from 1973 to 1974. Nelson's first exposure to silversmithing came in the summer of 1974 when he was looking for a job. Charlie Platero, Jr., a high-school friend and silversmith, taught him some basic techniques and got him a job in production work. "It took longer for me to make one small ring than for others to produce five," Nelson recalls. "I cared too much about the quality rather than the quantity." From 1975 to 1978, Nelson attended the University of New Mexico in Albuquerque on an academic scholarship, studying mechanical and civil engineering. He did not take any jewelry courses although he continued to experiment on his own. Just short of completing his degree, he took a job in 1977 in television production where he stayed for the next ten years, first with the local affiliate of NBC and then with ABC in Albuquerque. He returned to jewelry full-time in 1987.

For Nelson, jewelry is the medium he uses to create art. A careful craftsman, he describes the process he follows to make his jewelry. "I design and create on the workbench. I begin with a two-dimensional design initially centered around a geometric shape or stone. Opposing geometric shapes are used to complement one another." Once he sets the general design, Nelson balances the construction with multicolored stones and pieces of gold and metal. He combines highly polished surfaces with textured, engraved, or stamped surfaces. He uses oxidation, as a painter would use brush strokes, saying, "Often the oxidation of metal is used to highlight small details or to emphasize the shadowing effects of light and dark, negative and positive space. At times, a piece will call for a type of 'kinetic' movement in the form of a stone-drop or many silver dangles." The design aspects of his *Galaxy* pin include the large arc that balances the triangle, the negative space of the small cutout areas, and the textured gold squares with stone insets. *Galaxy* suggests unlimited possibilities, something Nelson has continued to explore in his modern and thoughtful jewelry. His jewelry has won many awards and has been collected by the San Diego Museum of Man and the Wheelwright Museum of the American Indian in Santa Fe.

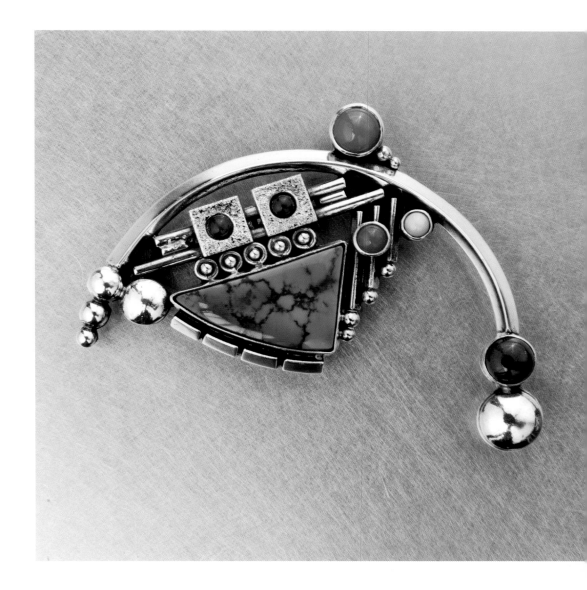

OPPOSITE: L. Eugene Nelson, Navajo. Sterling silver fabricated bolo tie with stone inlay and gold accents. Collection of Norm and Chris Byrd.

ABOVE: L. Eugene Nelson. Sterling silver *Galaxy* pin with coral, Turquoise Mountain turquoise, Sleeping Beauty turquoise, lapis, and gold accents. Collection of Norm and Chris Byrd.

WHILE MANY SOUTHWESTERN INDIAN jewelers are self-taught or have learned their skills from other family members, a large number of artists have graduated from the Institute of American Indian Arts in Santa Fe. More recently, many younger jewelers have been taking courses through the Poeh Arts Program at the Poeh Center in Pojoaque, just north of Santa Fe. Established in 1988 by the Pueblo of Pojoaque, the Poeh Center is the first tribally owned and operated center dedicated to preserving and perpetuating the cultural life and art forms of the eight northern Pueblos of New Mexico: Taos, Picuris, San Juan, Santa Clara, San Ildefonso, Nambe, Pojoaque, and Tesuque. From

its original mission of offering courses in traditional art forms, such as drum making and hide tanning that have direct application to tribal ceremonies, the Poeh Arts Program has expanded to include a range of courses in contemporary art, including jewelry. A sleek gallery showcases the work of faculty and students and is becoming a destination for those interested in contemporary Native American art. The Poeh Arts Program counts among its students and faculty a number of contemporary jewelers who have crossed the threshold from more traditional Native jewelry into sculptural jewelry.

David Gaussoin has been one of the pioneers of sculptural jewelry. In 2001, he set up the wax-casting program for the Poeh Arts Program, where he has taught casting and jewelry techniques to many jewelers. With his brother, Wayne Nez, he has mounted fashion shows, designing and sewing the clothes that complement their modern jewelry. He has demonstrated and lectured at museums throughout the Southwest, including the Heard Museum, the Museum of Arts and Culture, the Idyllwild Arts Foundation, the San Diego Museum of Man, and the Institute of American Indian Arts. He earned a degree in 1999 from the Anderson School of Business at the University of New Mexico. Gaussoin has won many awards for his innovative jewelry that can be playful and serious, traditional and innovative at the same time. An imaginative designer, Gaussoin has been a spokesperson for crafting new traditions in Southwestern Indian jewelry. "Tradition is about innovation," he says. "Native Americans are about using and adapting what's new, including new materials and techniques as they become available, as well as new designs."[26]

Gaussoin's bracelet, part of his *Satellite* series, exemplifies his ability to blend the old and the new in his jewelry. Of the bracelet series, he says, "All of them are one of a kind and different in design, yet the basic form is somewhat similar. I like to combine the top piece, which is progressive in

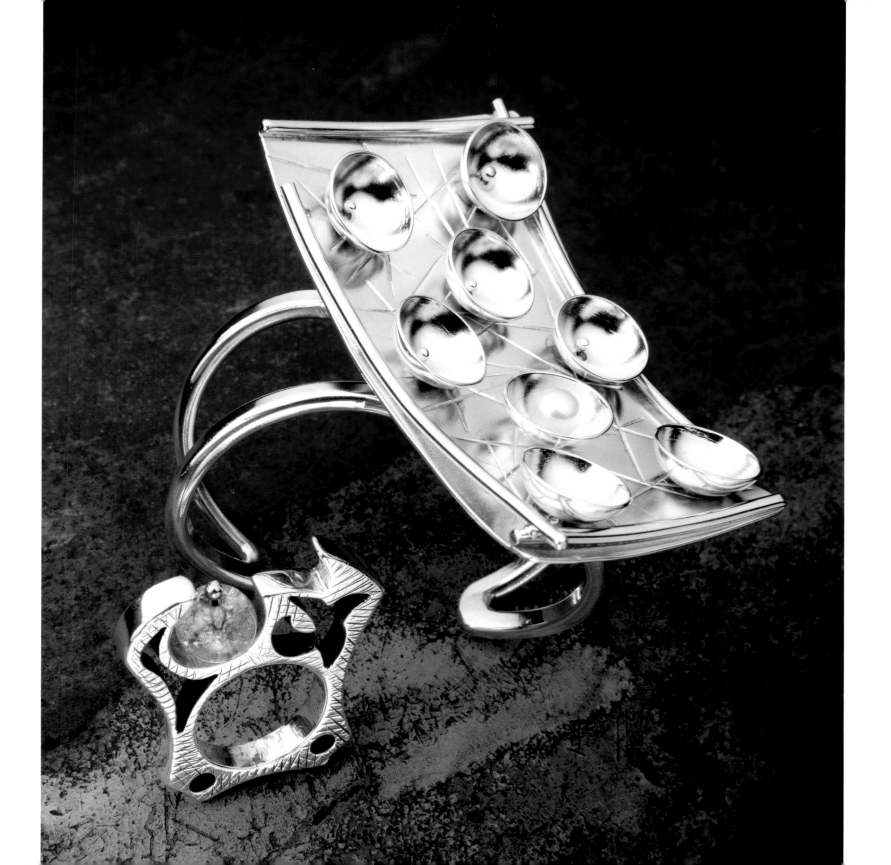

design, with the bottom band, which is a take-off on the old-style Navajo turquoise bracelets my mother and great-uncles used to make. This one has a lot of movement, with the natural cultured pearl representing the moon."[27] The ring is part of Gaussoin's *Chopper* series, which grows out of his fascination with motorcycles and tattoo art. "I wanted to make this piece look very sharp and dangerous on the exterior, yet very comfortable and beautiful to wear," he says. "I guess this goes back to my basic philosophy of living in balance, as a traditional Native American living in a modern world."

As a child, Gaussoin learned jewelry making from his mother, Connie Tsosie Gaussoin, one of the first contemporary women jewelers to gain national recognition in the early 1970s. Of Navajo and Picuris Pueblo descent, Tsosie Gaussoin comes from a long line of artists, including silversmiths, painters, weavers, and sculptors. Her father, Carl Tsosie, worked for Maisel's in Albuquerque. She says, "He made Fred Harvey-type jewelry for the tourists. My uncle, Thomas Tsosie, used bellows. Both my father and my uncle knew how to make the old-style traditional Navajo jewelry."[28] An accomplished silversmith, Tsosie Gaussoin expanded her own knowledge of jewelry techniques through courses at Pueblo V Design Institute, the Institute of American Indian Arts, Navajo Community College, and the College of Santa Fe. Besides teaching her sons—Jerry Jr., David, and Wayne Nez—Connie has taught at the Poeh Center, the Eight Northern Indian Pueblo Council vocational program, and the Wheelwright Museum of the American Indian. In 2005, she received the City of Santa Fe Mayor's Award for Arts Education.

Connie crafts both classic and contemporary works in metal. Her *Kiva Seed Bowl* has a traditional ladder that descends into the kiva, or ceremonial chamber. The top of the bowl is decorated with a crescent moon, dragonflies, and Pueblo stars. Horizon symbols and feathers are attached to the bowl. On Picuris Feast Days and other special occasions,

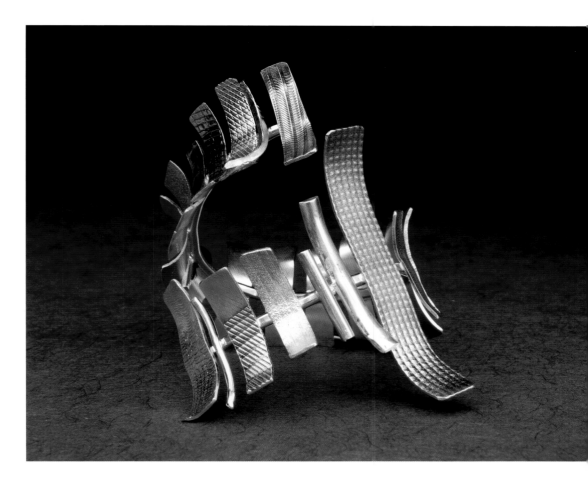

the Gaussoin family travels from Santa Fe to Picuris Pueblo in northern New Mexico where Tsosie Gaussoin has an ancestral home. Her bracelet is entitled *My Road to Canyon de Chelley*. The different patterns on the bars of silver are achieved by hand-stamping and texturing. They represent the tire tracks made in dirt roads on the way to Canyon de Chelly. Located in northeastern Arizona on the Navajo Reservation, Canyon de Chelly contains prehistoric architectural ruins and artifacts and is a National Monument under the U.S. Park Service.

OPPOSITE: Connie Tsosie Gaussoin, Picuris Pueblo, Navajo. Sterling silver *Kiva Seed Bowl* with Italian coral, Lone Mountain turquoise, and a 14k gold feather. Courtesy of the artist.

ABOVE: Connie Tsosie Gaussoin. Sterling silver fabricated bracelet. Collection of Helene Singer Merrin.

ABOVE: David Gaussoin, Picuris Pueblo, Navajo, French. 14k gold squash blossom pin. Private collection.

RIGHT: David Gaussoin. Sterling silver tufa-cast pendant with 14k gold accents and Russian pyrite. Private collection.

OPPOSITE: Wayne Nez Gaussoin, Picuris Pueblo, Navajo, French. Sterling silver bracelet. Collection of Helene Singer Merrin.

Early on, Tsosie Gaussoin encouraged her sons, David and Wayne Nez, to experiment with materials and designs in their jewelry. The family has traveled extensively in Europe, incorporating many of their experiences into their art. David, in particular, has been influenced by the minimalist aesthetic of Norwegian and Finnish jewelers. Although he has been making jewelry since he was eight years old, David recalls that he received a lot of criticism from collectors when he started breaking away from traditional styles and materials. "Collectors and other jewelers questioned our techniques and stones, but now our jewelry is being accepted," he says.

David's signature *Squash Blossom* pin exemplifies his belief that innovation does not diminish tradition. He says, "I carve the pin in wax and cast it in 14k gold, using a centrifugal casting machine. I do these [pins] to honor the squash blossom of the past. . . . I have a garden every summer in which I grow corn, squash, beans, strawberries, etc. So I study the flowers and plants while I am out there."[29] Similarly, his *Rain Pendant,* an abstract interpretation of the way rain clouds build before a storm, also incorporates the traditional cloud or step design on the left. He chose Russian Pyrite for the face, saying, "It is a naturally occurring rainbow-colored pyrite." The 14k gold wires suspended on the front of the figure suggest falling rain.

Wayne Nez Gaussoin, the youngest jeweler in the family, received an Associate of Fine Arts degree from Santa Fe Community College in 2003. He has taken photography at the Institute of American Indian Arts and classes toward a Bachelors of Fine Arts degree at the School of the Art Institute of Chicago. Wayne fuses his interest in photography, music, and fashion into his abstract jewelry that has gained an appreciative audience.

In 2006, Wayne, David, and Connie received the King Fellowship from the School of American Research in recognition of their collective efforts to write a new chapter in the history of Southwestern Indian jewelry.[30]

Fritz J. Casuse is an innovative jeweler who initially took courses at the Poeh Center and has returned as an instructor. A 1996 graduate of the Institute of American Indian Arts in two-dimensional and three-dimensional art forms, Casuse is well known for his sculptural jewelry. His success has been all the more impressive, as he did not take his first jewelry course until 1995. In 2006, he won a fellowship from the Southwestern Association for Indian Arts, just two years after his first Indian Market. Adept at painting, sculpture, ceramics, beadwork, and photography, Casuse has brought a multidisciplinary approach to his work.

As a child, Casuse exhibited a talent for art, which his father encouraged. "I remember my father, who was a carpenter and a welder, and the teachings he passed on to me," Casuse says. "He was able to create so many useful things with his knowledge. A lot of times, instead of playing with the neighborhood kids or riding a bike, I would sit with my father at the kitchen table and talk. This memory helps me to draw upon my imagination. At that table we shared many adventures. He's been my inspiration."[31] His father died when Casuse was fifteen years old, causing the family to move from Twin Lakes to Tohatchi, New Mexico. At Tohatchi High School, Casuse took classes in drawing and ceramics, later enrolling at New Mexico State University in Las Cruces in a ceramics program. Casuse recalls the time, "I was discouraged by my art instructor, who thought my work was too stereotypical." Casuse dropped out of college and went to work for a graphic design company in Gallup, creating designs for coffee mugs and t-shirts. In 1993, he enrolled at the Institute of American Indian Arts. As an instructor at the Poeh Arts Program, Casuse encourages creativity in his students. He says, "Art should be fun. I teach them the basics of cutting, filing, soldering, how to transfer a design to metal, but I also want them to feel free."[32]

Like many artists, Casuse has given titles to his sculptural jewelry. Some are descriptive, such as *Butterfly* for his tufa-cast ring in silver and 14k gold with a black Tahitian pearl. He says, "I made the ring first in copper before I carved it in tufa." The gold shot balls that accent the ring are a signature design that Casuse adds to his jewelry. *Calla* is the name he gives to his ring with coral, a Tahitian pink pearl, and five diamonds that won a blue ribbon at the 2005 Heard Museum Indian Market and the 2005 Santa Fe Indian Market. The bracelet is entitled *Inner Beauty* and is fabricated in sterling silver with three diamonds. "The bracelet is like our body," Casuse states. "The crossed silver wires

LEFT: Fritz J. Casuse in front of the Poeh Center, Pojoaque, New Mexico.

OPPOSITE: Fritz J. Casuse, Navajo. On left, sterling silver and gold tufa-cast ring with Tahitian pearl; on right, sterling silver fabricated bracelet with diamonds and coral; in foreground, gold tufa-cast ring with coral, diamonds, and a pearl. Collection of the artist.

represent the rib cage, which holds the inside together. The coral is the heart, and the three diamonds represent our life—the past, present, and future."

Nizoniful, or *beautiful*, is the playful Navajo/English title Casuse gives to his perfume-vial ring crafted in 18k yellow and white gold. He uses a hollow-form technique for the flask, which has a removable top with diamonds inlaid in the stopper. Blue, yellow, and pink diamonds accent the sculptural shape of the ring, which won Best of Classification at the 2006 Heard Museum Indian Market and the 2006 Santa Fe Indian Market.

Like Casuse, Cody Sanderson is an innovative metalsmith, who has drawn on a rich background of life experience and education for his sculptural and often humorous jewelry. His multifunctional tea infuser bracelet exemplifies his inventiveness and his tongue-in-cheek approach to his work. The tea infuser and the foot, which he modeled after his own foot, can be worn as a pendant, while the chain is a separate link bracelet. Sanderson says, "My pieces are visually digestible. It is what it looks like. In this case, it's a tea infuser/pendant/bracelet."[33]

Sanderson's road to jewelry was circuitous and didn't begin until he was thirty-seven years old. After graduating from Window Rock High School in 1982, he attended Mesa Community College in Arizona for two years. From 1985 to 1990, he served in the Navy. After the military, Sanderson returned to work as a chiropractic therapist in Window Rock, Arizona, for three years before moving to Santa Fe, where he was the night manager for a gallery. His foray into the jewelry world began in 1994 when he worked as a road salesman for eight years for M. M. Rogers, a fine jewelry company in Albuquerque. "I started thinking about how the jewelry was made," he recalls. "Pretty soon, I had bought a workbench and an acetylene torch and set up shop in my kitchen."[34]

To get started on his career in jewelry in November 2001, Sanderson made hinged money clips. When he had

enough orders, he quit his job to devote himself full-time to jewelry. Initially, he enrolled in a jewelry-making class taught by Sabra Sowell at Santa Fe Community College. He also took a course in casting from David Gaussoin at the Poeh Center, only to return later to teach casting himself. Originally from Window Rock, Sanderson is of Navajo and Nambe descent on his mother's side and Hopi and Pima heritage on his father's side. "My primary medium is sterling silver and 18k gold, but I also enjoy working in aluminum, copper, and stainless steel," he says. "Some of my designs involve intricate mechanisms and over fifty solder joints. Fabricating a final piece may include bending, casting,

OPPOSITE: Fritz J. Casuse, Navajo. 18k white and yellow gold perfume vial ring with colored diamonds. Courtesy of the artist.

ABOVE: Cody Sanderson, Navajo, Hopi, Pima, Nambe. Sterling silver tea-infuser bracelet. Collection of Martha H. Struever.

bution to parents. Now in the public domain, the film was rediscovered in the 1970s and has become a cult classic. With the pun intended, Sanderson has cut and inlaid the coral branches in wild disorder, the way coral grows on a reef, to match the chaotic flames he cuts out with a handsaw on the base of the bracelet. He has stamped classic Navajo designs on the inside of the bracelet.

IN OCTOBER 2000, Lois Sherr Dubin led a group of Southwestern Indian artists on a privately sponsored cultural and artistic exchange to Canada. Included in the group were jewelers Jesse Monongya, Vernon Haskie, Carlton Jamon, Marian Denipah, Steve LaRance, Myron Panteah, James Little, Lee Yazzie, and Veronica Poblano. As part of the trip, the group flew to the Queen Charlotte Islands, also called *Haida Gwaii (*islands of the People). The trip inspired Poblano to develop the design for her celebrated torque necklace. "The necklace reminds me of the waves and the movement of the ocean in Canada," she says. "Everything flowed together. I wanted to reproduce that somehow."[35] A gifted lapidarist, Poblano found a design that would yield an unlimited number of sculptural shapes and colors. lightweight and elegant, the torque neckwear has become a signature piece for Poblano. "My old designs were more horizontal and vertical," Poblano says. "Now my designs are more elaborate and fluid. My pieces have a lot of movement because life is like that."[36] Well known for the quality and uniqueness of the stones she uses, Poblano combines the bubblegum pink of cobalt calcite druzy from South Africa with the rare Peruvian blue opal in her necklace. Ultimately a colorist, Poblano is at home in the world of exotic stones that she has combined and inlaid in striking patterns.

The daughter of Leo Poblano, the famous Zuni carver, Poblano inherited an innate talent for working with stone. As a young boy at Zuni, Leo had taken part in the archaeological excavation of the ancient village of Hawikuh during

ABOVE: Cody Sanderson, Navajo, Hopi, Pima, Nambe. Sterling silver and 18k gold cast and fabricated Lego bracelet. Collection of Mark Del Vecchio.

OPPOSITE: Cody Sanderson. Sterling silver bracelet with coral. Courtesy of the artist.

forging, fusing, hammering, or stamping. I devote one day out of my week to experiment with new mediums and techniques." Just four years after he began making jewelry, Sanderson received a fellowship in 2005 from the Southwestern Association for Indian Arts.

Sanderson's originality has put him on the contemporary jewelry map. He has culled ideas for his jewelry from everywhere. He cast his sterling silver and 18k gold Lego bracelet entitled *Child's Play* from his children's plastic Lego blocks. He linked the individual blocks to each other with hinges, in the way that the plastic blocks interlock with each other. The name Lego is a derivative of a Danish phrase that means to "play well," an apt description for the way Sanderson approaches his jewelry. Another bracelet, *Reefer Madness*, is a humorous interpretation of the effects of marijuana. *Reefer Madness* is the title of a 1936 movie that warned of the dangers of smoking marijuana and was intended for distri-

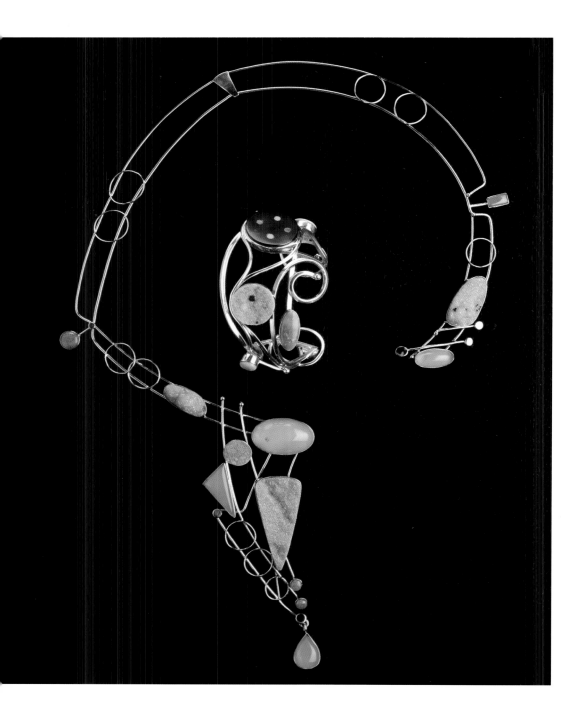

the 1917-1923 expedition led by Frederick Webb Hodge for the Heye Foundation. Founded in 1200, Hawikuh was the largest village at Zuni Pueblo and the first village that the Spanish explorers saw. It is located twelve miles southeast of the present-day Zuni Pueblo. During the excavation of Hawikuh, many examples of prehistoric mosaic jewelry were uncovered, pointing to its long history in the Southwest. By the 1930s, Leo Poblano was part of the revival of mosaic jewelry at Zuni Pueblo and would become well known for his inlaid Shalako, Rainbow God, and Knife-Wing figures, as well as his figurative sculptures of Zuni men and women carved from turquoise, coral, jet, and other stones. He also developed a style of inlaying circles of color into his fetish carvings.

Although she was barely ten years old when her father died in 1959 while fighting a fire in California, Poblano started helping her mother carve fetishes to provide food for the family. By the time she was fourteen, Joe Tanner recognized her talent, giving her materials and the freedom to choose her subjects. Tanner would later employ Poblano to inlay pieces cast by Preston Monongye. In 1987, after her mother's death, Poblano moved with her children to Solana Beach, California, and worked as a hairdresser. On the weekends, she showed her jewelry at local craft fairs, quickly developing an appreciative audience. In 1992, Poblano had to move her family back to Zuni precipitously to address legal challenges to her family's property rights and her own inheritance. Back at Zuni, she began devoting herself full-time to her art and today has a home and studio/gallery on her family's land. In 1993, she won a fellowship from the Southwestern Association for Indian Arts, which allowed her to buy a modern lapidary system. Initially a self-taught jeweler, Poblano has studied twice at the Revere Academy of Jewelry Arts in San Francisco and plans to go again. She says, "There is always something new to learn."

While Poblano has received international recognition for her modern sculptural jewelry—her work has been

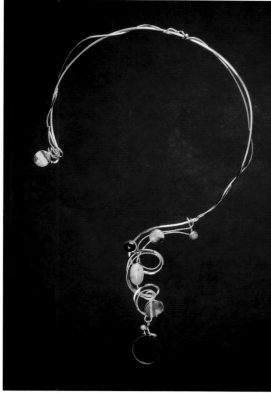

OPPOSITE: Veronica Darquise Poblano, Zuni. 14k gold torque neckwear and bracelet with Peruvian blue opal and cobalt calcite druzy. Courtesy of the artist.

ABOVE and **LEFT:** Veronica Darquise Poblano. Sterling silver torque neckwear with inlay of Kingman turquoise, Fox turquoise, Orville Jack faustite, black pen shell, and sugilite. The circle pendant is black jade. Courtesy of the artist.

213

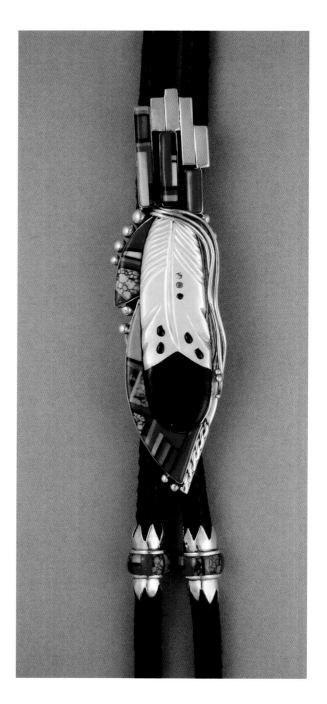

exhibited widely in Japan—she is also conscious of sustaining the legacy of her father. In 1999, through a grant from the Four Times Foundation, she established the Leo Poblano Memorial Mentorship Program. She has also recently returned to carving pieces that are evocative of her father's classic Zuni style. Her *Eagle Feather in Elegance* bolo illustrates her lapidary skills and the architectural structure of her jewelry. She inlays the feather with small dots of color, a technique perfected by Leo half a century ago. She frames the feather with irregular cuts of turquoise and coral on one side and her characteristic twisted wire motif on the other. On the top of the feather, she adds a stylized head-dress of asymmetrical cuts, a contemporary interpretation of a classic Zuni design.

Poblano's three children, all taught by her, have each established their own unique styles of jewelry. The oldest, Brad Poblano, has carved out a niche, fabricating and inlaying tiny crayons and pencils in imaginative colors and patterns. Jovanna Poblano and her husband, Daniel Chattin, collaborate on contemporary necklaces that combine hand-carved shell and stone beads and Corn Maiden carvings by Daniel with intricate beaded elements by Jovanna. She designs and strings the eclectic necklaces, which may include unusual Czechoslovakian glass beads interspersed with more traditional Southwestern materials.

Dylan Poblano, the youngest of Poblano's children, has emerged as one of the most innovative jewelers in the new generation. During the family's hiatus in Solana Beach, California, Dylan was exposed to another world quite distinct from his Zuni culture. After high school, he studied jewelry at the Fashion Institute of Technology in New York City for two years, where he was introduced to a wide range of techniques, designs, and materials. He is adept at drawing, mechanical drafting, lost-wax casting, sculpture, and painting—all of which play a part in his unique designs. Of his *Zuni to Paris* bracelet, he says, "During my time in New

York, I was inspired by the fashion industry and my friends who always talked about Paris as the fashion center of the world. I wanted to make something fun and whimsical."[37] Like Veronica, Dylan's jewelry is very architectural in construction. In his bracelet, he joins sheets of metal to each other at different angles, pushing the bracelet shape over the top into sculpture. The metal has been a canvas for his writings, which cover much of the surface and are interrupted by free-form designs. Highly polished surfaces reflect the patterns of densely textured planes. "Writing is another form of

artistic freedom," he says. Inspired since childhood by Andy Warhol's life and work, Dylan is a fan of popular culture and often scribbles his personal reflections on contemporary subjects on his jewelry.

Dylan's bold and imaginative designs have earned him the title of "a postmodern Zuni jeweler" by his collectors. In a nod to the tradition of inlay at Zuni Pueblo, he goes beyond the classic styles of channel inlay and sculptural inlay to combine glass and other materials with traditional stones. The patterns in his link bracelet and ring are miniature abstract

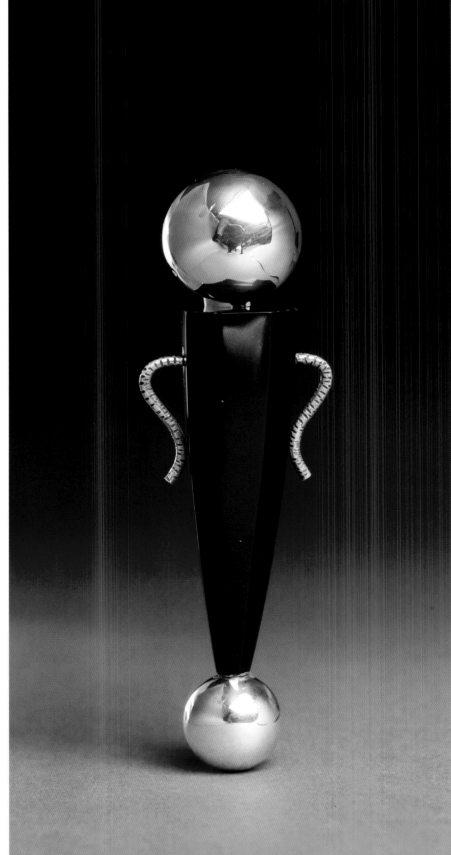

ABOVE: Dylan Poblano, Zuni. Sterling silver constructed bracelet with gold accent. Courtesy of Wright's Indian Art, Albuquerque, New Mexico.

RiGHT: Dylan Poblano. Sterling silver pendant with black marble. Courtesy of Wright's Indian Art, Albuquerque, New Mexico.

paintings. His pendant, carved from black marble, is a tribute to the Art Deco movement in its stylized, elegant shape. The pendant is also part of a series of planetary necklaces, inspired by his interest in astronomy and the galaxies, called *September Moon*. The large silver ball on the top represents the sun, and the smaller silver ball on the bottom is the moon.

In 2002, Dylan was selected to participate in *Changing Hands: Art Without Reservation*, an exhibit mounted by the Museum of Arts & Design in New York City. In an essay for the catalogue, David Revere McFadden, curator of the Museum of Arts & Design, wrote, "Poblano sees his own niche as that of an international artist with a goal of transforming tradition itself."[38] In his artist's statement in the catalogue, Dylan presented another point of view about his work, saying, "My work has a lot to do with today's society and life in this country, particularly in its diversity. Basically, my work is inspired by the younger generation. I try to fill in the gap where nontraditional things appeal to people my own age."[39] In 2007, Dylan expanded his artistic vision, writing, "My work is a tribute to the Zuni tradition of jewelry. I utilize all the basic techniques of jewelry making to create my own expression of the modern experience, and I try to keep my jewelry wearable. The designs still have to be functional. I hope my jewelry will attract new collectors of any age."[40]

AS SOUTHWESTERN INDIAN JEWELERS settle into the twenty-first century, they have at their disposal a plethora of materials and tools to create whatever designs they can envision. The various Indian markets across the country foster an exchange of ideas among jewelers, who may choose to create out of their tribal tradition, or not.

Maria Samora, of Taos Pueblo heritage, crafts beautiful sculptural jewelry that appears deceptively simple but is a technical achievement. In her artist's statement she says, "Growing up in Taos, New Mexico, has provided me with a cultural and creative richness. Life in Taos is simple and

ART TO WEAR

In 2006, Liz Wallace made her first tiara, entitled *Pet-su-melli*, which is Washoe for wild rose. The tiara is the first in a series that will represent the ethno-botanical plants of tribes in the Southwest. "I want to celebrate the native flora in noble materials and showcase how beautiful they can be," she says.[41] Inspired by the Art Nouveau period, Wallace fabricated the roses with the *plique-à-jour* enamel technique and made the stems flexible so that they move gently to catch light reflections.

Courtesy of Wheelwright Museum of the American Indian, Santa Fe.

beautiful, and I believe that my jewelry is a personal expression of this simplicity. The purpose of my art is to accentuate the body and capture the movement of the human form, enhancing one's personal beauty and grace with sophistication and elegance. My designs appeal to the senses and come to life on the body."[42] For her lily pad bracelet, Samora alloyed the 18k gold from 24k gold nuggets. From the hand-rolled sheet metal, she cut out each component with a handsaw, soldering the individual elements together before setting the diamonds in their bezels. "There are eight different components to the bracelet," she says. The bracelet won a First Place and an Honorable Mention at the 2006 Heard Museum Indian Market.

After graduation from Taos High School, Samora studied fine arts and photography at Pitzer College in California for a year and a half before leaving to travel for six months through South America. Back in Taos, she enrolled in some jewelry courses at the University of New Mexico in Taos and began making jewelry as a hobby when she was twenty. In 1998, she received a scholarship to the Taos Institute of Art to study with master goldsmith Phil Poirier. "On the first day, I learned as much as I had in three previous courses," she says. "I asked him if he needed an apprentice." That same year, Samora began her apprenticeship with Poirier, which continues today. Her first assignment was less than glamorous, however. "I had never worked in gold before," she recalls. "My first job was making 2,000 gold jump rings for chains." From Poirier, Samora learned all the techniques required for working in gold and silver. She was also exposed to the designs and methods used by the Etruscans, Egyptians, and Greeks that inspire much of Poirier's own jewelry.[43]

In 2006, Samora made her first *Lattice* bracelet, entitled *Persistence of Light,* from 750 hand-built tiny squares of gold that have been individually set in a network of interlocking sterling silver bands. The row of diamonds, hammer-set in thick-gauge bezels, accents the repeating designs of gold and silver. Behind the illusion of elegant simplicity is a feat of engineering, as each small square of gold moves gracefully and effortlessly with its owner, creating a ripple of light. An avid outdoors enthusiast, Samora draws her inspiration from the beauty of nature. She also stays grounded in her Taos heritage with daily visits from her father, Doroteo "Frankie" Samora, who turned 100 years old in 2006, just six months after Samora had her first child. Every day, he leaves Taos Pueblo to visit his daughter and grandson, reinforcing Samora's philosophy that beauty resides in the smallest gestures and the simplest patterns of nature, and jewelry can express that beauty.[44]

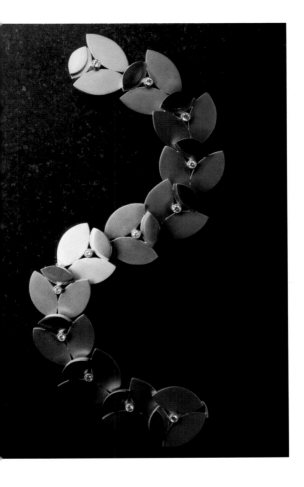

AT THE 2007 SANTA FE Indian Market, Myron Panteah displayed a quotation by Hirotoshi Itoh, a renowned Japanese metalsmith and professor of art at the Tokyo National University of Fine Arts and Music until his death in 1998. The statement, which has inspired Panteah in his art, includes the aphorism: "Love the metal, and it will love you back." In the twenty-first century, Southwestern Indian jewelry remains a dialogue between the silversmith and the silver, the lapidary and the stone, the artist and his or her vision. With all of the sophisticated equipment available to jewelers today, the act of creating beauty out of rough stones and flat sheets of metal is still a private affair that can be lonely and tedious, physically demanding and challenging. The global market for Southwestern Indian jewelry has been a catalyst for creativity, supporting jewelers in their exploration of new designs and new techniques—some of which perpetuate their Native cultures and others that break away entirely from cultural themes. What is a constant is that Southwestern Indian jewelers are crafting new traditions, perhaps unknowingly, each time they strike the metal with a hammer.

Notes

introduction

1 Darryl Dean Begay, e-mail to the author, April 22, 2006.

2 The four sacred mountains are to the east, Blanca Peak in Colorado; to the south, Mount Taylor in New Mexico; to the west, San Francisco Peaks in Arizona; to the north, Hesperus Peak in Colorado.

3 Carl Rosnek and Joseph Stacey, *Skystone and Silver* (Englewood Cliffs, New Jersey: Prentice-Hall, Inc., 1976), 115.

4 Paula A. Baxter with Allison Bird-Romero, *Encyclopedia of Native American Jewelry* (Phoenix: The Oryx Press, 2000), 188.

5 Jon Bonnell, telephone conversation with author, November 16, 2006.

6 *Skystone and Silver*, 115.

7 Harvey Begay, telephone conversation with author, November 14, 2006.

8 Ibid.

9 *Skystone and Silver*, 107.

10 Ibid., 108.

11 Georgia Loloma, e-mail to author, December 19, 2006.

12 Jerry Jacka, telephone conversation with author, December 19, 2006.

13 In 1988, Jerry Jacka and his wife Lois Essary Jacka published *Beyond Tradition—Contemporary Indian Art and Its Evolution*; in 1989, they won an Emmy for their video based on *Beyond* Tradition. See Suggested Readings on page 230 for other works by Jerry Jacka.

14 See Diana F. Pardue, *Shared Images—The Innovative Jewelry of Yazzie Johnson and Gail Bird* (Santa Fe: Museum of New Mexico Press, 2007) for a brief biography of Gail Bird and Yazzie Johnson.

15 Gail Bird, correspondence with author, 2007.

16 Gail Bird, interview with author in studio, July 26, 2007.

17 Gail Bird, "Southwest Jewelry," *Changing Hands: Art Without Reservation, l, Contemporary Native American Art from the Southwest* (London: Merrell Publishers Limited, 2002, in association with the American Craft Museum), 68.

CHAPTER 1

1 Arthur Woodward, *Navajo Silver* (Flagstaff: Museum of Northern Arizona, 1938), 23.

2 John Adair, *The Navajo and Pueblo Silversmiths* (Norman: University of Oklahoma Press, 1944). John Adair is considered the authority on the beginnings of Navajo silverwork. He bases his dates on oral interviews with informants who knew the early silversmiths.

3 Henry Greenberg and Georgia Greenberg, *Power of a Navajo—Carl Gorman: The Man and His Life* (Santa Fe: Clear Light Publishers, 1996).

4 Ibid., 8.

5 Paula A. Baxter with Allison Bird-Romero, *Encyclopedia of Native American Jewelry* (Phoenix: Oryx Press, 2000), 151.

6 Cippy CrazyHorse, telephone conversation with author, March 7, 2007.

7 Irma Bailey, *Joe H. Quintana—Master in Metal—Selections from the Irma Bailey Collection* (Santa Fe: Museum of Indian Arts and Culture, 2004), 3. This catalogue accompanied an exhibition of Quintana's work mounted by the Museum of Indian Arts and Culture in 2004.

8 Baxter and Bird-Romero, 19.

9 Mike Bird-Romero, telephone conversation with author, April 6, 2007.

10 McKee Platero, conversation with author, September 15, 2007.

11 McKee Platero, interview with author, Gallup, New Mexico, July 27, 2006.

12 Paul Zolbrod, *Diné bahané—The Navajo Creation Story* (Albuquerque: University of New Mexico Press, 1984), 36.

13 Perry Shorty, interview with author, Shiprock, New Mexico, July 26, 2006.

14 See Arthur Woodward, *Navajo Silver*, for a brief history of the evolution of the concha.

15 It is generally agreed that traders introduced the term *squash blossom* in order to make the style appear more authentic and native. The actual blossom of the squash does not resemble either the pomegranate or the fluted bead associated with squash blossom necklaces. Nevertheless, the term has stuck to the style.

16 Allison Lee, interview with author, Albuquerque, New Mexico, July 6, 2006.

17 Vernon Haskie, interview with author, Lukachukai, Arizona, June 15, 2006.

18 Frank McNitt, *The Indian Traders* (Norman: University of Oklahoma Press, 1962), 68.

19 Ibid., 210.

20 Dexter Cirillo, *Southwestern Indian Jewelry* (New York: Abbeville Press, 1992), 79–82. "In a cash-poor society, this form of exchange allowed the Navajo to weather the lean months before the harvest or the shearing of sheep earned him enough money to clear his debt. It was understood that an individual could redeem his jewelry for ceremonial occasions and that it would be returned afterward to remain his bond until his bills were paid. Later regulations were passed

specifying the length of time a trader had to keep the jewelry before it was legal to release it for outside sale, at which point it became "dead pawn." "Old pawn" generally refers to jewelry made before 1900, but the pawn system continues today on the Navajo Reservation and in border towns like Gallup, New Mexico, and Flagstaff, Arizona. Buyers of dead-pawn jewelry may have to sign a document indicating that they will return the piece to the original owner if he or she returns with the money to buy it back."

21 Deborah Slaney, *Blue Gem, White Metal—Carvings and Jewelry from the C. G. Wallace Collection* (Phoenix: Heard Museum, 1998). A good overview of C. G. Wallace's influence on the evolution of Zuni jewelry.

22 Mike Tharp, "You Can't Beat Something with Nothing," *Arizona Highways*, vol. L, no. 8 (August 1974), 37.

23 A *Kachina* is a spirit that is a mediator between this world and the world of the gods. Another spelling for Kachina is *Katsina* (*Katsinam*, plural). *Katsina* is a phonetic approximation of the Hopi word for Kachina.

24 Liz Wallace, telephone conversation with author, January 24, 2007.

25 Liz Wallace, interview with author, Santa Fe, New Mexico, April 26, 2006.

26 Charles Supplee, telephone conversation with author, March 7, 2007.

27 Tom Bahti, *Southwestern Indian Ceremonials* (Las Vegas, Nevada: KC Publications, 1974, 3rd ed.), 28–29.

28 Ibid., 18.

29 Darryl Dean Begay, correspondence with author, January 28, 2007.

30 Darryl Dean Begay, correspondence with author, January 29, 2007.

31 Steve LaRance, telephone conversation with author, February 12, 2007.

32 www.nau.edu/library/speccoll/exhibits/traders/oralhistories/interviews.html

33 To see a history of the Tanner family, read the entire oral interview at www.nau.edu/library/speccoll/exhibits/traders/oralhistories/textfiles/tanner-joe.txt. All quotes are from this interview unless otherwise stated.

34 Baxter and Bird-Romero, 111.

35 Barton Wright, *Clowns of the Hopi* (Flagstaff: Northland Publishing, 1994), 68.

36 Lee Yazzie, telephone conversation with author, February 7, 2007.

37 Gene Waddell, telephone conversation with author, February 7, 2007.

38 Jesse Monongya, telephone conversation with author, February 8, 2007.

39 Ric Charlie, telephone conversation with author, March 23, 2007.

40 Marian Denipah, interview with author, Flagstaff, Arizona, October 4, 2006.

41 Steve LaRance, telephone conversation with author, February 12, 2007.

42 Anthony Lovato, interview with author, Santo Domingo Pueblo, July 7, 2006.

43 Eddie Two Moons Chavez, telephone conversation with author, March 29, 2007.

44 Baxter and Bird-Romero, 94.

45 Gerald Lomaventema, telephone conversation with author. In 2005, Lomaventema received a fellowship from the Southwestern Association for Indian Arts.

46 Margaret Nickelson Wright, *Hopi Silver* (Flagstaff, Arizona: Northland Publishing, 1972, 4th ed. 1989), 38. This book also provides a good overview of the overlay technique.

47 Fred Kabotie (1900–1986) and Paul Saufkie (1898–1993) went on to teach a generation of artists at Hopi, including their sons, Michael Kabotie and Lawrence Saufkie, both highly respected jewelers.

48 Roy Talahaftewa, telephone conversation with author, February 20, 2007.

49 Norbert Peshlakai, telephone conversation with author, March 20, 2007.

50 Norbert Peshlakai, correspondence to author, January 17, 2007.

51 See Tricia Loscher, *Old Traditions in New Pots—Silver Seed Pots from the Norman L. Sandfield Collection* (Phoenix: Heard Museum, 2007).

52 Darrell Jumbo, telephone conversation with author, March 22, 2007.

53 Jared Chavez, correspondence with author, October 26, 2005.

54 Jared Chavez, telephone conversation with author, April 2, 2007.

55 Kee Yazzie Jr., telephone conversation with author, March 9, 2007.

56 Kee Yazzie Jr., interview with author, Winslow, Arizona, October 5, 2006.

57 Arland Ben, interview with author, Estancia, New Mexico, July 7, 2006.

58 Arland Ben, telephone conversation with author, March 27, 2007.

59 Arland Ben, telephone conversation with author, August 2, 2007.

60 Myron Panteah, telephone conversation with author, March 28, 2007.

61 Myron Panteah, interview with author, Zuni Pueblo, New Mexico, May 16, 2006.

62 Julius Keyonnie, interview with author, Winslow, Arizona, October 5, 2006.

63 Susan Brown McGreevy, *Indian Basketry Artists of the Southwest* (Santa Fe: School of American Research, 2001), 32.

64 Eric Othole, telephone conversation with author, April 4, 2007.

65 www.patpruitt.com.

66 Pat Pruitt, interview with author, Laguna Pueblo, New Mexico, July 28, 2006.

CHAPTER 2

1 A comprehensive reference on turquoise is Joseph E. Pogue, "The Turquois," *National Academy of Science: Memoirs* 12, pt. 2 (1915) that was reissued by the Rio Grande Press with additional material in 1972. Two more recent and excellent short surveys of turquoise are Arnold Vigil, *The Allure of Turquoise* (Santa Fe: New Mexico Magazine, 1995) and Joe Dan Lowry and Joe P. Lowry, *Turquoise Unearthed—An Illustrated Guide* (Tucson: Rio Nuevo Publishers, 2002).

2 Paul G. Zolbrod, *Diné bahanè—The Navajo Creation Story* (Albuquerque: University of New Mexico Press, 1984), 90.

3   See Erna Fergusson, *Dancing Gods: Indian Ceremonials of New Mexico and Arizona* (Albuquerque: University of New Mexico Press, 1931; fifth paperback printing, 1990); and Gladys A. Reichard, *Navaho Religion—A Study of Symbolism* (Princeton, New Jersey: Princeton University Press, Bollingen Series XVIII, Mythos series, 1990).

4   Fred M. Blackburn and Ray A. Williamson, *Cowboys and Cave Dwellers* (Santa Fe: School of American Research, 1997), 75–76.

5   *The Allure of Turquoise*, 18.

6   Ibid., 20.

7   *Turquoise Unearthed*, 8.

8   Cheryl Yestewa, personal statement.

9   Gene Waddell, interview with author, Tempe, Arizona, February 7, 2007.

10 Gene Waddell, telephone interview with author, May 16, 2007.

11 Raymond Yazzie, from an oral interview collected by Northern Arizona University. See www.nau.edu/library/speccoll/exhibits/traders/oralhistories/textfiles/yazzie-r.txt.

12 Raymond Yazzie, from correspondence with author, May 23, 2007.

13 For a full discussion of Santo Domingo beadwork and mosaic, see *Southwestern Indian Jewelry* (New York: Abbeville Press, 1992), 19–53.

14 Angie Reano Owen, telephone conversation with author, May 7, 2007.

15 For more information on Angie Reano Owen, please see article by Dexter Cirillo, "Back to the Past—Tradition and Change in Contemporary Pueblo Jewelry," *American Indian Art Magazine* 13 (Spring 1988): 46–63. Owen is also discussed in *Southwestern Indian Jewelry* (New York: Abbeville Press, 1992), Chapter One.

16 Angie Reano Owen, telephone conversation with author, May 7, 2007.

17 Charlie Bird, telephone conversation with author, June 5, 2007.

18 For a more complete biography of Charlie Bird, see *Southwestern Indian Jewelry*, 49–53.

19 Jimmie Harrison, telephone conversation with author, October 3, 2007.

20 Jake Livingston, interview with author, Houck, Arizona, June 8, 2007.

21 Tom Bahti, *Southwestern Indian Ceremonials* (Las Vegas, Nevada: KC Publications, 1970), 10.

22 Dale Edaakie, personal biographical statement. For information on Dennis and Nancy Edaakie, see *Southwestern Indian Jewelry*, 93–95.

23 Gomeo Bobelu, artist's statement.

24 Carl Rosnek and Joseph Stacey, *Skystone and Silver: The Collector's Book of Southwest Indian Jewelry* (Englewood Cliffs, New Jersey: Prentice-Hall, 1976), 107.

25 Ibid., 107.

26 Verma Nequatewa, interview with author, Hotevilla, Arizona, October 5, 2006.

27 For more biographical information on Sonwai and examples of jewelry by Nequatewa and Honhongva, see *Southwestern Indian Jewelry*, 155–157.

28 Annie Osburn, "Verma Nequatewa [Sonwai]," *Indian Artist*, Spring 1998, 39.

29 Ken Romero, telephone conversation with author, June 12, 2007. Other information from interview with author, Albuquerque, July 6, 2006.

30 Don Supplee, interview with author, Phoenix, October 3, 2006. The Jacka photograph appeared on the cover of the April 1979 issue of *Arizona Highways*, vol. 55, no. 4.

31 See *Southwestern Indian Jewelry*, 165–168, for biographical information on Charles Supplee.

32 Charles Supplee, telephone conversation with author, March 7, 2007.

33 See www.eddie2moons.com for information.

34 Eddie Two Moons Chavez, interview with author, Albuquerque, July 6, 2006.

35 Carl Clark, personal statement sent to author, October 25, 2006.

36 Carl and Irene Clark, interview with author, Phoenix, October 3, 2006.

37 The Mailman's reared Jesse, his sister Peggy, and his brother Kenneth. The fourth child, Michael, was adopted by a family in Flagstaff, Arizona.

38 Jesse decided to spell his name *Monongya* after his Hopi grandfather, David Monongya. Preston always spelled his last name Monongye. The name means *green lizard* in Hopi.

39 Jesse Monongya, telephone conversation with author, June 25, 2007.

40 Susan Peterson is the author of many books on Pueblo pottery, including *The Living Tradition of Maria Martinez* and *Pottery by American Indian Women*. Marjorie Raike, a collector, first told Monongya about the Bowerbird, a species indigenous to Australia and New Guinea.

41 Jesse Monongya, telephone conversation with author, July 7, 2007.

42 Benson Manygoats, interview with author, Tohatchi, New Mexico, September 19, 2005.

43 Benson Manygoats, telephone conversation with author, June 27, 2007.

44 Alvin Yellowhorse and Bryon Yellowhorse, interview with author, Lupton, Arizona, May 16, 2006.

45 Alvin Yellowhorse, telephone conversation with author, June 28, 2007.

46 Alvin Yellowhorse, from a personal statement sent to author.

47 Bryon Yellowhorse, telephone conversation with author, June 28, 2007.

48 Walter Ben Hunt, *Indian Silversmithing* (New York: Bruce Publishing, 1960).

49 Richard Chavez, telephone conversation with author, July 26, 2006.

50 Raymond Sequaptewa, Sr., interview with author, Tuba City, Arizona, October 4, 2006.

51 Michael Garcia, telephone conversation with author, July 2, 2007.

52 Michael Garcia, telephone conversation with author, July 2, 2007.

53 Michael Dukepoo, telephone conversation with author, July 3, 2007.

54 Ernest Benally, telephone conversation with author, July 3, 2007.

55 Melanie Kirk-Lente, interview with author, Isleta Pueblo, July 7, 2006.

56 Vernon Haskie, interview with author, Lukachukai, Arizona, May 15, 2006.

57 See: oncampus.richmond.edu/~melson/233/toelken.html for a discussion of stories related to the horned toad and coyote.

58 Phil Loretto, various telephone conversations with author in 2006 to 2007, and personal statement sent to author, February 1, 2007.

59 The Spanish brought coral trade beads into the Southwest that were in circulation among Native American tribes by the eighteenth century. However, coral would not become a regular component in Southwestern Indian jewelry until the mid-twentieth century. See Carl Rosnek and Joseph Stacey, *Skystone and Silver: The Collector's Book of Southwest Indian Jewelry* (Englewood, New Jersey: Prentice-Hall, 1976).

CHAPTER 3

1 For a chronology of the Santa Fe Railway, see Marta Weigle and Barbara A. Babcock, eds., *The Great Southwest of the Fred Harvey Company and the Santa Fe Railway*, (Phoenix: Heard Museum, 1996).

2 Daniel Sunshine Reeves, interview with author, May 17, 2006, Tohatchi, New Mexico; telephone conversation with author, July 24, 2007.

3 See Kathleen L. Howard and Diana F. Pardue, *Inventing the Southwest—The Fred Harvey Company and Native American Art* (Flagstaff: Northland Publishing, 1996) for more information on Schweizer and the Fred Harvey Company.

4 John Adair, *The Navajo and Pueblo Silversmiths* (Norman: University of Oklahoma Press, 1944), 25.

5 Margery Bedinger, *Indian Silver—Navajo and Pueblo Jewelers* (Albuquerque: University of New Mexico Press, 1973), 112. Her source was an early history of New Mexico published in 1907.

6 Laurence D. Linford, *A Measure of Excellence—Award-winning Indian Art and Artists from the Gallup Ceremonial—First Annual Edition* (Gallup: Inter-tribal Indian Ceremonial Association, 1991), vii.

7 Cindra Kline, *Navajo Spoons—Indian Artistry and the Souvenir Trade, 1880s—1940s* (Santa Fe: Museum of New Mexico Press, 2001), 20–24.

8 Adair, 53.

9 Kline, 18.

10 Edison Cummings, interview with author, Phoenix, October 10, 2006.

11 Amelia Joe-Chandler, interview with author, Cortez, Colorado, May 15, 2006.

12 Linda Lou Metoxen, telephone interview with author, August 1, 2007.

13 Thomas Curtis, Sr., conversation with author, Santa Fe, August 18, 2007.

14 Jennifer Curtis, interview with author, Albuquerque, July 6 2006.

15 Jared Chavez, interview with author, San Felipe Pueblo, September 27, 2005.

16 Jared Chavez, written explanation of the iconography in the *Commemoration Box* sent to author.

17 Clarence Lee, personal biographical statement sent to author.

18 Duane Maktima, telephone conversation with author.

19 Duane Maktima, telephone interview with author, August 1, 2007.

20 Cheyenne Harris, interview with author, Tempe, Arizona, October 2, 2006.

21 Martha Hopkins Struever, *Loloma* (Santa Fe: Wheelwright Museum of the American Indian, 2005), 26.

22 Carl Rosnek and Joseph Stacey, *Skystone and Silver* (Englewood Cliffs, New Jersey: Prentice-Hall, 1976), 108.

23 Ken Romero, interview with author, Albuquerque, July 6, 2006.

24 Lyndon Tsosie, interview with author, Gallup, May 17, 2006.

25 Eugene Nelson, interview with author, Albuquerque, July 7, 2006. Statement also sent to author.

26 Kay Lockridge, "Creative Clan," *The New Mexican*, August 13, 2006, E-2.

27 David Gaussoin, e-mail correspondence to author, August 12, 2007.

28 Connie Tsosie Gaussoin, interview with author, Santa Fe, April 26, 2006. David and Wayne Nez Gaussoin were also interviewed at that time.

29 David Gaussoin, e-mail to author, August 28, 2006.

30 In January 2007 in honor of its centennial, the School of American Research formally changed its name to the School for Advanced Research on the Human Experience.

31 Fritz J. Casuse, personal statement.

32 Fritz J. Casuse, interview with author, Santa Fe, April 26, 2006.

33 Cody Sanderson, telephone conversation with author, August 12, 2007.

34 Cody Sanderson, interview with author, Santa Fe, April 27, 2006.

35 Veronica Poblano, interview with author, Zuni Pueblo, May 16, 2006.

36 Virginia Campbell, "Elegance in Design," *Southwest Art*, August 2007, 179.

37 Dylan Poblano, telephone conversation with author, September 5, 2007. Interview with author, Zuni Pueblo, May 16, 2006.

38 David Revere McFadden, "Changing Hands: A Metaphor For Our Times," *Changing Hands: Art Without Reservation, 1, Contemporary Native American Art from the Southwest* (London: Merrell Publishers Limited, 2002), 23.

39 Ibid., 75.

40 Dylan Poblano, written correspondence with author, September 6, 2007.

41 Liz Wallace, interview with author, Santa Fe, April 26, 2006.

42 Maria Samora, correspondence given to author in personal interview, Taos, July 5, 2006.

43 See www.poirierstudio.com for information on Phil Poirier and his jewelry.

44 Doroteo "Frankie" Samora was born on February 9, 1906, and he passed away on May 22, 2007 at the age of 101. He was a respected elder at Taos Pueblo.

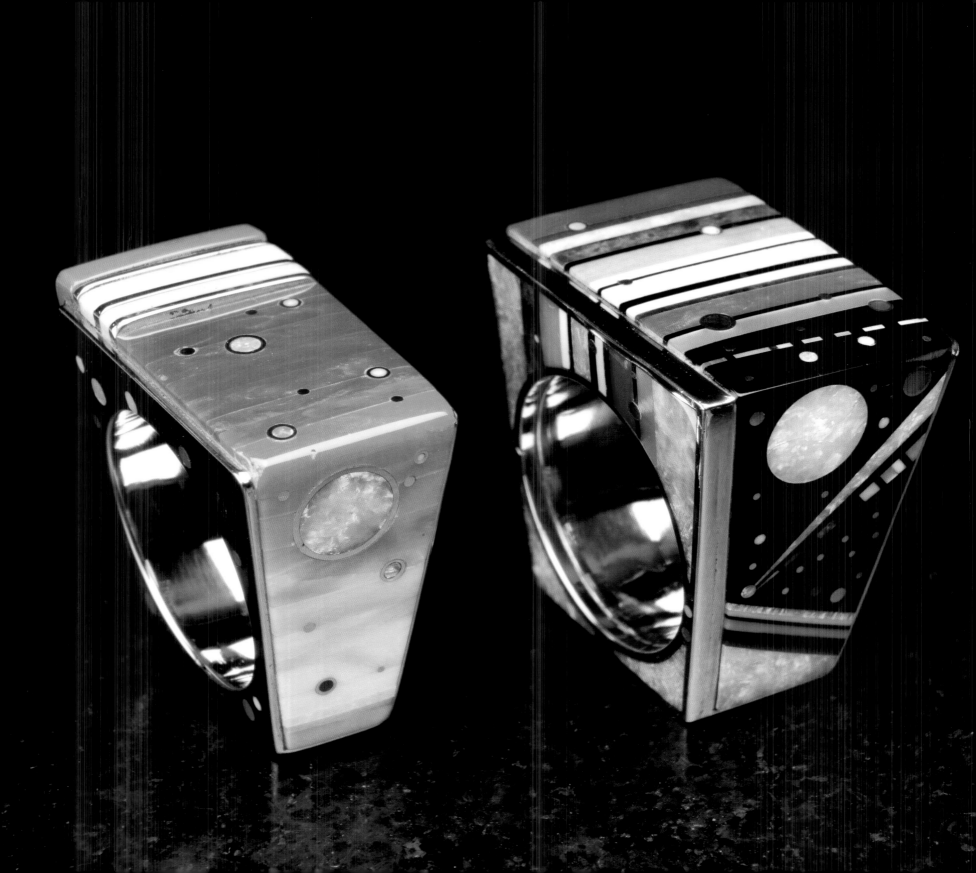

GLOSSARY

One of the joys of collecting contemporary Southwestern Indian jewelry is the opportunity to meet the artists at galleries, museum shows, and Indian markets. As the number of jewelers has increased over the last two decades, so too have the opportunities for artists to exhibit their work. National and regional competitions now fill almost every weekend of the year, affording jewelers and collectors many chances to meet each other. It can be challenging, though, to face the array of jewelry presented at a given market and to feel confident in making an informed selection. Like any field of art, Southwestern Indian jewelry comes with its own vocabulary of techniques, materials, and motifs. To make better informed purchases, collectors need to know how jewelry is made and to be able to recognize the different materials used. Artists are eager to talk about their work and to answer questions about their techniques and the stones they have selected. After all, they have spent endless hours alone creating a piece of jewelry with the goal of sharing their talent and vision with an appreciative audience. This glossary offers an overview of frequently used terms. It is not intended to be exhaustive, but rather to be a quick reference tool for readers.

LEFT: Jesse Lee Monongya, Navajo, Hopi. 14k gold inlaid rings, *Day* (left) and *Night* (right). Collection of Marcia Docter.

TECHNIQUES

Southwestern Indian jewelers craft their art by hand. They hammer decorations into silver, cut stones from rough rock, and grind, buff, and polish the final product. This list includes basic techniques used by jewelers plus some recent innovations.

ANNEAL

A process of heating and cooling metal to make it less brittle and easier to work.

APPLIQUÉ

An overlay technique of soldering cutout designs to a metal base.

CABOCHON

A stone that is cut in a convex or domed shape and polished before it is set. The shape of a cabochon may be oval or round, while its base is flat.

CASTING

The process of making jewelry by pouring molten metal into a mold in which a design has been carved.

Tufa, a porous soft stone formed by volcanic ash, is a popular material for casting that imparts a textured surface to the metal.

In *lost-wax casting*, a wax model is placed in a cylinder and covered with a plaster compound, called the *investment*, that hardens into a mold around the wax. The cylinder is then placed in a kiln and heated until the wax melts, leaving a cavity into which liquid metal is forced, taking the shape left by the wax mold.

CLUSTER WORK

A grouping of multiple stones cut and polished in the same shape and set in bezels around a center stone or design. The Zuni are considered masters of cluster work, which they began doing in the 1930s.

Needlepoint refers to long, slender stones that are sharp at either end.

Petit Point stones may be oval or pear-shaped and are usually distinguished from regular cluster work by their smaller size.

DOMING

The process of shaping seed pots, buttons, beads, and conchas by hammering silver into a hole, usually in wood, of a given size.

HYDRAULIC FORMING

The method of shaping metal under pressure. The artist makes a die that is placed in a cylinder with a sheet of metal on top. The pressure of the hydraulic press forces the metal to take the shape of the die. Hydraulic forming is a recent innovation in Southwestern Indian jewelry making and is used by some artists to form flatware and hollowware objects, such as the stems of goblets.

INLAY

A technique of gluing stones, shells, and other materials into a base in figurative or abstract patterns.

In *channel inlay*, pre-cut stones are placed into metal compartments soldered to a base and then ground down to a flat plane. The metal dividers are integrated into the design.

Raised inlay refers to stones that are placed perpendicular to a base and rise above the surface of the metal, sometimes in irregular sculptural patterns. *Pillow inlay* (or *corn-row inlay*) refers to multiple stones of the same size, cut as cabochons.

In *etched inlay*, designs are carved into inlaid stones.

Chip inlay refers to small particles of stones that are glued onto a metal surface.

MOKUME GANE (also called Marriage of Metals)

A process of laminating different metals to each other to achieve a variegated pattern. *Mokume Gane* is a recent innovation in Southwestern Indian jewelry.

MOSAIC

An overlay technique of creating a design on top of a shell or cottonwood base. Small cuts of rough stones and shells are glued to the base and each other with epoxy. The materials are then ground down to an even plane. The final step is buffing and polishing the mosaic.

OVERLAY

A technique, originated by the Hopis in the late 1930s, in which designs are cut out of one piece of silver that is then soldered to another solid piece of silver. The bottom sheet is blackened through oxidation, making the designs stand out in relief.

REPOUSSÉ

A process of hammering metal from one side to create a raised design on the other side.

ROCKER ENGRAVING

A process of decorating silver by moving a chisel back and forth repeatedly over metal to create fine-line designs. Practiced by First Phase Navajo silversmiths, it is a traditional technique that has been revived by some contemporary silversmiths.

STAMPWORK

A technique for decorating silver by repeatedly hammering a punch or die (a metal rod with a design imprinted on the end) into the metal. Designs may be abstract or representational. Some designs, such as animals, often require multiple stamps in their execution. Silversmiths like to collect old stamps, as well as to make their own.

STONES AND MATERIALS

Many of the materials in Southwestern Indian jewelry have religious and ceremonial significance. For the Navajos, jet, white shell, turquoise, and abalone are associated with their four sacred mountains to the north, east, south, and west, respectively. For all of the tribes, turquoise is an emblem of the sky and a talisman of good fortune. Today's jewelers have built on the time-honored turquoise and shell with an array of materials selected for their rich colors and aesthetic appeal. Improved lapidary equipment has made it possible for jewelers to craft the designs they envision. This is a short list of some of the stones and materials used in contemporary jewelry.

BLACK STONES

Jet, a hard form of fossil coal, was used by the Anasazi and Hohokam in their jewelry. Jet can be carved and polished to a high sheen and is used frequently in contemporary inlay.

Obsidian, a volcanic glass, has also been incorporated into jewelry for centuries. *Onyx, black marble*, and *Black Wyoming jade* are other black stones utilized by contemporary jewelers.

CORAL

The Spanish brought coral into the Southwest in the form of trade beads. In the 1930s, traders introduced small quantities of coral to Zuni artisans. Coral, however, was not widely used in jewelry until the 1950s. Coral ranges in color from pale pink, called *Angel Skin*, to deep red, also known as *Oxblood*. Coral has been imported primarily from Italy, Japan, and the South Pacific and has become increasingly rare and expensive, as beds are depleted from over-fishing and pollution.

DRUZY (or Drusy)

An aggregate of tiny crystals that form on a stone.

FOSSILIZED IVORY (also called Ancient Ivory)

Fossilized ivory comes from prehistoric walrus and mastodon tusks and ranges in color from cream to yellowish brown depending on the length of time it has been in the ground.

GARNET

A semiprecious dark red stone found on the Navajo Reservation and in other parts of the Southwest. Garnets were first used in jewelry around 1885.

GREEN STONES

Malachite, a medium to dark green stone with random stripes of black, has been a traditional stone for fetish carvings and inlay for decades.

Chrysoprase, mined in Arizona but often imported from Australia, became popular in jewelry in the 1990s for its bright apple-green color.

Gaspeite, a vivid green mineral, is the latest arrival to jewelry. Discovered in 1966 on the Gaspé Peninsula in Quebec, Canada, gaspeite is also mined in Australia and is prized for its color and rarity.

LAPIS LAZULI (or Lapis)

A medium to dark blue stone, sometimes flecked with gold, *lapis* has been used in inlay since around 1970.

Denim Lapis came into vogue in the 1990s; it is dyed to simulate a pale denim color.

METALS

Sterling silver (an alloy of 92.5 percent silver with 7.5 percent copper) is the most commonly used metal in Southwestern Indian jewelry.

Coin silver is silver that has been melted down from coins and contains a higher percentage of copper, roughly 10 percent.

Ingot silver refers to silver that has been cast into a slug that can then be rolled and hammered to the desired thickness. Historically, ingot silver would have been melted from coins. Some contemporary silversmiths melt scrap silver into ingots for storage.

Sheet silver was introduced by traders in the late 1920s. Sheet silver comes in different gauges from 14 to 32, the lower number being heavier and thicker.

Gold was used sporadically in Indian jewelry in the 1950s and 1960s. Since the 1970s, jewelers have increasingly used gold in their jewelry. A current trend is for jewelers to alloy their own gold to get a desired color.

OPALS

Used in jewelry since the 1980s, opals come in many colors and are appreciated for their iridescent qualities. The ironstone matrix in *Yowah* and *Boulder opals* from Queensland, Australia, gives them a striking blue-green color.

SHELLS

In prehistoric jewelry, shells were fashioned into bracelets, beads, and pendants. They serve as a base for mosaic overlay and are also cut into small tabs for use in mosaic.

The *spondylus*, or *spiny oyster* shell, is widely used, especially at Santo Domingo Pueblo, for its rich orange-red color. The *purple spiny oyster* is also popular in jewelry.

Mother-of-pearl and *abalone* are popular in mosaic and inlay because of their iridescence and various shades of color.

Pen shell, with its mottled brown exterior, has replaced the endangered tortoiseshell.

Heishi (which means shell) necklaces are frequently made from *melon*, *clam*, and *olive* shells.

Green snail and *cowrie* shells form the base for mosaic in bangle and cuff bracelets, respectively.

SUGILITE

A purple stone that was discovered in 1944 but not mined in any quantity until 1979, when a large deposit was found in the Kalahari Desert in South Africa. Also called Royal Lavulite, *sugilite* has been used in Southwestern Indian jewelry since 1981. *Gel sugilite* is a rare translucent variation.

TURQUOISE

The centerpiece of Southwestern Indian jewelry, turquoise has been used in jewelry and mined in the Southwest for centuries. A hydrous phosphate of copper and aluminum, turquoise varies in color from sky blue to indigo to green, and is named for the mine from which it comes. Arizona, New Mexico, Colorado, and Nevada have all produced high-grade turquoise over the years (see page 8). However, as American mines have been depleted or have closed for economic reasons, China has taken up the slack, providing much of the turquoise used in Southwestern Indian jewelry. In its natural state, the majority of turquoise mined is relatively soft and may be treated in some way to make it useful for jewelry:

Stabilized turquoise has been infused with a liquid resin to harden it so it may be worked. While a dye is not added, the process of stabilizing the stone can intensify the color. At juried Indian markets, artists are required to identify the type of turquoise they use. Stabilized turquoise is accepted as long as it is disclosed.

Treated turquoise has been artificially dyed.

Reconstituted turquoise is an amalgam of particles that have been mixed with glue and formed into a block that can be cut.

Natural turquoise can be gem-quality, which means it has a true color that does not have to be enhanced, and it is hard enough to be cut and polished without stabilization. Natural turquoise is becoming increasingly rare, constituting a small fraction of turquoise on the market. Collectors and artists alike may request a letter of authenticity from a seller of natural turquoise.

WOOD

Ironwood, a dense, brown hardwood found in the Sonoran Desert, was introduced into Southwestern Indian jewelry in the 1950s.

Cocobolo wood is a variegated reddish to deep mahogany wood from Central America.

Ebony is sometimes used in inlay for its deep black color and ability to take a high polish.

TERMS AND MOTIFS

Southwestern Indian jewelry is unique because much of it is based on the cultural heritage of the individual artist. This section includes some terms that reflect specific tribal beliefs as they are appropriate to the jewelry.

ANASAZI

A Navajo name meaning "The Ancient Ones," who were the precursors of the *Pueblo* cultures. Also called *Ancestral Pueblo* peoples, the Anasazi inhabited the Four Corners area (where Utah, Colorado, New Mexico, and Arizona meet) from circa 100 B.C. to 1300 A.D. *Pueblo* is Spanish for village, and is the generic term used to describe the Pueblo tribes that live in New Mexico and Arizona.

BEAUTY WAY (also called the Blessing Way)

A Navajo ceremony to restore balance and harmony to an individual.

CONCHA (or Concho)

A round or oval-shaped plaque of silver that is typically decorated with stampwork and may be set with stones. Contemporary concha belts often have distinct designs on each concha.

CORN

As a centerpiece of Pueblo ceremonial life, corn motifs are popular in jewelry.

The *corn leaf* design is a curved shape formed by repoussé that appears on belt buckles and concha belts.

Corn Maidens, the divine figures who watch over the crops, are interpreted in pins, bolo ties, pendants, and necklaces as abstract female shapes inlaid with stones.

Corn row refers to an inlay of matching cabochon stones shaped like corn kernels.

DINÉ

The Navajos call themselves *Diné*, which means *The People.*

FETISH

A stone or shell carving of a zoomorphic subject. Initially, fetishes of different animals and birds were carved for their talismanic properties. Today, most fetishes are carved as miniature sculptures prized for their detail and realism.

FIRST PHASE SILVERWORK

Silverwork that was produced by Navajo silversmiths from 1868 to 1900 and characterized by deep chisel and stampwork and simple bezel-set stones.

HARVEY HOUSE JEWELRY (also termed Tourist Jewelry)

Lightweight silver jewelry decorated with "Indian" motifs and sold to tourists at the Harvey Houses during the era of railroad travel to the West in the early twentieth century.

HOGAN

A traditional Navajo home used for ceremonies. Built in an octagonal shape, the *hogan* is supported by four poles that represent the four sacred mountains that circumscribe the Navajo Nation: Hesperus Peak (north) in Colorado; Mount Blanca (east) in Colorado; Mount Taylor (south) in New Mexico; and the San Francisco Peaks (west) in Arizona. The domed shape of the hogan represents the sky, and the floor is Mother Earth.

HÓZHÓ

A Navajo word for *balance and harmony. Ho'zhojii* is Navajo for the Beauty Way/Blessing Way ceremony. To live in balance and harmony is the fundamental principle underlying the Navajo way of life. The phrase *Walk in Beauty* is another way to express the meaning of hózhó.

KACHINA

A spirit intermediary. The Hopi word for spirit is *Katsina* and the plural is *Katsinam. Kachina* is the more conventional term for the figures that are carved out of cottonwood and represent the more than 400 Katsinam that constitute the complex religious and ceremonial life of the Hopi. Kachina figures have become a popular motif in jewelry.

KIVA

A special meeting room, either underground or above ground, used for religious purposes and entered by a ladder.

The *kiva-step* design represents the ladder and is a popular motif in jewelry.

The *step design* is also referred to as a *cloud design.*

KNIFE-WING FIGURE

A Zuni animal spirit and a popular motif in mosaic jewelry since the 1930s, the figure is portrayed as a man with outstretched feathered arms.

KOKOPELLI (also called the Humpbacked Flute Player)

A fertility symbol, this figure is ubiquitous on rock art throughout the Southwest and is frequently depicted in overlay jewelry.

MIMBRES

A prehistoric culture that inhabited southern New Mexico and developed a sophisticated ceramic tradition from approximately 550 A.D. to 1150 A.D. Their figurative and geometric patterns have inspired contemporary jewelers.

NAJA

A crescent-shaped pendant that is suspended from a *squash blossom* necklace. Originally of Moorish origin, the Spanish used the *naja* on horse bridles as a protective amulet and introduced it into the Southwest.

PETROGLYPHS

Prehistoric carvings of human, animal, and abstract designs found on rocks throughout the Southwest.

PREHISTORIC

Generally understood as the time before the arrival of the Spanish to the Southwest in the early sixteenth century.

RAINBOW FIGURE

A guardian spirit with a curved body like a rainbow, popular in inlaid jewelry since the 1930s, especially among the Zuni.

SANDPAINTING

A dry painting of colored sand created by a Navajo medicine man for the purpose of healing.

SHALAKO

One of six giant *Kachinas* that appear at the Zuni Winter Solstice ceremony as messengers of the gods. Like the *Knife-Wing* figure, the *Shalako Kachina* is another subject the Zuni portray in colorful inlaid jewelry.

SQUASH BLOSSOM NECKLACE

A silver bead necklace with flowerlike pendants attached on either side and a *naja* in the center. The design was inspired by decorations on the clothing of Spanish and Mexican gentlemen. Traders coined the name *squash blossom*.

TABLITA

A wooden headdress with a cutout step design worn by Pueblo women at dances. Often painted turquoise to symbolize the sky, tablitas are often decorated with butterfly and dragonfly motifs, emblems of rain.

TURTLE

A symbol of Mother Earth and associated with long life and water. At Pueblo dances, men wear a turtle-shell rattle tied to one leg as a percussive instrument. Turtle dances are held each year at San Juan Pueblo and Taos Pueblo. In jewelry, the turtle has become a popular subject for inlay.

YEI

A Navajo deity. *Yeibichai* are masked dancers who impersonate the *Yei*.

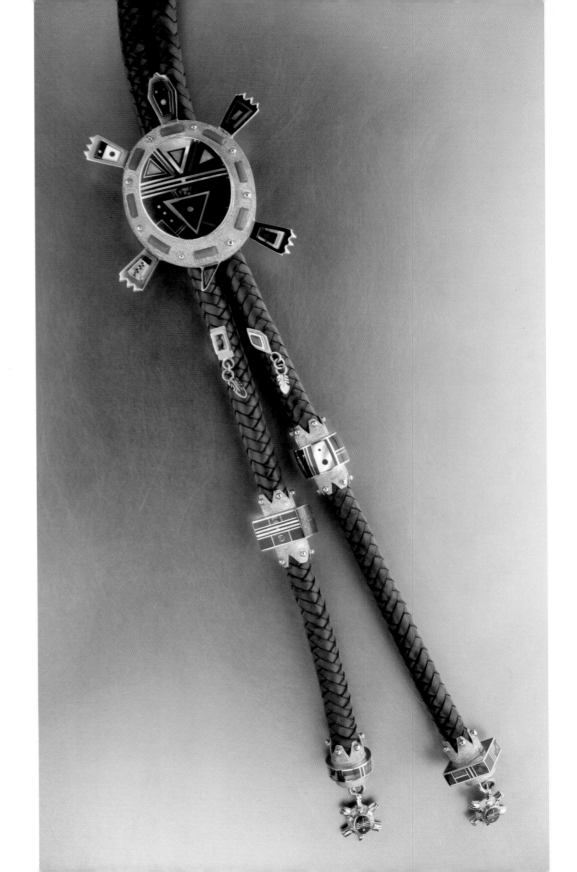

RIGHT: Benson Manygoats, Navajo. 14k gold bolo tie inlaid with coral, lapis, turquoise, mother-of-pearl, Acoma jet, and opals. Collection of Mr. and Mrs. N. Smith.

SUGGESTED READINGS

Adair, John. *The Navajo and Pueblo Silversmiths*. Norman: University of Oklahoma Press, 1944.

Arizona Highways: Vol. 50 (August 1974); Vol. 51 (March 1975); Vol. 52 (August 1976); Vol. 55 (April 1979); *Turquoise Blue Book and Indian Jewelry Digest* (1975).

Bahti, Tom. *Southwestern Indian Ceremonials*. Las Vegas, Nevada: KC Publications, 1974.

Bauver, Robert. *Navajo and Pueblo Earrings 1850–1945*. Los Ranchos de Albuquerque, New Mexico: Rio Grande Books, 2007.

Baxter, Paula A. *Southwest Silver Jewelry*. Atglen, Pennsylvania: Schiffer Publishing Ltd., 2001.

Baxter, Paula A. with Bird-Romero, Allison. *Encyclopedia of Native American Jewelry— A Guide to History, People, and Terms*. Phoenix: The Oryx Press, 2000.

Bedinger, Margery. *Indian Silver—Navajo and Pueblo Jewelers*. Albuquerque: University of New Mexico Press, 1973.

Bird-Romero, Allison. *Heart of the Dragonfly*. Albuquerque: Avanyu Publishing, 1992.

Blackburn, Fred M. and Williamson, Ray A. *Cowboys and Cave Dwellers— Basketmaker Archaeology in Utah's Grand Gulch*. Santa Fe: School of American Research Press, 1997.

Chalker, Kari, ed. *Totems to Turquoise—Native North American Jewelry Arts of the Northwest and Southwest*. New York: Harry N. Abrams, Inc. Publishers, 2004.

Cirillo, Dexter (in collaboration with Nancy Pletka Benkof). *Across Frontiers— Hispanic Crafts of New Mexico*. San Francisco: Chronicle Books, 1998.

Cirillo, Dexter. "Back to the Past: Tradition and Change in Contemporary Pueblo Jewelry." *American Indian Art* 13 (Spring 1988): 46–63.

Cirillo, Dexter. *Southwestern Indian Jewelry*. New York: Abbeville Press, 1992.

Dubin, Lois Sherr. *Jesse Monongya—Opal Bears and Lapis Skies*. New York: Hudson Hills Press, 2002.

Dubin, Lois Sherr. *North American Indian Jewelry and Adornment—From Prehistory to the Present*. New York: Harry N. Abrams, Inc. Publishers, 1999.

Fergusson, Erna. *Dancing Gods: Indian Ceremonials of New Mexico and Arizona*. Albuquerque: University of New Mexico Press, 1931; fifth paperback printing, 1990.

Greenberg, Henry and Greenberg, Georgia. *Power of a Navajo—Carl Gorman: The Man and His Life*. Santa Fe: Clear Light Publishers, 1996.

Howard, Kathleen L. and Pardue, Diana F. *Inventing the Southwest—The Fred Harvey Company and Native American Art*. Flagstaff: Northland Publishing, 1996.

Iverson, Peter. *Diné—A History of the Navajos*. Albuquerque: University of New Mexico Press, 2002.

Jacka, Jerry and Jacka, Lois Essary. *Beyond Tradition—Contemporary Indian Art and its Evolution*. Flagstaff: Northland Publishing, 1988.

Jacka, Jerry and Jacka, Lois Essary. *Enduring Traditions—Art of the Navajo*. Flagstaff: Northland Publishing, 1994.

Jacka, Jerry and Jacka, Lois Essary. *Navajo Jewelry—A Legacy of Silver and Stone*. Flagstaff: Northland Publishing, 1995.

Jernigan, E. Wesley. *Jewelry of the Prehistoric Southwest*. Santa Fe: School of American Research, 1978.

Kline, Cindra. *Navajo Spoons—Indian Artistry and the Souvenir Trade, 1880s–1940s*. Santa Fe: Museum of New Mexico Press, 2001.

Loscher, Tricia. *Old Traditions in New Pots—Silver Seed Pots from the Norman L. Sandfield Collection*. Phoenix: Heard Museum, 2007.

Lowry, Joe Dan and Lowry, Joe P. *Turquoise Unearthed—An Illustrated Guide*. Tucson: Rio Nuevo Publishers, 2002.

McFadden, David and Taubman, Ellen, general editors. *Changing Hands—Art Without Reservation, I—Contemporary Native American Art from the Southwest*. London: Merrell Publishers, 2002.

McNitt, Frank. *The Indian Traders*. Norman: University of Oklahoma Press, 1962.

Osburn, Annie. *Visions of Sonwai—Verma Nequatewa*. Hotevilla: Sonwai, Inc., 2007.

Pardue, Diana F. *Shared Images—The Innovative Jewelry of Yazzie Johnson and Gail Bird*. Santa Fe: Museum of New Mexico Press, 2007.

Pardue, Diana F. *The Cutting Edge—Contemporary Southwestern Jewelry and Metalwork*. Phoenix: Heard Museum, 1997.

Reichard, Gladys. *Navajo Religion—A Study of Symbolism*. Princeton: Princeton University Press, Bollingen Series XVIII, Mythos Series, 1990.

Roessel, Jr., Robert A. *Pictorial History of the Navajo from 1860 to 1910*. Rough Rock, Navajo Nation, Arizona: Navajo Curriculum Center Rough Rock Demonstration School, 1980.

Rosnek, Carl and Stacey, Joseph. *Skystone and Silver: The Collector's Book of Southwest Indian Jewelry*. Englewood Cliffs: Prentice-Hall, 1976.

Schaaf, Gregory. *American Indian Jewelry I, 1,200 Artist Biographies*. Santa Fe: Center for Indigenous Arts and Cultures Press, 2003.

Slaney, Deborah C. *Blue Gem, White Metal-Carvings and Jewelry from the C. G. Wallace Collection*. Phoenix: Heard Museum, 1998.

Struever, Martha Hopkins, with the assistance of Jonathan Batkin and Cheri Falkenstien-Doyle. *Loloma—Beauty is His Name*. Santa Fe: Wheelwright Museum of the American Indian, 2005.

Tisdale, Shelby J. *Fine Indian Jewelry of the Southwest—The Millicent Rogers Museum Collection*. Santa Fe: Museum of New Mexico Press, 2006.

Vigil, Arnold, ed. *The Allure of Turquoise*. Santa Fe: New Mexico Magazine, 1995.

Weigle, Marta and Babcock, Barbara A., eds. *The Great Southwest of the Fred Harvey Company and the Santa Fe Railway*. Phoenix: Heard Museum, 1996.

Woodward, Arthur. *Navajo Silver*. Flagstaff: Northland Press, 4th printing, 1974. Originally published by the Museum of Northern Arizona in August 1938 as *Museum of Northern Arizona Bulletin* No. 14.

Wright, Barton. *Clowns of the Hopi*. Flagstaff: Northland Publishing, 1994.

Wright, Margaret Nickelson. *Hopi Silver*. Flagstaff: Northland Publishing, 1972; 4th ed., 1989.

Zolbrod, Paul G. *Diné bahanè—The Navajo Creation Story*. Albuquerque: University of New Mexico Press, 1984.

ARCHIVAL PHOTOGRAPH REFERENCES

Pages 26: Palace of the Governors (MNM/DCA, #044519); 27: National Museum of the American Indian, Smithsonian Institution (P21241); 28: Palace of the Governors (MNM/DCA, #016333); 29: top, Palace of the Governors (MNM/DCA, #130163); bottom, Palace of the Governors (MNM/DCA, #3197); 42: Palace of the Governors (MNM/DCA, #167028); 46: left, Palace of the Governors (MNM/DCA, #127458); 47: Palace of the Governors (MNM/DCA, #16480); 49: bottom, Palace of the Governors (MNM/DCA, #55864); 51: School for Advanced Research (SAR.1978-1-105); 65: Palace of the Governors (MNM/DCA, #4578); 71: right, Palace of the Governors (MNM/DCA, #86991); 74: Southwest Museum of the American Indian, Autry National Center (#2005.87.1); 75: Northern Arizona University, Cline Library, Special Collections and Archives (HCPO.PH.2003.1HC 5.32); 99: left, Palace of the Governors (MNM/DCA, #4235); right, Palace of the Governors (MNM/DCA, #128725); 106: top, Arizona State Museum, University of Arizona (#39221); 115: Palace of the Governors (MNM/DCA, #71137); 126: Denver Public Library, Western History Collection (#GB-5482); 136: right, Palace of the Governors (MNM/DCA, #71067); 168: left, Palace of the Governors (MNM/DCA, #177688); right, Palace of the Governors (MNM/DCA, #1507); bottom, Palace of the Governors (MNM/DCA, #015780); 170: Palace of the Governors (MNM/DCA, #132439).

OTHER PHOTOGRAPHER CREDITS

62 and 63: Bill Faust
66: Rebecca T. Begay
84: Bruce Hucko
100: Mike Waddell
107 and 109: Elena Gomez
116 and 117: David H. Davis
123 and 147: TedJerome.com

129: Jerry Jacka Photography
164: Fotolux Inc.
169: Light Language Studios
186, 196, and 197: Peter Jacobs, Fine Arts Imaging
214: TedJerome.com
218: Kevin Rebholtz

ARTISTS

This list includes all of the artists who appeared in *Southwestern Indian Jewelry*, as well as those who are in *Southwestern Indian Jewelry—Crafting New Traditions*.

Aguilar, Marie (b. 1924, Santo Domingo Pueblo)

Aguilar, Tony (b. 1919, Santo Domingo Pueblo)

Aiula, Horace (1901–1978, Zuni); also spelled Iule

Beck, Victor (b. 1941, Navajo)

Begay, Darryl Dean (b. 1973, Navajo)

Begay, Harvey (b. 1938, Navajo)

Begay, Kenneth (1914–1977, Navajo)

Begay, Rebecca (b. 1976, Navajo)

Ben, Arland (b. 1962, Navajo)

Benally, Ernest (b. 1959, Navajo)

Bird, Charlie (b. 1943, Laguna/Santo Domingo Pueblo)

Bird, Gail (b. 1949, Laguna/Santo Domingo Pueblo)

Bird-Romero, Mike (b. 1946, San Juan Pueblo/ Taos Pueblo)

Bobelu, Gomeo (b. 1964, Zuni)

Boone, Lena (Zuni)

Calabaza, Jimmy (b. 1949, Santo Domingo Pueblo)

Casuse, Fritz (b. 1969, Navajo)

Cate, Joe (1944–2007, Santo Domingo Pueblo)

Cate, Rosey (b. 1948, Santo Domingo Pueblo)

Charlie, Ric (b. 1959, Navajo)

Chavez, Eddie Two Moons (b. 1953, Chiricahua Apache)

Chavez, Jared (b. 1982, San Felipe Pueblo, Navajo, Hopi/Tewa)

Chavez, Petra (b. 1951, Santo Domingo Pueblo)

Chavez, Richard (b. 1949, San Felipe Pueblo)

Chavez, Ronald (b. 1958, Santo Domingo Pueblo)

Clark, Carl (b. 1952, Navajo)

Clark, Irene (b. 1950, Navajo)

Cordalis, Rita Joe (b. 1954, Navajo)

Coriz, Frank (Santo Domingo Pueblo)

Coriz, Rita (Santo Domingo Pueblo)

CrazyHorse, Cippy (b. 1946, Cochiti Pueblo)

Crispin, Virginia (Santo Domingo Pueblo)

Cummings, Edison (b. 1962, Navajo)

Curtis, Jennifer (b. 1964, Navajo)

Curtis, Sr., Thomas (b. 1942, Navajo)

Day, Chalmers (b. 1956, Hopi)

Deleosa, Juan (1882–1940s, Zuni); also spelled de Dios and Didedios

Denipah, Marian (b. 1959, Navajo/San Juan Pueblo)

Deyuse, Leekya (circa 1889–1966, Zuni)

Dukepoo, Causandra (b. 1976, Taos Pueblo)

Dukepoo, Michael (b. 1971, Hopi/Yaqui/Laguna Pueblo)

Edaakie, Dale (b. 1957, Zuni)

Edaakie, Dennis (b. 1931, Zuni)

Edaakie, Nancy (Zuni)

Eustace, Christina (b. 1954, Zuni/Cochiti Pueblo)

Garcia, Barbara (Santo Domingo Pueblo)

Garcia, Michael (b. 1953, Pascua Yaqui)

Garcia, Raymond (Santo Domingo Pueblo)

Gaspar, Dinah (b. 1945, Zuni)

Gaspar, Pete (b. 1938, Zuni)

Gaussoin, Connie Tsosie (b. 1948, Navajo/Picuris Pueblo)

Gaussoin, David (b. 1975, Navajo/Picuris Pueblo/French)

Gaussoin, Wayne Nez (b. 1982, Navajo/Picuris Pueblo/French)

Golsh, Larry (b. 1942, Pala Mission/Cherokee)

Harris, Cheyenne (b. 1963, Navajo/Northern Cheyenne)

Harrison, Jimmie (b. 1952, Navajo)

Haskie, Vernon (b. 1968, Navajo)

Honanie, Watson (b. 1953, Hopi)

Honhongva, Sherian (b. 1960, Hopi)

Jackson, Tommy (b. 1958, Navajo)

Jim, Thomas (b. 1955, Navajo)

Joe-Chandler, Amelia (b. 1962, Navajo)

Johnson, Yazzie (b. 1946, Navajo)

Jumbo, Darrell (b. 1960, Navajo)

Kabotie, Michael (b. 1942, Hopi)

Kagenveama, Bennett (b. 1964, Hopi)

Kaskalla, Roderick (b. 1955, Zuni)

Keyonnie, Julius (b. 1964, Navajo)

Kirk-Lente, Melanie (b. 1971, Isleta Pueblo)

Kirk-Lente, Michael (b. 1975, Isleta Pueblo)

LaRance, Steve Wikviya (b. 1958, Hopi/Assiniboine)

Lee, Allison (b. 1958, Navajo)

Lee, Clarence (b. 1952, Navajo)

Lee, Russell (b. 1976, Navajo)

Little, James (b. 1947, Navajo)

Livingston, Jake (b. 1945, Zuni/Navajo)

Loco, Jan (b. 1949, Warm Springs Apache)

Loloma, Charles (1921–1991, Hopi)

Lomaventema, Gerald (b. 1967, Hopi)

Loretto, Phil (b. 1951, Jemez/Cochiti Pueblo)

Lovato, Anthony (b. 1958, Santo Domingo Pueblo)

Lovato, Calvin (b. 1958, Santo Domingo Pueblo)

Lovato, Charles (1937–1989, Santo Domingo Pueblo)

Lovato, Julian (b. 1925, Santo Domingo Pueblo)

Lovato, Pilar (b. 1960, Santo Domingo Pueblo)

Lovato, Ray (b. 1946, Santo Domingo Pueblo)

Lovato, Sam (b. 1935, Santo Domingo Pueblo)

Maktima, Duane (b. 1954, Hopi/Laguna Pueblo)

Manygoats, Benson (b. 1967, Navajo)

Martza, Leonard (b. 1928, Zuni)

Metoxen, Linda Lou (b. 1964, Navajo)

Monongya, Jesse (b. 1952, Navajo/Hopi)

Monongye, Preston (1929–1987, adopted
    Hopi/Mission)

Naktewa, Walter (Zuni); also spelled Nakatewa
    and Nahktewa

Navasya, Phil (b. 1944, Hopi)

Nelson, Eugene (b. 1954, Navajo)

Nequatewa, Verma (b. 1949, Hopi)

Nez, Al (b. 1959, Navajo)

Nez, Gibson (b. 1944, Navajo/Jicarilla Apache)

Nez, Mike (Navajo)

Nez, Rita (Navajo)

Ohmsatte, Silas (1939–1990s, Zuni)

Othole, Eric (b. 1977, Zuni/Cochiti Pueblo)

Owen, Angie Reano (b. 1946, Santo Domingo Pueblo)

Panteah, Myron (b. 1966, Zuni/Navajo)

Peshlakai, Norbert (b. 1953, Navajo)

Platero, McKee (b. 1957, Navajo)

Poblano, Dylan (b. 1974, Zuni)

Poblano, Veronica (b. 1951, Zuni)

Poseyesva, Phil (b. 1958, Hopi)

Pruitt, Pat (b. 1973, Laguna Pueblo/Chiricahua Apache)

Quandelacy, Andres (Zuni)

Quandelacy, Barlow (Zuni)

Quandelacy, Dickey (b. 1953, Zuni)

Quandelacy, Ellen (1924–2002, Zuni)

Quandelacy, Faye (b. 1958, Zuni)

Quandelacy, Georgia (b. 1957, Zuni)

Quandelacy, Stewart (Zuni)

Quintana, Joe H. (1915–1991, Cochiti Pueblo)

Reano, Angie (Santo Domingo Pueblo)

Reano, Charlene Sanchez (b. 1960, San Felipe Pueblo)

Reano, Charlotte (b. 1950, Santo Domingo Pueblo)

Reano, Daisy (Santo Domingo Pueblo)

Reano, Denise (Santo Domingo Pueblo)

Reano, Frank (b. 1962, Santo Domingo Pueblo)

Reano, Joe (Santo Domingo Pueblo)

Reano, Joe B. (Santo Domingo Pueblo)

Reano, Percy (b. 1951, Santo Domingo Pueblo)

Reano, Rose (Santo Domingo Pueblo)

Reano, Terry (Santo Domingo Pueblo)

Reeves, Daniel Sunshine (b. 1964, Navajo)

Romero, Ken (b. 1956, Laguna/Taos Pueblo)

Rosetta, Johnny (b. 1949, Santo Domingo Pueblo)

Rosetta, Marlene (b. 1948, Hopi)

Rosetta, Mary (b. 1930, Santo Domingo Pueblo)

Rosetta, Ray (b. 1929, Santo Domingo Pueblo)

Samora, Maria (b. 1975, Taos Pueblo)

Sanderson, Cody (b. 1964, Navajo/Hopi/Pima/Nambe)

Sequaptewa, Sr., Raymond (b. 1948, Hopi)

Shorty, Perry (b. 1964, Navajo)

Smokey (b. 1956, Zuni)

Supplee, Charles (b. 1959, Hopi/French)

Supplee, Don (b. 1965, Hopi/French)

Talahaftewa, Roy (b. 1955, Hopi)

Tewa, Bobbie (b. 1948, Hopi/San Juan Pueblo)

Todacheene, Andrew (b. 1955, Navajo)

Tracey, Ray (b. 1953, Navajo)

Tsabetsaye, Edith (b. 1940, Zuni)

Tsosie, Lyndon (b. 1968, Navajo)

Tsosie, Richard (b. 1953, Navajo)

Vicenti, Edison (b. 1945, Zuni)

Vicenti, Jennie (b. 1944, Zuni)

Wallace, Liz (b. 1975, Navajo/Washoe/Maidu)

Weebothie, Lee (b. 1927, Zuni)

Weebothie, Mary (1933–1997, Zuni)

Yazzie Jr., Kee (b. 1969, Navajo)

Yazzie, Lee (b. 1946, Navajo)

Yazzie, Leo (b. 1940, Navajo)

Yazzie, Raymond (b. 1959, Navajo)

Yellowhorse, Alvin (b. 1968, Navajo)

Yellowhorse, Bryon (b. 1972, Navajo)

Yestewa, Cheryl (b. 1958, Hopi/Navajo)

Yunie, Albenita (b. 1944, Zuni)

JEWELRY SOURCES

Following is a select list of regional, national, and international galleries and museum shops that carry Southwestern Indian jewelry. Noteworthy Indian markets are also included.

REGIONAL: SOUTHWEST

ARIZONA

Bahti Indian Arts
Tucson, Arizona
www.bahti.com

Blue-Eyed Bear
Sedona, Arizona
www.blueeyedbear.com

Cameron Trading Post
Cameron, Arizona
www.camerontradingpost.com

Faust Gallery
Scottsdale, Arizona
www.faustgallery.com

Garland's Indian Jewelry
Sedona, Arizona
www.garlandsjewelry.com

Grey Dog Trading Company
Tucson, Arizona
www.greydogtrading.com

Heard Museum Shop
Phoenix, Arizona
www.heardmuseumshop.com

Hoel's Indian Shop
Sedona, Arizona
www.hoelsindianshop.com

Many Horses Trading Company
Sonoita, Arizona
520-455-5545

McGee's Indian Art Gallery
Keams Canyon, Arizona
www.hopiart.com

Medicine Man Gallery
Tucson, Arizona
www.medicinemangallery.com

Morning Star Traders and Antiques
Tucson, Arizona
www.morningstartraders.com

Museum of Northern Arizona Museum Shop
Flagstaff, Arizona
www.musnaz.org

Navajo Arts and Crafts Enterprise
Window Rock, Arizona
www.navajoartsandcraftsenterprise.com

River Trading Post
Scottsdale, Arizona
www.rivertradingpost.com

Sedona Indian Jewelry
Sedona, Arizona
www.sedonaindianjewelry.com

Turkey Mountain Traders
Scottsdale, Arizona
www.turkey-mountain.com

Waddell Trading Company
Scottsdale, Arizona
www.waddelltradingco.com

COLORADO

Elk Ridge Art Company
Evergreen, Colorado
www.elkridgeart.com

Ivory's Trading Co. & Gallery
Ouray, Colorado
www.ivorystradingandgallery.com

Mudhead Gallery
Denver, Colorado
www.mudheadgallery.net

Notah Dineh Trading Company and Museum
Cortez, Colorado
notah@fone.net

Southwest Traditions
Boulder, Colorado
www.southwesttraditions.com

Toh-Atin Gallery
Durango, Colorado
www.toh-atin.com

NEVADA

Indian River Gallery
Las Vegas, Nevada
www.indianrivergallery.com

NEW MEXICO

Bahti Indian Arts
Santa Fe, New Mexico
www.bahti.com

Bien Mur Indian Market Center
Albuquerque, New Mexico
www.bienmur.com

Blue Rain Gallery
Santa Fe, New Mexico
Taos, New Mexico
www.blueraingallery.com

Case Trading Post Museum Shop
Wheelwright Museum of the American Indian
Santa Fe, New Mexico
www.casetradingpost.com

Christopher's Enterprises
Albuquerque, New Mexico
christopherindianart@msn.com

Desert Son of Santa Fe
Santa Fe, New Mexico
505-982-9499

The House of Lyndon
Gallup, New Mexico
505-879-0413

Indian Pueblo Cultural Center
Albuquerque, New Mexico
www.indianpueblo.org

Institute of American Indian Arts Museum Store
Santa Fe, New Mexico
www.iaia.edu

Keshi
Santa Fe, New Mexico
www.keshi.com

Legends Santa Fe
Santa Fe, New Mexico
www.legendssantafe.com

Millicent Rogers Museum
Taos, New Mexico
www.millicentrogers.org

Joe Milo's White Water Trading Company
Vanderwagen, New Mexico
www.joemilo.com

Museum of Indian Arts and Culture
Santa Fe, New Mexico
www.indianartsandculture.org

Packards on the Plaza
Santa Fe, New Mexico
www.packards-santafe.com

Palace of the Governors Museum Shop
Santa Fe, New Mexico
www.palaceofthegovernors.org

The Rainbow Man
Santa Fe, New Mexico
www.therainbowman.com

Richardson's Trading Company
Gallup, New Mexico
www.richardsontrading.com

River Trading Post
Santa Fe, New Mexico
www.rivertradingpost.com

Shiprock Trading Company
Santa Fe, New Mexico
www.shiprocktrading.com

Martha Hopkins Struever
www.marthastruever.com

Tanner Chaney
Albuquerque, New Mexico
www.tannerchaneygallery.com

Tanner's Indian Arts
Gallup, New Mexico
505-863-6017

Wright's Indian Art
Albuquerque, New Mexico
www.wrightsgallery.com

Yazzie's Indian Art
Gallup, New Mexico
www.yazzieindianart.com

UTAH

Twin Rocks Trading Post
Bluff, Utah
www.twinrocks.com

NATIONAL

Abby Kent Flythe Fine Art
Spotsylvania, Virginia
540-895-5012
abbykentflythe@aol.com

American Indian Art Gallery
Centreville, Delaware
www.americanindianartgallery.com

Autry National Center/Southwest
Museum of the American Indian
Los Angeles, California
www.autrynationalcenter.org

Four Winds Gallery
Naples, Florida
www.fourwindsnaples.com

Four Winds Gallery
Pittsburgh, Pennsylvania
www.fourwindsgallery.com

Home and Away
Kennebunkport, Maine
www.homeandawaygallery.com

The Indian Craft Shop
Washington, D.C.
www.indiancraftshop.com

The Indian Store
Los Gatos, California
www.theindianstore.com

Katy's American Indian Arts
Madison, Wisconsin
www.katysamericanindianarts.com

National Museum of the
American Indian
Washington, D.C.
New York, New York
www.nmai.si.edu

River Trading Post
Dundee, Illinois
www.rivertradingpost.com

Tribal Expressions
Arlington Heights, Illinois
www.tribalexpressions.com

Urban Spirit Gallery
New York, New York
www.urbanspiritgallery.com

White River Trader
Eiteljorg Museum, Indianapolis
www.whiterivertrader.com

INTERNATIONAL

Four Winds Gallery, Sydney
Sydney, Australia
www.fourwindsgallery.com/au

Funny Co., LTD.
Osaka and Tokyo, Japan
www.funny-western.co.jp

God Trading, Inc.
Tokyo, Japan
81-3-3770-7271

INDIAN MARKETS

The following markets are annual
events. The month in which they occur
is in parentheses.

Autry National Center Intertribal Arts
Marketplace
Los Angeles, California
www.autrynationalcenter.org
(November)

Eight Northern Indian Pueblos Arts
and Crafts Show
www.eightnorthernpueblos.com (July)

Eiteljorg Museum Indian Market
Indianapolis, Indiana
www.eiteljorg.org (June)

Gallup Inter-Tribal Indian Ceremonial
Gallup, New Mexico
www.gallupintertribal.com (August)

Heard Museum Guild Indian
Fair and Market
Phoenix, Arizona
www.heardmuseum.org (March)

Museum of Indian Arts and Culture
Native Treasures Indian Arts Festival
Santa Fe, New Mexico
www.nativetreasurerssantafe.org (May)

Museum of Northern Arizona
Heritage Program-Indigenous Festivals
Hopi Festival of Arts and Culture (July)
Navajo Festival of Arts and Culture
(August)
Zuni Festival of Arts and Culture (May)
Flagstaff, Arizona
www.musnaz.org

Navajo Nation Fair
Window Rock, Arizona
www.navajonationfair.com (September)

Pueblo Grande Museum Indian Market
Phoenix, Arizona
www.pgindianmarket.com (December)

Red Earth Native American
Cultural Festival
Oklahoma City, Oklahoma
www.redearth.org (Summer)

Santa Fe Indian Market
Santa Fe, New Mexico
www.swaia.org (August)

Acknowledgments

There are many challenges in writing a book on contemporary Indian art, one of which is simply geography. There are over eighty artists in this book spread across reservations, towns, and cities in New Mexico and Arizona. The jewelry selected for photography has come from the artists, as well as collectors, museums, and galleries located throughout the United States and abroad. Add to that the fact that Addison Doty, the photographer, is based in Santa Fe, the publisher is located in New York City, and I live in Colorado, and you begin to see the logistical puzzle. It has taken the collective effort of many people to make *Southwestern Indian Jewelry—Crafting New Traditions* happen.

Between the fall of 2005 and 2007, I made nine research trips from Colorado to New Mexico and Arizona to interview artists on the reservations, in their studios, at museums, and during Indian markets. I thank all of the jewelers for the time they have given to this project, from completing questionnaires to being interviewed to proofing their profiles. Without exception, all have been committed to getting the facts right, and to sharing their own creative journeys for future generations to study.

There are dozens of collectors who have generously loaned their jewelry for photography, and I thank all of them for the efforts they have made to travel long distances, to meet deadlines, and to share their knowledge with me. I especially want to acknowledge JoAnn and Bob Balzer, Marcia Docter, Dan and Jan Hidding, Hiroumi Imai, Chris Klein, Sam and Judy Kovler, Donald and Noël Neely, Tristine Smith, and Dr. Gregory Schaaf. I am grateful to Marti Struever for her support, and for introducing me to Dale Edaakie and Raymond Sequaptewa, Sr. I am also indebted to Ruth Schultz for her insights into contemporary jewelry gleaned from twenty years of receiving jewelry for judging at the Santa Fe Indian Market. A special thanks to Joe Tanner for sharing his experience as a trader working with Zuni and Navajo jewelers in the 1960s and 1970s. For the information on Fred Peshlakai and the early history of Navajo silverwork, I thank Lauris Phillips and Art Tafoya.

There are many gallery owners who have also contributed to this book, and I wish to recognize the special efforts of the following people: John Krena of Four Winds Gallery shared dozens of photographs of McKee Platero's work with me, charting his evolution as an artist. Bill Faust of Faust Gallery went out of his way to provide the photographs of Ric Charlie's work. Jed Foutz of Shiprock Trading Company directed me to Perry Shorty, and Susan Garland of Garland's Indian Jewelry put me in touch with Cheryl Yestewa. Wayne Bobrick of Wright's Indian Art was always available to answer my questions about artists. Gene Waddell has supported this project from beginning to end, introducing me to Gerald Lomaventema and Don Supplee, and filling in the gaps on turquoise mining. With characteristic generosity, Gene Waddell and his son Mike flew Lee Yazzie to the Lone Mountain Mine in Nevada to take the photographs included here. It was a special moment for Lee Yazzie, who has used Lone Mountain turquoise for more than thirty years, but had never seen the mine. I also wish to thank Taka Kitaura of Funny Co., LTD for our conversations and e-mail correspondence about the Japanese market for Southwestern Indian jewelry.

For some of my research, I have drawn on historical material from the photo archives of several museums and universities. I am especially appreciative of the efforts of Daniel Kosharek and Lou Stancari, photo archivists at the Palace of the Governors and the National Museum of the American Indian, Smithsonian Institution, respectively. Similarly, a number of pieces have come from museum collections, and I thank the following individuals for their help: Cheri Falkenstien-Doyle, curator, Wheelwright Museum of the American Indian; Twig Johnson and Toni Liquori, curator and photo archivist respectively, Montclair Art Museum; Tricia Loscher, curator, Heard Museum North; Kelly Rushing, registrar, Eiteljorg Museum of American Indians and Western Art; and Jennifer Day, registrar, Indian Arts Research Center, School for Advanced Research.

To organize the photography of approximately 350 pieces of jewelry, we had to find a central location in Santa Fe where jewelers and collectors could drop off jewelry to be photographed. Jonathan Batkin, director of the Wheelwright Museum of the American Indian, gave us the green light to use the museum's Case Trading Post, for which I am ever grateful. My deepest appreciation goes to Robb Lucas, director of the Case Trading Post, and his staff members, Joretha Hall and Connie Campbell, who spent a year checking the jewelry in and out and safeguarding it. We all breathed a huge sigh of relief when the last piece of jewelry was safely back in the hands of its owner.

For the splendid photography in this book, I wish to thank Addison Doty for his consummate professionalism and talent. For more than a year, Addison juggled a busy schedule of his own with the complex logistics of this book, photographing each piece of jewelry with great care and artistic sensibility. During the 2006 Santa Fe Indian Market, he worked around the clock to photograph award-winning pieces as quickly as I could borrow them from the artists. Besides the studio photography, Addison made three trips of his own throughout the Southwest, one of which was thwarted by a late spring snow storm, to photograph the artists' portraits and to take the stunning landscape shots that open each chapter.

Many thanks to my agent, Sarah Jane Freymann, who believed in my first book on this subject and was willing to go to bat again and convince Rizzoli International Publications that *Southwestern Indian Jewelry—Crafting New Traditions* was worth publishing. It has been a total pleasure for me to work with my editor, Sandy Gilbert, and I am deeply grateful for her incomparable ability to steer a long-distance project with patience and good humor. And to Susi Oberhelman, the designer, many thanks for creating such a beautiful and balanced book from an unexpectedly lengthy text and more photographs than she anticipated. She has been the wizard who makes us all look good.

And to my husband, Dennis Cirillo, my thanks and my love for making every day of our life together a memorable one.

RIGHT: Jimmy "Cá Win" Calabaza. Santo Domingo Pueblo. Necklace (detail) with Kingman turquoise beads. Courtesy of the artist.

Index

Adair, John, 29, 34, 168–69
Alvarado Hotel Indian Building
    (Albuquerque), *168, *170
Anasazi (Ancestral Pueblo
    people), 7, 84, 98, 106,
    112, 144
ant motifs, 52–54, *54
Apaches, 8, 25, 131; Mescalero,
    8, 25, *26, 27
Arizona Highways, 18, 79, 89,
    104, 126, 135, 147, 151, 162
Arritt, Susan, 99–100
arrowhead motifs, 65, *78, 79, *134,
    135, *160, 162
Art Nouveau, 52, 217
Atencio, Luteria, 34
Aztecs, 99

Bahti, Tom, 54, 55
Bailey, Irma, 30
Barber, Charles, 39
basketry, 75, 90–91
Bauver, Bob, 52
Baxter, Paula, 34, 72
beadwork: silver, 27, *28, 42, *42,
    43; stone, 49, 98, *98, 109, 237
Bean Dance, 72, 74
bear motifs, 76, *77, *85, *128, 129,
    *134, 135, *135, 157
Beauty Way, 115, *115, 132–33
Begay, Bobby, 66
Begay, Darryl Dean, *5, *10, 11, *11,
    56, *56, 63–66, *64–67, *171
Begay, Harvey A., *14, 15, 129, *129
Begay, Kenneth, 11, *12, *13,
    13–16, 18, 22, 28, 117, 129,
    165, 175, 193
Begay, Rebecca, 63–66, *64–66
Begay, Whitehair, 66
Ben, Arland F., 84–89, *86, *87
Benally, Ernest, *153, 153–57
Bird, Charlie, 95, 112, *113

Bird, Gail, 18–22, *19, *20, *22, *23,
    *41, 165
Bird, Lorencita, 34
bird motifs, 72–74, *73, 80, *80,
    115, *116, *117, 117–18, 136, *137.
    See also hummingbird motifs
Bird-Romero, Allison, 34, 72
Bird-Romero, Mike, 29, 34, *35,
    84, *171, 176, *176
blacksmithing, 27
Bobelu, Gomeo Zacharias, 119,
    *119
Bonnell, John, 15
Bonnell, Jon, 175
Boomer, John, 78
Bosque Redondo Indian
    Reservation, 25–27, *26, 28, 47
bowguards (ketohs), 29–30, *31
boxes, sterling silver, *10, *10, *11,
    182–85, *184, 196, *196–97
Branson, Oscar, 109
brass, *33, 34, 41
bridles, 27, *28, 42, 48, 170
Brookins, Jacob, 188
Burbank, E. A., 47
butterfly motifs, 49–52, *50–53,
    *64–65, *65, *152, *153, 155, *156,
    157, *185, *206, *207
buttons, silver, 27, 28, 170

Cabochons, 60, *102, 104
Calabaza, Jimmy, 98, *98, 237
canteens, silver, 28, 30, *30, 170,
    182, 188–89, *190
Carson, Kit, 26
Castellani, Fortunao Pio, 132
cast jewelry, 126, *127, 129, *129.
    See also tufa casting
Casuse, Fritz J., *206–8, *207–9
Cates, Christopher, 41
Cerrillos Mining District, 99
Chaco Canyon, 98–99, *99

Chaco Culture, 7
*Changing Hands: Art Without
    Reservation I* (New York City,
    2002), 22, 194, 217
Changing Woman, 66, 106
Charlie, Ric, *62, 63, *63, 68
Chattin, Daniel, 214
Chavez, Eddie Two Moons,
    70–72, *71, 129–31, *131
Chavez, Jared J., *81, 83, 182–85,
    *184, *185
Chavez, Richard I., 83, 135, *146,
    *147, 147–48, 165, *185
Chee, Mark, 34
chess set, sterling silver,
    177–81, *178
Chicago World's Fair (1893), 28
Chicago World's Fair (1933), 15
Chiricahua Apache, 8, 70–72, *71
Chon, Atsidi (Ugly Smith), 27
chrysoprase, 141, 165
cicada motifs, *53
Clark, Carl, *132, 132–33, *133
Clark, Irene, *132, 132–33, *133
cloud motifs, 70, *70, *85, 88, 98
cluster work, 48, *48
coin silver, 28–29, *38, 39, *39, 40
Colton, Harold, 74–75
Colton, Mary Russell, 74–75
concha belts, 27, *28, 30, *33, 34, 40,
    48, *64–65, *65, 182; brass, *33,
    34; conceptual, *19, 19–21, *20*;
    history of, 41–42; hollow ware,
    189, *191; inlaid, 60, *61, 68, *69,
    104, 115, *153, *154, *158, *159, *194,
    195; overlay, 76, *77, 84, *85*;
    stainless-steel, *94–95, 95*;
    stamped, *79, 79–80, *81, 83*;
    tufa-cast, 68, *69, 76, *77,
    194, 195; variation of designs
    within, 61, 158
copper, 34, 41; in silver alloys, 39

coral, *49, 69, 112, *160, *161, 165,
    211, 223n.59
corn and cornstalk motifs, 55, *56,
    56–58, *64–65, *65, 70, *70, 74,
    *74, 177
Corn Dance, 55, 70, 98, 106
Cornett, Joe, *188, 189–93
Corn Maidens, *16, 18, 70, *156, 157
Cotton, C. N., 47, *48, 169
CrazyHorse, Cippy, 29, 30–34, *32,
    *33, *171
cross motifs, *32, 47, 68
Crow Mother, *72, 72
Cummings, Edison, *172–74,
    173–75
Curtis, Jennifer, 182, *183
Curtis, Thomas, Sr., 182, *183

Deleon, Thane, 143–44
Delicate Arch, *96–97
Denipah, Marian, 68, *68, 210
Deyuse, Leekya, 49, *49, 103
d'Harnoncourt, René, 16
diamonds, 129, 131, 136, 141, 165
Dodge, Henry L., 27
dragonfly motifs, *3, *43, 49–52,
    88, *151, 151
Draper, Teddy, Jr., *158, 196
druzy quartz, 131
Dubin, Lois Sherr, 210
Dukepoo, Causandra, *153, 155
Dukepoo, Michael, *153, 154
Duran, Anthony, 34

Eagle motifs, 76, *77
Edaakie, M. Dale, *118, 118–19
Eight Northern Indian Pueblos
    Arts and Crafts Show, 8
Eiteljorg Museum of American
    Indians and Western Art
    (Indianapolis), 8
European influence, 130, 189, 204

Fetishes, 49, *49
Fire God figures, 54–55, *55
First Phase silverwork, 27–29, *28,
    37, 78, 175; contemporary
    silversmiths inspired by
    (revival style), 29–42, *30–45
flatware, sterling silver, *174, 175,
    175, 193
Frazetta, Frank, 83
fur traders, 42

Gallup Inter-Tribal Indian
    Ceremonial, 8, 170
Garcia, Michael, *150, 151, *151, 153
garnets, 54
gaspeite, 165
Gaussoin, Connie Tsosie, *200,
    *202, *203, 203–4
Gaussoin, David, *200, 200–203,
    *201, *204, *209
Gaussoin, Wayne Nez, *200, 200,
    *203, *204, *205
Gemological Institute of
    America, 129, 157, 165
Geronimo, 70–72, *71
Gill, Delancy, *71
goblets, sterling silver, *180, 181,
    189, *190
gold, 42, 66, *67, 121, 132, 165;
    overlay designs, 86, *86, *87
Golsh, Larry, 135
Gorman, Carl, 28
Gorman, R. C., 28
granulation, 132

Hair pick, *195, 195
hand motifs, 86, *86, *87
Harris, Cheyenne, 189–94,
    *192, 193
Harrison, Jimmie, *114, 114
Harvey, Fred, Company, 48,
    167–70, *170

Haskie, Vernon, 42, *45*, *158–61*, *158*–62, 210
Hattie, Anita and Buddy, 48
Hawikuh, 210–12
Heard Museum (Phoenix), 18–19, 78–79
Heard Museum Guild Indian Fair and Market (Phoenix), 8
height bracelets, *16*, *120*, *121*, 194–95
heishi necklaces, 109
Heye, George Gustav, 98–99
hogans and hogan motifs, *176*, *177*, 177, *196*, *197*
Hohokam Indians, 106, *106*, 109
"holiday" pins, *118*, 118–19
Honhongva, Sherian, 121–23
Hopi Arts and Crafts Co-op Guild, 75
Hopi Craftsman Exhibit, 74
Hopi Pu'tavi Projects, Inc., 75–76
Hopi Reservation, *24*, 56, 59, 68, 70, 126, *126*
Hopis, 8, 55, 58, 68; brass traditions of, 34; clan symbols of, 75; Crow Mother of, *72*, 72; naming ceremony of, 56–58; overlay tradition of, 74–75; silversmithing taught to, 27; tablitas of, *51*
Hopi Silvercraft Guild, 75
Hopi Silver Project, 75
Houser, Allan, 70
Hoyungwa, Manuel, 104
hózhó concept (balance and harmony), 56, 153, 162, 196
Hubbell, Dorothy, 54
Hubbell, Juan Lorenzo, *47*, 47–48, 75, 168, 169
Hubbell Trading Post (Ganado, Ariz.), 41, 47, 47–48, 54
Hubert, Virgil, 75
Hueros, Charley, *42*
hummingbird motifs, 56, *56*, 64–65, *65*, *156*, *157*
Hunt, W. Ben, 147

Indian Art of the United States (New York City, 1941), 16

Indian Art Travel Seminars, 41
Indian market competitions, 8
inlay, 112–65; beveled, *150*, *151*; channel, 115; cluster work, 48, *48*; corn row, *139*, 141, *152*, *153*; etched, 115, *118*, 118–19, *119*; figurative, *118*, 118–19, *119*, 133–37, *134–38*, *142*, *143*, 144; flat, *50*, 55, 58, 61, 112–15, *132–39*, 132–44, *142–45*; micro-fine intarsia, 132, *132*, *133*; minimalist approach to, 146–51, *147*–51; mosaic-style, *49*, 104, *104*, *105*, 114–18, *116–19*; raised (sculptural), *16*, *17*, 18, *52*, *53*, 59, *59*, 60, *60*, 61, 112–15, *120*, *121*–31, *122–31*, *139*, *140*, *141*, *146*, *147*, 147–48, *160*, *161*, 162–65, *163*, *164*, 194–99, *194–99*, 214, *214*, *215*, 215–17, *224*; stone-on-stone, 114, *114*, 115, 135, *140*, 141; tufa casting and overlay combined with, *76*, 77; wavy cornrow, *142*, 144
insect motifs, *19*, 21, 37, 52–54, *54*. *See also* butterfly motifs; dragonfly motifs; ladybug motifs
Institute of American Indian Arts (Santa Fe, N.M.), 16, 200
ironwood, 15, 165
Itoh, Hirotoshi, 219
ivory, fossilized (ancient ivory), 165

Jacka, Jerry, 18
Jackson, W. H., 65
jade, 99, 165
Jamon, Carlton, 210
Joe-Chandler, Amelia, 176–81, *177–79*
Johnson, Harold "Cal," 60
Johnson, Yazzie, 18–22, *19*, *20*, *22*, *23*, 165
Jumbo, Darrell, 80, *80*, *171*, 186, *186*

Kabotie, Fred, 16, 75, *75*
Kachinas and Kachina motifs, 8, 18, 49, *51*, 72–74, *73*, *74*, 76, *77*, 104, *105*, 121, *156*, *157*, 221n.23

ketohs (bowguards), 29–30, *31*
Keyonnie, Julius, 90, *90–91*, *91*
Kirk-Lente, Melanie, *156*, *157*, 157
Kirk-Lente, Michael, *156*, *157*, 157
Klaus, Ted, 59
Kline, Cindra, 170, 173
Knife-Wing figures, 49, *49*
Kokopelli figures, 76, *77*
Koyemshi (Mudheads), 58, *58*

Ladybug motifs, 46, *46*, *140*, 141
Lanyade, 27
lapis lazuli, 135, 165
LaRance, Steve Wikviya, 56–58, *57*, 68, *68*, *69*, 210
Lauren, Ralph, 34
leatherwork, 41, 78
Lee, Allison, 42, *44*
Lee, Clarence, *171*, 186–88, *187*, 188
Lee, Russell, 186–88, *187*, 188
Lego bracelet, 210, *210*
Lewis, Greg, 95
lightning motifs, 76, 77, 86, *86*, *129*, 129, 137
Little, James, 135, 210
Livingston, Irene Owens, 117
Livingston, Jake H., 115–18, *116*, 117
Loloma, Charles, 11, 13, *16*, 16–18, *17*, 19, 22, 63, 70, 103, *120*, 121–23, *125*, 129, 135, 151, 165, 194–95, 198
Loloma, Georgia, 18
Lomaventema, Gerald, 72–74, *73*, 74
Loretto, Philip C., 162–65, *163*, 164
lost-wax casting, 126
Lovato, Anthony, 70, *70*
Lovato, Julian, 34
Lowry family, 100
Luna, Anastascio, 34–37

Maktima, Duane, 76, 84, 89, 188–89, *189–91*
Malone, Bill, 41
Manygoats, Benson, 46, *46*, 137–41, *139*, *140*, 229
Martza, Leonard, 49, *52*

McFadden, David Revere, 217
McGreevy, Susan, 91
McKibbon, Teal, 34
McNitt, Frank, 47, 48
Mescalero Apaches, 8, 25, 26, 27
Metoxen, Linda Lou, *180*, *181*, 181
Mexico, 7, 25–26, 34, 41, 42, 48, 99
micro-fine intarsia inlay, 132, *132*, *133*
migration motifs, 83, 85
Mimbres pottery, 21, 112
miniature pots, 78, 78–79, 182, *183*, 186, *186*
minimalist jewelry, 146–51, *147–51*
Mitten Butte, *136*, 136–37, *137*
mokume gane, *92*, 93
Monongya, Jesse Lee, *front cover*, 1, 61–63, 114, 133–37, *134–38*, 210, *224*
Monongye, Preston, 58, *58*, 59, *59*, 60–63, 114, 135, 212
Monument Valley, 63, 133, *136*, 136–37, *137*, *142*, *143*, 144
Moore, J. B., 47, 48, 75, 78
Moorish designs, 41
Morsea, Kathryn, 52
mosaic, *107–11*, 109–12, *113*, 115, 153, *155*, 212; shells decorated with, 106, *107*, *108*, 109, *110*, 111, *111*, 112; -style inlay, *49*, 104, *104*, *105*, 114–18, *116–19*
Mudheads, 58, *58*
multiple-band bracelets, 34, *35*
Museum of Arts & Design (New York City), 22, 194, 217
Museum of Modern Art (New York City), 16
Museum of Northern Arizona (Flagstaff), 74–75; Annual Hopi, Navajo, and Zuni Festivals of Arts and Culture, 8

Naja pendants, 27, *28*, 42, *42*, *43*
Namingha, Dan, 104
naming pieces of jewelry, 22
nativity scene, 188, *188*
Navajo Reservation, 7, 47, 56, 177

Navajos, 7; brass and copper traditions of, 34; creation story of, 37, 55, 66, 90, 98, 133; dwellings of (*see* hogans and hogan motifs); healing ceremonies of, 42, 63, 114, 115, 118, 133; *hózhó* concept of, 56, 153, 162, 196; relocated to Bosque Redondo, 25–27, *26*, 47; silversmithing traditions of, 27–29, 30, 34, 37, 41–42; stone and shell associations for, 66–68; textiles of, 46, *46*, 47–48, 78, 144, 169; trading posts and, 47–49
Nelson, L. Eugene, *171*, *198*, 198–99, *199*
Nequatewa, Verma, *72*, 72, 121–23, *121–23*
New, Lloyd Kiva, 16
Newspaper Rock, *84*, 84
Night Chant, 63

Opals, 56, *57*, 135, *157*, 165
Othole, Eric, *92*, 93
overlay, 74, 74–75, 76, 77, 78, 82, 83–91, *85*–88, *86*, 91. *See also* mosaic
Owen, Angie Reano, *106*–9, *109*, *111*, 112
Owen, Rena, 109

Panteah, Myron, *88*, 89, 89–90, *175*, 175, 210, 219
patinas, colored, *62*, 63
pawn system, 49, 220–21n.20
pearls, 22, *23*, 165
perfume-vial ring, *208*, 209
Peshlakai (Slender-Maker-of-Silver), 15, 27, *27*–28, *28*
Peshlakai, Clyde: family of, *29*
Peshlakai, Fred, 13–15, 28
Peshlakai, Norbert, *78*, 78–80, *79*, 84, *171*
Peterson, Jack, 18
petroglyphs and petroglyph motifs, 7, 21, *82*, 83, *84*, 84–88, *89*, 90, *141*, *143*, 144, *175*, 175

Plains Indians, 34, 65
Platero, McKee, 29, 34–37, *36, 37, 42*
Platero, Vincent, 86
plique-à-jour enameling, 52, 217, *217*
Poblano, Brad, 214
Poblano, Dylan, 214–17, *215, 216*
Poblano, Jovanna, 214
Poblano, Leo, 210–12, 214
Poblano, Veronica Darquise, 58, *58,* 210–14, *212–14*
Poeh Center and Arts Program (Pojoaque, N.M.), 200, *207*
Poirier, Phil, 218
pomegranate motifs, 41, 42, *43, 44*
Pooyouma, Gene, 59
pottery motifs, 21, 49, 75, 112, 136, 157, *157*
prayer sticks, 42, 45, 118
precious stones, 129, 165. *See also* diamonds
Primero, Narbona, *29*
Pruitt, Pat, 93–95, *93–95*
Pueblo architectural motifs, *124–28, 125–126*
Pueblo Bonito, 98–99, *99*
Pueblo Design Inlay©, 123–25
Pueblo tribes, 7–8
Pueblo V Design Institute, 76, 84, 89, 189
purses, sterling silver, *172, 173, 176, 176*

Quintana, Joe H., 29–30, *31*
Quintana, Terecita, 29

Reano, Clara Lovato, 109, 111
Reano, Frank, *111,* 112
Reano, Joe I., 109
Reeves, Daniel Sunshine, 169, *169*
repoussé, 30, *30, 36*
reticulation, 86
revival style, 29–42, *30–45*
ring holders, 176–77, *179*

rocker engraving, 37
Romero, Ken, 123–26, *124, 125,* 195, *195*

Samora, Maria, 217–18, *218, 219*
Sanchez Reano, Charlene, *110, 111,* 111–12
Sanderson, Cody, 30, *30,* 209–10, *209–11*
Sandfield, Norman L., 78–79
sandpainting, 115, *115,* 133, 177, *178*
Sani, Atsidi (the Old Smith), 27, 95
Santa Fe Indian Market, 8, 170
Santa Fe Railway, 48, 167, *168,* 169
Santo Domingo Pueblo, 7, 55, 70, 99, 106, 109, 115
Saufkie, Paul, 75, *75*
Schweizer, Herman, 167–70
Scott, Ray, 83
sculptural jewelry, 194–219, *194–219. See also* inlay—raised
seed pots, *78,* 202, 203
Seppa, Heikki, 188, 193
Sequaptewa, Raymond, Sr., 148, *149*
serpent motifs, 72, *73, 85,* 148, *149*
Shalako ceremony, 54–55
shell, *106,* 106–12, *118,* 118–19, 165; heishi necklaces, 109; mosaic designs on, 106, *107, 108,* 109, *110,* 111, *111,* 112. *See also* inlay
Shorty, Perry, 37–41, *38–40, 171*
signing jewelry, 15
Sikyatala, 27
silver and silversmithing, 27–91; beadwork, 27, 28, 42, *42, 43;* coin, 28–29, 38, *39, 39, 40;* First Phase, 27–29, *28,* 37, 78, 175; as inlay foundation, 112, 115; objects, 169, *169,* 170–89, *171–90;* revival style, 29–42,

30–45; sterling, 39; trading posts and, 47–49, 58–61. *See also* overlay; stampwork; tufa casting
Slender-Maker-of-Silver (Peshlakai), 15, *27,* 27–28, *28*
Snowman, A. Kenneth, 52
Soleri, Paolo, 16, 162
Southwestern Association for Indian Arts, 22, 41, 89, 147, 151, 158, 193, 207, 210, 212
Spain, 7, 25, 41, 42, 68, 99
spiny oyster shell, 165
spiral motifs, 86, *86, 88,* 90
spirit pendants, 70, *70*
spoons, sterling silver, 170–72, *171*
squash blossom, 220n.15; necklaces, 42, *42–45,* 48, 182; pin, 204, *204*
Stacey, Joseph, 18
stainless steel, 93–95, *93–95*
stampwork, *4,* 30, *33,* 34, *36, 44,* 76, 77, *78, 79,* 79–80, *81, 82, 83,* 168, *168,* 182, *183;* early Navajo, 41–42
Stevens, Fred, 115, *115*
Struever, Martha Hopkins (Marti), 41
sugilite, 165
Supplee, Charles, 52–54, *54,* 126, 129, 130, *130*
Supplee, Don, 126–29, *127, 128*
swastika motifs, 170
sweating, 34

Tablita headdresses, 49, *51,* 55, 98, 119, *119*
Talahaftewa, Evangeline, 75
Talahaftewa, Roy, 75–76, *76, 77*
Tanner, Joe, 58–61, 103–4, 212
Taos Pueblo, 8, *65,* 125; trade fairs at, 64–65, *65*
tea-infuser bracelet, 209, *209*
teapots, sterling silver, *173, 175*–76, *177,* 180, 181

textiles, 75; Navajo, 46, *46, 47–48,* 78, 144, 169
tiara, 217, *217*
toad imagery, 158–62, *160*
torque neckware, 210, *211, 212*
Touraine, Pierre, 126–29, 130, 165
tourist trade, 15, 30, 34, 48, 167–72, *168*
Tracey, Ray, 137–41, *143*
Traders: Voices from the Trading Post, 58
trading posts and traders, 47, *47–49,* 58–61, 169–70; pawn system of, 49, 220–21n.20
truck, sterling silver, 186, *187*
Tsosie, Lyndon B., *194,* 195–98, *196, 197*
Tsosie Gaussoin, Connie, 200, *202, 203,* 203–4
tufa casting, *10, 11, 11, 54,* 56–58, *56–59,* 59, 62–74, *63–66, 68–72,* 131, *131, 133, 194, 195, 196, 196, 197, 206, 207;* overlay and inlay stone work combined with, *74,* 74–75, *76, 77*
turquoise, 8, 37, 86, 97–105, *100,* 106, 112, 165; beadwork, 98, *98, 237;* fossil, 104, *104;* mining and brokering of, 8, 99–103; natural and nugget, 101, *101, 102. See also* inlay
Turquoise Museum (Albuquerque), 100
turtle motifs, *1, 87, 88, 137, 138, 139, 141, 229*

United Indian Traders Association, 58

Vessels, silver, *4, 59, 78, 78–79,* 182–85, *183, 184. See also* canteens
Vicenti, Edison, 48, *48*
Vicenti, Jennie, 48, *48*

Waddell, B. C., 103
Waddell, Gene, 61, *100,* 101–3, 126
Wallace, Alan, 52
Wallace, C. G., 37, 49, *50,* 54, 103, 119
Wallace, Liz, 52, *52, 53,* 171, 217, *217*
Walpi, 126, *126*
wedding baskets, 90–91
Wheelwright Museum of the American Indian (Santa Fe): spoon exhibition at, 170–73, *171*
White Hogan (Scottsdale, Ariz.), 15, 175
White-Shell Woman, 66, 106
Wittick, Ben, 27, *28,* 47
Woodward, Arthur, 27
Wright, Frank Lloyd, 16

Yazzie, Colina, 41, *103,* 104
Yazzie, Harry, 193
Yazzie, Kee, Jr., *4, 82,* 83–84, *85, 171*
Yazzie, Lee A., *2–3, 59, 59*–61, *60, 61, 100,* 103, 104, 210
Yazzie, Raymond C., 41, 66, *102*–5, *103–4*
Yeibichai figures, 63, 114, *114*
Yei figures, 63, 86, 115, 117, 118, *132, 133, 180, 181*
Yellowhorse, Alvin, 141–44, *141–44*
Yellowhorse, Bryon, 141, *141,* 144, *145*
Yellowhorse, Elsie, 144
Yellowhouse, Frank, 141–43
Yestewa, Cheryl Marie, 101, *101*

Zuni Pueblo, 7, 49, 54, 59, 93, 115, 119, 212, 215
Zunis, 117–18; brass and copper traditions of, 34; cluster work of, 48, *48;* jewelry as window into ceremonial life of, 54–55, *55,* 58, *58;* silversmithing taught to, 27, 49